P. H. Woodward

Insurance in Connecticut

P. H. Woodward

Insurance in Connecticut

ISBN/EAN: 9783743327535

Manufactured in Europe, USA, Canada, Australia, Japa

Cover: Foto ©ninafisch / pixelio.de

Manufactured and distributed by brebook publishing software (www.brebook.com)

P. H. Woodward

Insurance in Connecticut

CONNECTICUT

BY

P. HENRY WOODWARD

1897

D. H. HURD & CO

BOSTON

CONTENTS.

CHAPTER I.

	PAGE
EARLY FIRE AND MARINE INSURANCE.	1–10

Poverty of the country after the Revolution—Mutual antipathies of the Colonies—Situation in Connecticut—Re-awakened energy—Policy written by Sanford and Wadsworth in 1794—The Hartford and New Haven Insurance Company in 1795—Ezekiel Williams, Jr., and local marine insurance—Its methods—Hartford conspicuous in insurance—The pioneers: Jeremiah Wadsworth, Peleg Sanford, Daniel Wadsworth, John Caldwell, John Morgan, Ezekiel Williams, Jr., John Chenevard, Michael and Thomas Bull, Hudson & Goodwin—The Hartford Insurance Company formed in 1803—Merger in the Protection in 1825—Thomas Scott Williams—The stock note method—The New Haven Company—Companies in Norwich, Middletown, New London and New Haven—The Napoleonic wars—The West India trade—Commercial distress after 1807—Our navy—Passage of early marine insurance.

CHAPTER II.

THE MUTUAL ASSURANCE COMPANY OF THE CITY OF NORWICH. . . .	10–11

The first incorporated insurance company of Connecticut—Incorporated May, 1795—The New London agency—Annual meetings held in the court house—A prosperous business—Secretaries from 1794 to 1876—Insurance exclusively on dwelling-houses since 1838.

THE MUTUAL ASSURANCE COMPANY OF NEW HAVEN	11
THE NORWICH FIRE INSURANCE COMPANY	11

Joseph Williams, Jr., first secretary and executive officer—Abandonment of marine business in 1818—Admitted into State of New York in 1849—Presidents from 1807 to 1868.

THE HARTFORD FIRE INSURANCE COMPANY.	12–21

Scarcity of securities—Its first investment—Rates empirical—Character—Cause of slow growth—Planting agencies—Corporate donations—Early salaries—Good and bad luck—No reserves laid by—General Nathaniel Terry and Walter Mitchell—Change of management and heavy losses in 1835—How a crisis was met—A series of fires—Eliphalet Terry—Increase of capital—Profits capitalized—Hezekiah Huntington—T. C. Allyn—George L. Chase—A more vigorous policy—Losses by the Chicago fire settled in full—One million dollars in fresh subscriptions—Mr. Chase and the Ocean Bank receivership—Successive offices—Builds in 1870 and enlarges in 1896—Officers—Present condition.

THE NEW HAVEN FIRE INSURANCE COMPANY.	21–22

Incorporated in 1813—Charter revoked in 1822.

THE MIDDLETOWN FIRE INSURANCE COMPANY.	22

Incorporated May, 1813—After a short existence its outstanding risks were assumed by the Ætna of Hartford.

CHAPTER III.

THE ÆTNA INSURANCE COMPANY OF HARTFORD 22–32

Curious origin—Organization—First officers—Henry L. Ellsworth—Reinsures risks of Middletown Fire Insurance Company—Early discussions and practices—Agency business pushed—Mobile, Alabama, in 1827—Distress following the English panic of 1825—Heroic action of directors—Isaac Perkins—The panic of 1837—An early journey—The early director—Three generations: Joseph, Junius S., and J. Pierpont Morgan—Inland insurance—President Brace and the New York fire of 1845—Turn of the tide—Passage of the half century—Failure of the Protection—The Ætna occupies the vacated field—Increases of capital—Sketch of Thomas K. Brace—Edwin G. Ripley—Thomas A. Alexander—Internal dissensions over reinsurance reserves—Beginning of classifications—Art—Outline charts—A book of instructions—The Chicago and Boston fires—Lucius J. Hendee—Jotham Goodnow—Erastus J. Bassett—Andrew C. Bayne—Present officers and condition—William B. Clark.

THE PROTECTION INSURANCE COMPANY OF HARTFORD 32–35

Initial advantages—Lineage—Organization—William W. Ellsworth—Thomas C. Perkins—Its widespread agency system—Ephraim Robins and his work—Head of the western department—Its Cincinnati office a Whig club room—List of successive officers—Mark Howard, first special agent—His courage—Apparent profits dissipated in dividends—W. B. Robins—Desperate expedients—Collapse—Residuary legatees.

CHAPTER IV.

THE SECURITY INSURANCE COMPANY OF NEW HAVEN. . . 35–36

THE CITY FIRE OF HARTFORD. . . 36

THE BRIDGEPORT FIRE AND MARINE INSURANCE COMPANY. . . 36–37

Bogus swapping of securities—Driven from New York and Massachusetts—Failure.

THE CITY FIRE INSURANCE COMPANY OF NEW HAVEN. 37

Double retirement.

THE CONNECTICUT FIRE INSURANCE COMPANY OF HARTFORD. 37–40

Conservative policy—Capitalization of profits—Benjamin W. Greene—Settlement of Chicago losses in 1871—Saving the plant—Increase of capital—John B. Eldridge—M. Bennett, Jr.—J. D. Browne—Present condition and officers.

THE PHŒNIX FIRE INSURANCE COMPANY OF HARTFORD. 40–44

Henry Kellogg, the founder—Organization—N. H. Morgan—Occupation of frontier and Pacific coast—Rapid growth—Increase of capital—Simeon L. Loomis—Governor Jewell amid the ruins of the Chicago fire—First payment of loss—Effect on the despairing multitude—Fresh capital—Successive locations—Asa W. Jillson—Henry Kellogg—D. W. C. Skilton—Statistics—Officers.

THE STATE FIRE INSURANCE COMPANY OF NEW HAVEN 45–48

Charter dormant—Nebulous assets—More vapor—Enter Benjamin Noyes—Unseen favors—Flight of the secretary—Elizur Wright hoodwinked—A new light—Certificates for show—Plausible phrases—The lion roused—Efforts to prosecute—Voluntary assignment—Suits on stock notes—An unparalleled shrinkage.

CHAPTER V.

	PAGE
THE MERCHANTS' AND THE NATIONAL OF HARTFORD . . .	49-52

Formation of the Merchants'—Lessons from the Protection—Monotonous prosperity—Entire assets in 1871 distributed to Chicago policy-holders—Revived in the Merchants'—Large over-subscription—Whole capital paid in cash—Boston fire of 1872—Mark Howard—James Nichols—Condition—Officers.

CHARTER OAK FIRE AND MARINE INSURANCE COMPANY OF HARTFORD.	52
THE HOME INSURANCE COMPANY OF NEW HAVEN.	53

Heavy losses and large dividends—Fluctuations of capital—Failure and local distress—Benjamin Noyes in a spasm of virtue.

THE NORTH AMERICAN FIRE INSURANCE COMPANY OF HARTFORD.	53-54
THE NEW ENGLAND FIRE AND MARINE INSURANCE CO. OF HARTFORD.	54
THE NORWALK MARINE AND FIRE INSURANCE COMPANY	54
THE THAMES FIRE INSURANCE COMPANY OF NORWICH.	54
THE UNION FIRE INSURANCE COMPANY OF HARTFORD.	54
THE PUTNAM FIRE INSURANCE COMPANY OF HARTFORD .	54
THE QUINNIPIAC INSURANCE COMPANY OF NEW HAVEN	55
THE ORIENT INSURANCE COMPANY OF HARTFORD	55

Succeeds the City Fire Insurance Company—Organized in November, 1871—Losses in Boston in 1872—Rapid recovery—Charles B. Whiting—Effects of the panic of 1893—Condition—Officers.

THE MERIDEN INSURANCE COMPANY.	56
THE ATLAS INSURANCE COMPANY	57
FOREIGN COMPANIES MANAGED IN AMERICA BY MARTIN BENNETT, JR.	57

CHAPTER VI.

MUTUAL INSURANCE COMPANIES	58

Age and assets—Needs which brought into being the oldest of the Mutuals.

THE WINDHAM COUNTY MUTUAL FIRE INSURANCE COMPANY	58

Formation, Progress and Economies—The rural director—Officers.

THE HARTFORD COUNTY MUTUAL FIRE INSURANCE COMPANY.	59

The premium note—A small beginning—A crisis met—Officers.

THE MIDDLESEX MUTUAL ASSURANCE OF MIDDLETOWN	60

Largest of Connecticut mutuals—Evolution of methods—Officers.

THE NEW LONDON COUNTY MUTUAL FIRE INSURANCE COMPANY .	60

Officers from 1840 to 1895.

THE STATE MUTUAL FIRE INSURANCE COMPANY OF HARTFORD	61

CHAPTER VII.

HARTFORD AND LIFE INSURANCE 61

    The pioneers—Curious opposition—Elder Swan denounces the pernicious novelty.

THE CONNECTICUT MUTUAL LIFE INSURANCE COMPANY OF HARTFORD . 62

    Origin—Restrictions of the charter—Organization—Guaranty fund—Severe economy —Dissensions—Battle—The premium note—Controversy with Superintendent Barnes of New York—Defiant attitude of the company—No forage for raiders—Distribution of savings—Voluntary renunciation of forfeitures—Rapid growth, 1863-67 · Outpour of paper money and land speculations—Refusal of the company to loan to speculators—Heedless legislation—Defeat of a desperate assault—Guy R. Phelps—James Goodwin—Succession of officers—Jacob L. Greene—John M. Taylor—The company first to foresee the fall in rates of interest—Its prudent action—Acrid criticism—Patrons protected—Hostility to the Tontine and other speculative schemes—Condition—Officers.

CHAPTER VIII.

THE AMERICAN NATIONAL LIFE AND TRUST COMPANY OF NEW HAVEN 69–81

    Professor Benjamin Silliman, president—Benjamin Noyes, secretary—Reckless assumptions as to rates of interest and mortality—Perplexity of commissioners over statements —Exclusion from New York and Massachusetts—Criticisms of Elizur Wright—Noyes in full control—Also first insurance commissioner of Connecticut—Building on leased land —Ideal figure-heads—A troublesome trustee—An honest agent—Sophistication of debts —An attack from Norwich—Under a new name—Looseness of new charter—Bogus subscriptions—Guaranty capital—Metempsychosis—A bad bargain—Trouble at Albany—John W. Stedman, commissioner—Frequency of complaints—A thorough investigation—Deficiency in assets—Trustee applied for—The commissioner beaten—Mythical securities—Unconscious shareholders—Something from nothing—Value of the building—Courage and persistence of Commissioner Stedman—Fight transferred to the legislature—Sudden conversions—The curtain lifted—Another trial—A phantom credit of $50,000—Nemesis—Departure from Connecticut—Purchase of a Washington charter—Dark seances—More phantom bonds—Clothing a corpse—A fresh start—Jersey justice—Noyes in prison—Talcott H. Russell appointed receiver—Efforts to collect the wreckage—Triumphal return—forlorn exit.

CHAPTER IX.

THE CONNECTICUT HEALTH INSURANCE COMPANY 81

    An impracticable scheme—Changes of plan—Slaves and coolies—Officers—James Dixon.

THE CHARTER OAK LIFE INSURANCE COMPANY OF HARTFORD . . 82–89

    Brilliant start—Gideon Welles—Selling stock notes—Their character—Successive officers—Stock notes paid in earnings—Beguiling Votes—Good work in the field—High tide—Weak management—Note of warning—Bad breaks—Allen, Stephens & Co.—Mining ventures—The Valley Road—A summer hotel—A hole in West Virginia—A costly office building—Entrance of Henry J. Furber—Secures control—His contract—Loopholes—Expert investigations—Deplorable discoveries—Exchange of bad debts for valuable real estate—Premature sales—Prevalent distrust—A special commission—Differing views of the Commissioner and of the commission—Mortgage of the building—Change of management—Marshall Jewell in control—Too late—The company changes from stock to mutual—Trial for conspiracy—Secret contracts of Wiggin and White—George M. Bartholomew, president—Final collapse.

CONTENTS

CHAPTER X.

THE ÆTNA LIFE INSURANCE COMPANY OF HARTFORD 90-94
A child of the Ætna Fire Insurance Company—Separation of control—Organization—General financial depression—War stimulus—Large increase of business—Rapid growth—Profitable investments—Early loans on Illinois Central lands—Other profitable loans—Death-rate small—Increases of capital—Eliphalet A. Bulkeley—Thomas O. Enders—Morgan G. Bulkeley—Other officers—The accident department opened January 1, 1891.

THE PHŒNIX MUTUAL LIFE INSURANCE COMPANY OF HARTFORD . . 94-99
Temperance and life insurance—Reformers—Public indifference—Abandonment of the temperance feature—Early officers—Panic of 1873—Excessive dividends to policy holders—Change of management in 1875—Painful discoveries—Payment of stock notes—The work of repair—Appearance of an adventurer—Suggested perils—Action of the legislature—Extinguishment of stock—The company becomes mutual—Its new building—Condition—Officers.

CHAPTER XI.

THE CONTINENTAL LIFE INSURANCE COMPANY OF HARTFORD . . . 99-101
Organization—Plots and counterplots—Capture—Spectral payments of stock notes—A bewildered commissioner—Bogus bank credits—Phantom bonds—Report of special commission—Filling a hole—A rude awakening—Further probing—Explosion—Appointment of receivers.

THE CONNECTICUT GENERAL LIFE INSURANCE COMPANY. . . . 101-103
Formed to insure impaired lives—Inherent difficulties—Abandonment of the scheme—Capital paid in cash—Organization—Corner turned in 1876—Tontine insurance—Complimentary banquet—Thomas W. Russell—Condition of the company—Officers.

THE HARTFORD LIFE AND ANNUITY INSURANCE COMPANY (NOW THE HARTFORD LIFE INSURANCE CO.). 103-106
Original scheme—Organization—Early losses—Change of policy—Prosperity—Another change—Recuperation—Plan of Henry P. Duclos—Officers—New building.

CHAPTER XII.

MISCELLANEOUS INSURANCE OF HEALTH, OF LIVE STOCK 106
THE TRAVELERS INSURANCE COMPANY OF HARTFORD. 106-112
Conception—Organization—Early difficulties and economies—The field unexplored—Facts and generalizations—Costliness of new truths—Gratuitous advertising through accidents—Wild competition—Absorption—Fatality among weaklings—No rival left—A secession in 1874—Jokes before the funeral—Establishment of life department in 1865—Its success—Increases of capital—Purchase of an historic mansion—Its enlargement—Character of loss-claims—Notable accidents—James G. Batterson—Rodney Dennis—Officers—Condition.

THE HARTFORD STEAM BOILER INSPECTION AND INSURANCE COMPANY. 112-117
Incoming of steam—Early boiler explosions—Recklessness of engineers—The Polytechnic Club—Foreign inspections—Evolution of a new idea—Charter—Organization—Lack of faith—Desertion of directors—J. M. Allen called—Acceptance—Public skepticism—Creation of a new demand—Economies—Thoroughness of inspections—Absence of losses—Changes of capital—Stock of $500,000 fully paid—The Locomotive—Preventive work—Indemnity—Plans for steam plants—The laboratory—Impartial attitude toward the trade—Statistics—Occasional casualties—J. M. Allen—Other officers.

INSURANCE IN CONNECTICUT LOCALIZED 117-118
Underwriting in Connecticut mostly confined to Hartford—Evolution of a century—Leadership, how gained—Cosmopolitanism—State commissioners.

POSTSCRIPT, JULY 1ST, 1897 118
Ætna Insurance Company—Hartford Life Insurance Company.

INSURANCE IN CONNECTICUT.

BY P. HENRY WOODWARD.

CHAPTER I.

FIRE INSURANCE.*

UNDERWRITING in Connecticut began in the last decade of the eighteenth century. Its early ventures were humble, for the country was poor and few could afford to take risks. Most of the large fortunes of the colonial period were scattered and lost during the Revolution. At the close of the struggle the stock of specie on hand went abroad to buy goods for which importers could find little else to offer in payment. Six years of unrest and anxiety followed, during which the work of repair progressed slowly. It was not till the adoption of the Federal Constitution in 1789, and the establishment of a mild but stable central government that our people threw off the weight of repression.

When Washington became the first president there was slight travel, or traffic, or social intercourse between residents of different states. Habits of isolation arose, not alone from difficulties of transportation, but from deep-seated though wholly irrational antipathies. The free commingling of troops from all the colonies during the war did little to arouse a spirit of nationality. Sons of Massachusetts and Connecticut, of Virginia and Carolina, were intensely loyal to their respective mothers, but hardly cared for brothers across the border, except as united in a common league to break the hated yoke of King George.

In Connecticut the industrial situation at the commencement of our story was simple. Manufactures, except for coarse articles of prime necessity, awaited birth among the unsuspected marvels of the future. A large majority drew support from agriculture. Commerce with the West Indies and with neighboring groups of islands carried off the surplus, giving not only employment, but practical education to many youth, born of the best blood of the commonwealth, who learned every part of the business from selling and buying cargoes to navigating ships, running blockades and eluding hostile cruisers. Hartford, New Haven, Middletown, New London and Norwich gathered the surplus products of surrounding districts, and distributed the goods purchased in exchange.

After 1789 the reawakened energies of our people found outlets in ever-multiplying activities. In 1792 the Hartford Bank and the Union Bank of New London were organized. The benefits were so quickly apparent that other towns hastened to pro-

---

* A few citations without change of verbiage have been incorporated in the following history from reports made from time to time by the writer.

vide like facilities. At Hartford insurance followed quickly in the wake of the new bank, initiated and largely carried on for half a generation by the same men.

Early in 1794 Sanford and Wadsworth opened an office for the purpose of insuring houses, furniture, merchandise, etc., against fire. Policy No. 2, issued February 8, 1794, insures the house of William Imlay for one year at the rate of one-half per cent.

As the evolution of a policy satisfactory to both parties making the contract, has been long and tedious, and is still incomplete, the first attempts in that line have a peculiar interest. It runs thus, pen-written words being reproduced in italics.

"No. 2.

WHEREAS *William Imlay, Esq., of Hartford*, or whom else it may concern, wholly or partly, Friend or Foe, doth make Assurance *on His House* against Fire, and all dangers of Fire; moreover against all Damage which on Account of Fire may happen, either by Tempest, Fire, Wind, own Fire, Negligence and Fault of own Servants, or of Neighbors, whether those nearest or furthest off; all external Accidents and Misfortunes; thought of or not thought of, in what manner soever the damage by Fire might happen; *for the space of one year commencing on the eighth day of February, 1794, and ending on the eighth day of February, 1795, both at twelve o'clock at Noon*, valuing specially and voluntarily the said *House at the Sum Insured*.—And the Assured, or whom it may concern, in case of Damage, or Hurt, shall need to give no Proof nor account of the Value; but the producing this Policy shall suffice. And in case it should happen that the said *House*, the Whole or Part, are burnt and suffer Damage, on that Account, we do hereby promise punctually to pay and ratify, within the space of three Months after the Fire shall have happened, due Notice having been given to us, and no Deduction to be made from the Sum assured except Two and an Half per Cent., provided said Loss amounts to Five per Cent., under which no Loss or Damage will be paid. And in case of a partial Loss, all that shall be found to be saved and preserved, shall be deducted, after the Deduction of the Charges paid for the saving and preserving; and concerning which the Assured shall be believed on his Oath, without our-alledging any thing against it. And so we the Assurers are contented, and bind Ourselves and Goods present and to come, renouncing all Cavils and Exceptions contrary to these Presents, for the true Performance of the Premises, the Consideration due unto us for this Assurance by the Assured, at and after the Rate of *one-half per cent.*

Reciprocally submitting all Differences to two Persons, One to be chosen by the Assured out of Three to be named by the Assurer, the other by the Assurer or Assurers, out of Three to be named by the Assured, who shall have full Power to adjust the same; but in case they cannot agree, then such two Persons shall choose a Third, and any two of them agreeing, shall be obligatory to both Parties.

In Witness Whereof, We the Assurers have subscribed our Names and Sums assured in *Hartford* the 8th Day of *February*, One Thousand Seven Hundred and *Ninety-four*.

£800 *Sanford & Wadsworth for the Hartford Fire Insurance Company.* } *Eight hundred Pounds.*

At no point can charges of evasion or ambiguity be brought against the document. In preparing the printed form, it was well understood that none but persons of good repute could buy indemnity. Sanford & Wadsworth either signed for themselves alone, or for a small coterie for whom they acted as agents. There was then no such chartered institution as the "Hartford Fire Insurance Company."

Jeremiah Wadsworth, John Caldwell, Sanford & Wadsworth, Elias Shipman and John Morgan, July 27, 1795, formed a copartnership "for the purpose of underwriting on vessels, stock, merchandise, etc., by the firm of the Hartford and New Haven Insurance Company." Obviously this is the partnership of the year before enlarged by the addition of Elias Shipman, of New Haven, who was made agent at that city. Between the others there had been, and continued to be, very close relations. They were together in many enterprises, both public and private. When the new member was taken in, the name was also expanded that it might cover with its comprehensiveness the entire field of operations. John Caldwell was appointed agent for

Hartford. Elias Shipman soon withdrew, establishing a separate business in New Haven. From the fall of 1797 this was carried on under the charter of the New Haven Insurance Company till it retired in 1833.

Local marine insurance soon became a separate branch of the business, crystallizing around Ezekiel Williams, Jr. It was carried on not by a definite association, but by distinct combinations, variable in *personnel* and in amounts written. Mr. Williams formed the groups, collected the premiums, kept the records, investigated claims and paid losses.

Owing to the excellence of its harbor most of the vessels covered by the policies thus issued sailed to and from New London. A smaller number hailed from Saybrook, Middletown, and the Connecticut River. With few exceptions they were bound to the West Indies and to the smaller groups in the same seas. There was some coastwise trade with Charleston, S. C. Rarely a ship cleared for an European port.

For the round trip the gross premiums often ran up to ten, twelve, fifteen and sixteen per cent., and in some cases even higher, according to the character of the voyage. Material rebates were frequently allowed if the vessel either touched only or avoided certain ports, and returned safely. For the premium the assured usually gave their notes, payable out of the profits or at the close of the venture.

The assurers agreed to bear "perils of seas, men of war, fires, enemies, pirates, rovers, thieves, jettisons, letters of mart, and counter-mart, surprizals, takings at sea, arrests, restraints, and detainments of all kings, princes, or people of what nation, condition or quality soever; baraty of the master (unless the assured be the owner of the vessel) and mariners, and all other losses, perils and misfortunes, that have or shall come to the hurt, detriment or damage of the said vessel or any part thereof, for which assurers are legally accountable."

Aside from the terminals named in the policy vessels were allowed, without prejudice, to sail to, touch and stay at any ports or places, if obliged by stress of weather, or unavoidable accident. In case of loss the assured abated two and one-half per cent., and payment was to be made within ninety days after proof, provided the loss amounted to five per cent., under which limit no liability was incurred unless in case of general average. Disputes were settled by arbitration, the decision being final.

The amounts written by the several assurers on a single vessel were very variable. Sometimes a dozen parties would join, taking from fifty to one hundred and fifty dollars each. Others freely wrote two, three, and as high as five and six hundred dollars. John Caldwell was, perhaps, the boldest operator. Quite a number ventured in once or twice and then retired permanently from the arena. A single hit cured them of the gambling propensity, if so harsh a word may be used in connection with a strictly legitimate business. When autumnal tempests were raging or wintry winds howling, the timid found a risk on a marine policy a dreadful hindrance to sleep.

The names that appear most frequently are John Caldwell, Michael and Thomas Bull, Asa and Dan Hopkins, Richard Alsop, Normand Knox, John Chenevard, E. Williams, Jr., Thomas Sanford, John Morgan, Hudson & Goodwin, William Howe, Samuel Lawrence, Gleason & Cowles, Hooker & Chaffee, Spencer Whiting, Daniel Jones, John Knox, Samuel Alcott, somewhat in the above order.

Wherever any line of effort attains paramount success, especially if it involves unusual difficulties and dangers, the inquirer will find that at the outset, or at some crisis in its development, or most often continuously, its destinies have been carried by men of strong character and marked ability. Experiments in underwriting have been freely made in nearly all the cities of the state. With the exception of a few mutual fire companies, outside of a single town, almost every venture has ended in disaster. In many instances the tradition of their existence has faded out, even in the communities where they once flourished. If questioned on the point the local antiquary looks blank and asks for time. Of them it can generally be said that they were managed with ordinary ability, and were destroyed by extraordinary calamities.

Hartford stands forth a conspicuous exception. Though in size but a speck on the map of the world, she has few rivals in underwriting, while the oldest, richest and biggest cities on the planet would be rash to claim superiority. To comprehend the situation as presented to-day we must review the history of the men who laid the foundations, and of their successors who have reared the superstructure.

The first avowed partnership formed for the purpose begins with the name of Jeremiah Wadsworth, an intimate associate of Robert Morris and Alexander Hamilton, and one of the best equipped financiers of the time. He was born in Hartford July 12, 1743, son of Rev. Daniel Wadsworth, pastor of the First Church. At the age of thirty he settled in his native town as a merchant, having made several voyages as master. By successive promotions he became, in the spring of 1778, commissary-general of purchases for the colonies. Later he accepted a similar position in the French army in America, and held it till our allies returned home. Under his roof Washington, Lafayette, Rochambeau, Ternay, and many other dignitaries were entertained.

Colonel Wadsworth was one of the founders of the Bank of North America in Philadelphia, in 1781-2, taking one hundred and four shares of $400 each. In 1785, on the urgent advice of Alexander Hamilton, he was elected president of the Bank of New York. He was a director in the first United States Bank, and was chiefly instrumental in organizing the Hartford Bank, of which he was elected president, but declined.

Besides filling minor positions Colonel Wadsworth served in the Continental Congress, in the convention called to ratify the Constitution, and three terms in the Federal Congress. Public-spirited and large-hearted, he was foremost in the enterprises which he believed would advance the prosperity of his neighbors and of the country. He died April 30, 1804. In our histories his eminent talents and services have received scant recognition.

Peleg Sanford, confidential clerk of Col. Wadsworth, formed a partnership with his only son Daniel, under the title of Sanford & Wadsworth. By mutual consent the firm was dissolved January 10, 1798. Mr. Sanford moved to New Haven, and died in April, 1801, on the passage from Charleston to New York.

Rich by inheritance and benevolent by nature, Daniel Wadsworth was chiefly noted among contemporaries for the grandeur of his belongings, and is chiefly remembered for the munificence of his public gifts. He furnished the site and a generous cash subscription for the Athenæum, where the literary, artistic and historical treasures of the city are largely collected. To this institution he bequeathed thirty paintings, several by eminent artists. His influence on the movements of business was more indirect than active. He died in 1848.

Major John Caldwell, a merchant extensively engaged in foreign and domestic trade, held a leading place in nearly all the local enterprises of his time. He built and owned ships, providing no small share of the cargoes to and from the West Indies, and the ports of other foreign lands. He was president of the Hartford Marine Insurance Company throughout its entire existence; first major of the Governor's Horse Guards, incorporated in 1788; and was elected twenty times to the legislature, which then met semi-annually. John Trumbull, the poet, John Caldwell and John Morgan constituted the commission for building the State House, begun in 1794. Major Caldwell was also a member of the commission that supervised the building of the bridge across the Connecticut in 1809. He was one of the founders of the Asylum for the Deaf and Dumb, the pioneer school in the United States for the education of this class of unfortunate children. Young men came from the West Indies to acquire a mercantile education in his house. Several, after returning home, became distinguished merchants. The firm of John Caldwell & Co. prospered for a long period, but later sustained ruinous losses in the Napoleonic wars and in the War of 1812. He lived twenty years after retirement from active work, passing away May 20, 1838, in his eighty-third year, having been born December 31, 1755. Six feet tall and of stalwart frame, he is still remembered as a genial and courtly gentleman of the colonial type. Col. Samuel Colt, inventor of the revolver, was the son of his daughter Sarah.

John Morgan, of the fifth generation from James, the emigrant ancestor, having graduated at Yale College in 1772, selected Hartford for a home, and became a leading merchant of the Connecticut Valley. By the largest subscription and by tireless efforts he pushed the construction of the bridge across the Connecticut, holding the presidency of the company from 1809 till 1820. The street thence to Main took his name. His operations were so extended that he made large importations in the first American craft to enter Chinese waters. He was devoted to Christ Church, and was largely instrumental in raising it from weakness to strength. Possessing a rich, well-trained voice, he not unfrequently read the service on Sundays. Outside, in excited talk, he now and then tore words from their decorous settings in the prayer-book to drop them quite unconsciously into bad company. Fellow-worshipers knew that no harm was meant and gently overlooked these aberrations of language. To the last Maj. Caldwell and John Morgan clung to the colonial style of dress, short breeches, long stockings, silver knee-buckles and ruffled shirt bosoms, which well became their high bearing and courtly manners. The large fortune of Mr. Morgan was lost in the business distress that long bore heavily on New England, during and after the War of 1812. He died in New York city, September 19, 1842, aged eighty-nine.

These men undoubtedly made up the partnership of 1794, known as the "Hartford Fire Insurance Company." When Elias Shipman was admitted in July, 1795, out of compliment to him and to express more accurately its enlarged scope of operations, the name was changed to the Hartford and New Haven Insurance Company, the word Fire being designedly omitted as excluding marine risks.

With the dissolution of the partnership of Sanford & Wadsworth in 1798, the Hartford and New Haven Insurance Company passed away. Caldwell and Morgan brought the weight of their wealth and influence to the aid of Ezekiel Williams, Jr., who as already described became the central figure for the next few years in the marine insurance of the Connecticut valley.

Ezekiel Williams, Jr., was born at Wethersfield, Conn., December 29, 1765. In both the male and female lines the descendants of Robert Williams, of Roxbury, Mass., the emigrant ancestor of Ezekiel, have in large numbers by character and talents won high position both in the professions and in business. His father, for twenty-two years sheriff of Hartford county, resigned in 1789. Silas Deane, chagrined that a townsman could surpass him in loyalty to the cause of independence, spoke sneeringly of his ardor as "boiling zeal." The zeal sprang from both temperament and training, for his father Rev. Solomon Williams for over half a century was pastor of the church in Lebanon, of which Gov. Jonathan Trumbull was a pillar. From the view-point of the king that church was one of the hottest nests of treason in America. William Williams, signer of the Declaration of Independence, was a brother of Ezekiel, Sr. "Rector" Elisha Williams, brother of Rev. Solomon, served as colonel in the field, as chaplain of a regiment, as judge of the superior court and as president of Yale College. Such fruit ripened on a single twig of the family tree. Ezekiel, Jr., graduated at Yale in 1785. He was postmaster at Hartford from 1795 till 1803. He married Abigail, daughter of Oliver Ellsworth, chief justice of the United States Supreme Court, and died October 18, 1843.

John Chenevard, son of John Michael Chenevard, of Geneva, was born in Hartford in 1733, about ten years after the arrival of his father in this country. Having been a member of the council from the charter of the city in 1788, till March, 1799, he was then elected alderman in place of John Caldwell, who had also served in one or other of the boards continuously during the same period. A thrifty merchant, he left, in 1805, an estate of over thirty thousand dollars.

Michael and Thomas Bull were the youngest sons of Caleb and Martha (Caldwell) Bull, who had twelve children that lived to marry. Six of the sons were original stockholders in the Hartford Bank. At this time, from numbers and standing, the family had wide influence.

Hudson & Goodwin published the Connecticut *Courant*, established in 1764, the oldest newspaper in the country. From the day the first number was issued, till the close of the War of 1812, the people of the state moved forward with singular unanimity, and the *Courant* voiced their convictions on matters of morals, religion and politics. Despite the increase in the number of competitors for popular favor, and the rivalry of an ever-growing body of literature, it still retains a large share of its ancient power. Mr. Goodwin's active connection with the paper lasted for seventy years. He died May 13, 1844, "the oldest man in the town," having been born in 1757. Mr. Hudson withdrew in 1815.

In Hartford the pioneers in underwriting gave the profession a character, which has clung to it through all vicissitudes of fortune. The early method of conducting the business involved a great deal of needless labor. Many policies bore from ten to fourteen signatures. In the first place these must all be procured. In case of a prosperous voyage, the distribution of the premiums called for an interview with each subscriber. Less cheerful was the presence of the broker when he went around to collect for losses. Some were not in, some not ready to settle, and frequent were the invitations to "come again." A single contract might impose on him twenty or more separate interviews, and each contract required a repetition of the same routine. A large part of the details could be avoided by a "pooling of issues." Accordingly, in October, 1803, a charter was procured for "The Hartford Insurance Company." * The capital was $80,000, with the privilege of increase to $150,000, divided into shares of $40 each. Twenty-five per cent. was paid in notes in two equal installments, and the remaining seventy-five per cent. in notes secured by mortgages on real estate, or by approved indorsements. John Caldwell, Jonathan Brace and Ephraim Root were authorized to call the first meeting of stockholders, and to appoint one of their number to preside thereat. The company was organized and ready for business within two months from the passage of the act of incorporation. John Caldwell was elected president, and Normand Knox, secretary. It opened an office on the south side of Pearl street, near Main, one door west of the Hartford

---

* Incorporated as "The Hartford Insurance Company," but called in early policies "The Hartford Marine Insurance Company." Its business was wholly marine.

Bank. Mr. Knox was also cashier of the bank from June, 1799, till July, 1814, when he resigned to take the presidency of the Phœnix Bank. The contract of the company follows mainly the forms in use, but explicitly excludes from responsibility individual shareholders:

"And the assured in this policy expressly agrees, and the Hartford Marine Insurance Company by their president undertake, that the joint stock and property of the said company, shall alone be responsible for any loss that may accrue upon this policy; and the assured, by accepting the signature of the president, gives credit thereby only to the said stock, and disavows having recourse to the person or separate property of any member of the company. And all suits to be brought, if any there shall be, shall be brought against the president who subscribes this policy, or his successor in office for the time being; and all recoveries had thereon, shall be conclusive upon the company, so far as to render the company's property liable thereby and no farther."

Mr. Williams continued for a short time to solicit business on the old plan, but, about the middle of June, 1804, gave up the unequal contest. Later, he succeeded Mr. Knox as secretary.

For ten years from 1807, Thomas Scott Williams, younger brother of Ezekiel, Jr., held the place. He was born at Wethersfield, Conn., June 26, 1777, graduated at Yale College in 1794, studied law, and, rounding out his education by a course in practical insurance, further dignified the family record by various services in the General Assembly, by representing the district in the Fifteenth Congress, by four years in the mayoralty of Hartford, and by eighteen on the bench,—thirteen as Chief Justice of Connecticut. All benevolent enterprises found in him an ardent friend. He died December 15, 1861.

The secretaryship must have possessed great attractions, for in 1817 Mr. Williams was succeeded by his brother-in-law, William W. Ellsworth, afterwards member of Congress and governor. In May, 1825, the stockholders were incorporated as the Protection Insurance Company. John Caldwell remained president till the company was merged in its successor.

Besides the companies located at Hartford and New Haven, the Norwich Marine and the Middletown Insurance Companies were chartered in 1803, and the Union of New London in 1805. The business of the five, by the several acts of incorporation, was confined wholly to marine insurance.

A practice, enjoined at first by the poverty of the country, prevailed for a long time from the case with which it allowed new ventures to be launched on a small investment of funds in hand. Nearly all early charters required a variable, but never a large percentage of the subscriptions to stock to be paid either at once or within a few weeks, leaving the balance to be represented by notes secured to the satisfaction of the directors. These obligations might or might not bear interest; but if they did it was expected that the payments, as they fell due, would be canceled by dividends. Still, both subscribers and the public looked upon the stock-notes as binding obligations, to be met to the last cent in case of necessity. Later in the development of the country, swindlers, ever on the alert not only to contrive new schemes of fraud, but to pervert existing customs to purposes of cheating, hit upon the device of starting bogus concerns on froth instead of cash. Of course these went to pieces in the first serious storm. Policy-holders, misled by lying statements, lost heavily. Educated by experience, the people became more careful, while, in state after state, this kind of cheats has been suppressed by law.

The capital of the New Haven Company, the first of the group, was fixed at not less than fifty thousand dollars, divided into shares of twenty-five dollars. Five dollars on each share were called for within thirty days from the time of subscription, five more by note of hand payable within sixty days, and the remaining fifteen were paid by stock-notes. While the shareholders were relieved from personal liability outside of the special investment, they were also required to insert in every policy a clause expressive of the fact.

Elias Shipman, who had acquired an appetite for insurance by his connection with the first group of underwriters in Hartford, procured the charter, and in January, 1798, was elected president. Austin Denison was appointed secretary. At the annual meeting a year later, the board declared a dividend of $3 a share out of the profits of the previous six months, or 30 per cent. on the cash actually paid in. The following July the dividend was increased to $5 a share, or 50 per cent. on the money invested. These were paid through the New Haven Bank, of which William Lyon, treasurer of the insurance company, was cashier. Mr. Shipman held the presidency about twenty-six years, and was succeeded by Gilbert Totten. In 1833 Timothy Dwight was elected president. Secretaries were Austin Denison, 1798-1812; John Shipman, 1812-1833; Elihu Sanford, 1833.

For reasons to be given presently, its early good fortune did not long continue. After a patient struggle with adversity, in 1831 the stockholders voted to suspend business for two years, or, until a special committee raised to consider the situation, with Timothy Dwight as chairman, should judge it expedient to call a meeting in order to resume. But the outlook did not improve. In January, 1833, the stockholders voted to cease the issue of further policies. No dividend had been paid for six years, and the committee reported that the prospect of making good past losses by future income was far from flattering. The affairs of the company were quickly settled, the sum of $7.25 on each share having been distributed the following July as a final dividend. After retirement from active operations, the organization was kept up nominally, with Timothy Dwight as an impressive figurehead, for the purpose of pressing claims against the government on account of French spoliations.

The capital of the Norwich was the same as that of the New Haven Company, the shares being $50 each.

Middletown secured more liberal terms. The capital of her company was $60,000, divided into shares of $50 each, on which $2.50 were paid at the time of subscribing, the same amount within thirty days after commencing business, and the other $45 in notes.

Benjamin Williams, who had written marine risks on his own account, was first president, holding the place till 1810, when he was succeeded by Ebenezer Sage. In 1819 Joseph Alsop became president, and soon after the company wound up its affairs. Secretaries were Asher Miller, Enoch Parsons, Chauncey Whittlesey and Samuel B. Redfield.

The capital of the Union Insurance Company at New London was fixed at not less than $100,000, with the privilege of increase to $150,000. By way of variety it was divided into shares of $200 each. Ten per cent. was called for in two installments of five per cent. each, and the other ninety per cent. in notes secured by mortgage on real estate or by personal indorsements.

Presidents were: Jared Starr, 1805-1818; Elihu Denison, 1818-1829; Coddington Billings, 1829-1831; Richard Law and Coleby Chew. Secretaries were: Job Taber, David Colt, Thomas S. Perkins, Coleby Chew and Joshua C. Learned.

The Ocean, of New Haven, incorporated in October, 1818, began business on a capital of $60,000 the following June, in its office on Union wharf. Roger Sherman was president and Truman Woodward secretary. Justus Harrison became secretary in 1832. Conditions were too unfavorable to permit the concern ever to gain a sure foothold. After a long infancy it passed away by a lingering death.

The marine companies that entered the field, near the beginning of the century, for a short time enjoyed great prosperity. With no experience to aid the managers in framing a system, they divided current earnings to the last penny, without a thought of building up reserves to carry them safely through seasons of possible disaster.

During the Napoleonic wars our carrying trade, stimulated for short intervals by abnormal profits, was vexed and robbed by Great Britain and France in turn, who both looked with equal contempt upon our rights and our power. As if this were not enough, our own government adopted a policy of retaliation, still more destructive to our commerce than the lawless acts of the belligerents.

New Haven, New London, Hartford and other towns of the lower Connecticut valley, had an extensive and, when let alone, a lucrative trade with the West Indies and other islands in the same seas. Exports embraced horses, cattle, hay, lumber, hoops, staves, flour, corn, corn-meal, potatoes, oats, beans, onions, tobacco, cheese, lard, beef, pork, butter, crackers, etc. Imports consisted mostly of sugar, salt, rum, and molasses. Horses which were rapidly used up on the sugar plantations, and for which there was a steady demand, and cattle, were driven across the country to the ports on the sound. A great deal of stuff from Massachusetts, Vermont and New Hampshire was floated down the river to Hartford, and either shipped direct, or carried around to New London in small craft, and there transferred to ocean freighters.

In Connecticut many young men of the highest promise, after leaving school, acquired on shipboard experience of great value to themselves and to the country. Bright boys were thrust into positions of responsibility, and often acquitted themselves admirably. Beset with perils from the utter disregard of England and France for neutral rights, they became skillful in eluding dangers which they were too weak to meet openly.

To masters thus trained wide latitude was given. Live stock was usually consigned to some dealer on the islands and the in-bound cargo to the captain. After the first landing he was authorized to sail to other ports at his discretion, according to the state of the market and the political outlook. Owners instructed captains to be careful not to get into difficulty by going into a blockaded port, or by taking on board contraband goods, and yet, ever ready to run risks for the chance of great gains, closed the letters with a saving clause, leaving the business of the voyage to be conducted as they should think "most for the interest of the concerned." Hostile cruisers could not find in the instructions a line or a hint to excuse seizure, partly because drawn up for their perusal. Trained amid perils and forced to meet ever changing conditions, masters became adroit diplomats as well as skillful sailors and traders.

The embargo of 1807 and the subsequent non-intercourse acts oppressed New England. Exports from the United States fell from $110,084,207 in 1807 to $22,430,960 in 1808. On imports the duties paid at New London dropped from $201,838 in 1807 to $98,107 in 1808; $58,417 in 1809, and $22,343 in 1810. Our vessels lay idle and rotting. In New England the commercial distress was the more unbearable because the people well knew that the restrictive policy of the government was more injurious to them than to the nations at which it was aimed.

Of course the fortunes of our marine insurance companies withered with the failure of foreign trade. Even war rates, though oppressive to the shipper, fell below the losses of insurers. Claims for French spoliation and other unlawful seizures gradually took the place of solid assets in the hands of the companies.

After long endurance, when at length the Federal government was driven into war, our sailors, trained in the merchant marine, electrified friends and astounded foes by the splendor of their naval victories. On the ocean where she was supposed to rule without a rival England was humiliated and beaten. Till then both at home and abroad the flag of the Republic had symbolized little but immaturity. Our small navy in the first real trial of its mettle both cemented the wavering sentiment of nationality and gave to the people faith in their destiny.

To the sorrow of marine underwriters the peace of 1815 failed to bring a speedy revival of prosperity. Foreign trade improved haltingly. Relapses so interrupted the course of recovery that at times the observer could hardly tell whether the movement was forward or backward. In the case of a people full of energy, enterprise and resources, there could be no doubt as to the final outcome. The strong can work and wait, certain that good times are ahead. But many cannot wait. The passage across the depressions, always broad and deep and rough beyond expectation, strews the graveyards of commerce with the bones of the weak. Crippled by seizures and spoliation, our marine companies yielded to the strain. The Norwich was saved by changing to fire insurance in 1818. Seven years later the Hartford came forth from the shadows of the dark valley reincarnate in the Protection. The others passed away silently, leaving few traces from which their troublous story can be told. Thus ended the first dynasty of marine underwriters in Connecticut.

CHAPTER II.

INSURANCE IN CONNECTICUT—Continued.

THE first incorporated insurance company in the state still exists, and in an age of countless changes has never departed from the simple plan of its founders. On the evening of December 29, 1794, a number of substantial citizens of Norwich met to consider plans for mutual protection against losses by fire. The old way of passing around the hat for the aid of the neighbor who had lost his house or barn, did not work fairly. The generous gave too much, but there were more who gave too little. At best the outcome was uncertain, and this gathering looked for something better.

On the 26th of January they met again. By-laws and a deed of settlement were approved. Each person joining the association agreed to pay on the sum insured for him a premium of one-half per cent. for the first year, one-third for the second and one-fourth thereafter. Profits were to be left in the treasury till they reached £2,000 ($6,666.66), after which the surplus was to be divided annually on equitable terms. Each person insured to an amount not exceeding £100 was entitled to one vote, for an insurance of £200 to two votes, and above that sum to one vote for each £200, but no incorporation could have more than one vote by any way or means whatever. The post-Revolutionary generation of Americans had a great dread of corporations, and as law-makers, in granting charters where abuses were likely to arise, insisted upon strict limitations. Similar fears cropped out in dealing with them as associates.

In case a single loss exhausted the money or property in the treasury, the members were bound to contribute pro rata, not exceeding one per cent. on the amounts insured for each, to make up the deficiency.

In May, 1795, the association was incorporated by the name of the Mutual Assurance Company of the City of Norwich, on the basis of the "deed of settlement." The company issued policies only from the home office and through its agency in New London. At the annual meeting in 1814 the auditors reported that not only was the guaranty capital of £2,000 fully made up, but after appropriating $1,054.27 to pay return premiums, a balance of $450.93 still remained in the treasury, subject to the order of the directors.

Annual meetings were held in the court-house at Norwich Town till, in 1825, it was voted to hold them alternately in the two societies, beginning at Chelsea the following year.

In general the business has been prosperous. The insured are all known to the managers and to a large extent to each other. At any time a person of doubtful reputation would have found it very difficult to secure one of its contracts. Yet, although hedged in by safeguards, the company has passed through seasons of adversity. In 1844 it lost $3,189 on nine policies, meeting the drain by borrowing $1,800 from the Savings Society. Three years passed before the impairment of $1,691 in the capital account was made good. Under the most careful management the business of fire insurance has from the outset been called to pass through seasons of calamity that set at defiance the laws of average. With the growth of population and wealth the recurrence of fiery seasons becomes more marked. Like certain comets astronomers know they must return, but when or whence the wisest cannot foretell.

Since 1838 the company has insured only buildings used exclusively for dwellings, and takes only $1,000 on any one risk. Policy No. 1 is still in force on the house of the late Benjamin Huntington. The first eight policies were issued to Christopher Leffingwell. The gross assets of the company are about $13,000 and the net about $12,000. It has no desire to extend its business or make large accumulations.

The secretary has always been the executive officer. For many years he received an annual salary of $60, and it now does not exceed $200.

Zachariah Huntington was chosen secretary in 1794; Thomas Tracy, in 1800; Levi Huntington, in 1807; John Fanning, in 1812; Joseph Williams, in 1813; J. W. Kinney, in 1834; John T. Adams, in 1835; G. B. Ripley, in 1836; Burrel Lathrop, in 1839; Henry B. Tracy, in 1841, and Asa Backus, the present incumbent, in 1876.

An association very similar was organized in New Haven in 1801, by the name of the Mutual Assurance Company. Elizur Goodrich was chosen secretary and Simeon Baldwin, treasurer. It soon passed out of existence.

Mention has already been made of the Norwich Marine Insurance Company, chartered in 1803. Having found the business unprofitable its name in 1818 was changed by act of legislature to The Norwich Fire Insurance Company, and the capital was increased from $50,000 to $100,000, with the privilege of a further increase to not more than $300,000.

The directors fixed the capital at $100,000, of which fifteen per cent. was paid in cash and the rest in stock notes. Joseph Williams, as secretary, was the active executive officer prior to the abandonment of marine business, and filled the position till 1854. Presidents, selected for high standing in the community and changed often, were not expected to become familiar with the *technique*. Till near the end of Mr. Williams' administration the company rested content with a narrow field of operations. Both agents and risks were carefully selected. On the whole the returns on the actual cash investment of the stockholder proved highly satisf--

tory. No attempt was made to lay by a surplus. As soon as a dollar reached the treasury it was looked upon as earned. No reserve was charged against it nor was such a charge required either by custom or law. When fortune smiled the directors met every few weeks to divide the balance on hand. No regularity as to time or amount governed the action of the board. Plenty followed famine, and famine plenty. Now stockholders rejoiced over abundant showers, and now lamented over withering droughts. But through both alike, every loss was met with scrupulous care. The company led off in limiting its insurance to seventy-five per cent. of property as valued. Single risks were restricted to $5,000. It was once its boast that for thirty years it had not had a trial at law.

In June, 1849, the company was admitted into the state of New York. The stock had been raised to $150,000. Of the assets about $20,000 were invested in bank stocks in Norwich and Hartford; $10,031 were reported as "cash on hand just received specially for investments;" $340 represented for several years the supposed value of twenty-three shares of turnpike stock; and the balance consisted of secured notes. The business of 1849, though not large, began to reflect the results of a more enterprising policy. Premiums reached $22,056.35 and interest $1,204.20. In losses were paid $11,270.38 and in dividends $11,000. As reported the gross assets continued to barely touch $150,000 till 1852, when they slightly overran the nominal capital.

Augustus Brewster was elected president in 1854, and Ebenezer Learned, Jr., secretary. Mr. Brewster, a man of force, was also president of the Norwich and Worcester Railroad. Mr. Learned graduated at Yale College in 1831, and was a lawyer.

In 1856 the stock notes were mostly taken up and the proceeds invested in securities. The capital was increased to $200,000 in 1860, and to $300,000 in 1864. Its losses in the Chicago fire of October, 1871, so largely exceeded its assets that no attempt was made to continue its existence, although it was the oldest stock fire company in the state and had always maintained a high reputation.

Presidents were Samuel Woodbridge, Simeon Thomas, 1807; Thomas Lathrop, 1810; Ebenezer Huntington, 1813; David Ripley, 1819; Charles P. Huntington, 1820; John Buswell, 1825; George L. Perkins, 1830; William Williams, Jr., 1836; Lewis Hyde, 1845; Charles Johnson, 1846; John G. Huntington, 1849; Samuel Morgan, 1853; Augustus Brewster, 1854, and Ebenezer Learned, 1864. Secretaries, Shubael Breed, Joseph Williams, 1814; Ebenezer Learned, 1854; John L. Dennison, 1864, and W. T. Steere, 1868.

THE HARTFORD FIRE INSURANCE COMPANY.

The Hartford Fire Insurance Company was incorporated in 1810, and since the Chicago fire of 1871, has ranked as the oldest stock insurance company in the state. The capital was placed at $150,000 with the privilege of enlargement to $250,000, divided into shares of fifty dollars each. Subscribers were required to pay five per cent. within thirty days from the passage of the act, and five per cent. more within sixty days. For the remaining ninety per cent. they were allowed to give notes secured by mortgage on real estate, or by satisfactory indorsements, payable thirty days after demand by the president and directors.

The subscribers met on the 27th of June at the inn of Amos Ransom, and organized by electing as directors Nathaniel Terry, Nathaniel Patten, David Watkinson, Daniel Buck, Thomas Glover, Thomas K. Brace, James H. Wells, Ward Woodbridge, and Henry Hudson. General Nathaniel Terry was chosen president, and Walter Mitchell appointed secretary.

In due time fifteen thousand dollars reached the treasury from cash payments on capital account. How to invest funds with a view both to safety and productiveness was then quite a novel question. Few were confronted with the difficulty, for the great majority had no surplus. Prosperous farmers bought more land or loaned to neighbors on mortgage. Prosperous merchants extended their trade. Of the well-nigh uncounted millions of securities now bought and sold at the centres of exchange, all but a tenuous fraction rest upon forms of enterprise then unknown. Brokers confined their dealings mostly to bonds of the United States and the several states, which moved sluggishly. Cities had not acquired the art of piling up big debts. The spirit of speculation found food by rushing singly and in widely ramifying combinations into dealings in wild lands.

At Hartford the Hartford Bank, established in 1792, loomed high amid the general bareness. At this time its capital exceeded half a million, and already it had won a reputation for strength that has never been clouded. Hence the board naturally turned to the bank. November 14, 1810, they voted that Nathaniel Terry and Nathaniel Patten be a committee to obtain by subscription or purchase, at discretion, a number of shares, not exceeding forty, in the stock of the Hartford Bank, and that the pecuniary funds of the company be transferred to them for the purpose. "Also, that they obtain a loan from said bank of such an amount as they shall judge requisite to effect said purpose."

As the par of the shares was then $400 and they commanded a premium of four per cent., the committee would have needed $16,640 had they decided to go to the limit allowed by the vote. November 27th, $16,224 were placed to their credit, the excess over $15,000 having been borrowed. But the matter was too vital for hurried action. After duly weighing the pros and cons, the committee on the 13th of December bought fourteen shares at $5,824, returning the balance to the treasury. October 29, 1817, the investment had grown to one hundred shares, bought at a total cost of $43,684.25. The company now holds five hundred and fifty-six shares of the bank stock (par reduced to 100) representing a cost of $63,962.75, considerably less than one-fifth of the dividends received upon it.

In 1810 fire insurance was supposed to be a matter of pure chance. No attempt had been made to generalize the laws underlying the business. Indeed the existence of such laws was unsuspected, except possibly by some deep thinker, who passed for a visionary. Facts were ungathered. Hardly a contribution had been made to the literature of the subject, which now loads the shelves of large libraries. Amid prevalent darkness pioneers could only experiment. Hence charges to the insured often bore no close or fair ratio to the cost. Some paid too little, and others too much. The rates must be low enough to attract patrons, and high enough to pay losses.

An address read before a meeting of agents held at Niagara Falls, June 9, 1885, by Charles B. Whiting, formerly secretary of the Hartford, and later president of the Orient, contains much curious information respecting this and other companies of the city.

Policy No. 1 of the Hartford covered a builder's risk of $4,000 for three months at twelve and one-half cents. No. 5 took $11,000 on a gin distillery at one and one-fourth per annum. No. 21, $20,000 on a stock of dry-goods at seventy-five cents. No. 22, $20,000 on a stock of hardware at twenty-five cents. Within a few weeks from birth the company was taking single risks thirty-three per cent. in excess of its entire cash assets.

The hazard was less than it seems, for the character of the insured, though unmentioned in the policy, formed one of the most important elements in the co tract. Every risk was accompanied by a survey of the property, and the written representations of the owner had the force of a guaranty. Persons desiring insurance solicited it as a privilege from the officers of the company, and, being required to carry themselves a material part of the hazard, the two parties to the agreement became partners in the venture. A man of bad reputation found difficulty in obtaining a policy on any terms. At first no commission was paid to agents, their compensation coming from the survey and policy fee, which varied with the labor, and was collected from the assured.

Then, too, the population was homogeneous and almost entirely of English parentage. The spirit of Puritanism still pervaded New England. Branded often by latter-day critics as cruel and ridiculed as narrow, it is admitted to have encouraged the growth of the rugged virtues. What will be the final product of the inflow and mixture of many races no one can foretell. Few will deny, however, that at the present stage of progress, the process has increased the perils of underwriting.

For nine months ended April, 1811, premiums were $2,784.51; interest and dividends, $638.53, making total income $3,423.04. The first full fiscal year ended April, 1812, with premiums of $3,542.25, and $956.03 interest, a total of $4,498.28. For the year ended April, 1820, the premiums were $5,258.48, and the interest $2,808.05; total, $8,066.53.

Why did the company grow so slowly during the first decade? Because money-making was a secondary consideration. The gathering at Ransom's Inn was made up of men of affairs, owners of stores, merchandise, shops and homes. Occasional fires fell crushingly upon sufferers. In an hour one might see the slow savings of a life—the support of age, the provision for children—swept away forever. Like the sword of Damocles, the threat hung by a thread. Nearly every one in trade or in the workshop had his property collected in one spot, liable to utter destruction in a single catastrophe. A sense of ever-present peril, a desire to avert the worst effects of calamity from the immediate sufferer by distributing the loss through the community, and a willingness to contribute fairly to the common fund, brought the company into existence. Doubtless the subscribers hoped to make a profit. Money set aside to guarantee the performance of hazardous contracts, entitled depositors to more than the ordinary rate of interest. Still dividends above the current rate were rather a matter of hope than faith. Not till long after the venture was launched and the hands that laid the keel had turned to dust, did its commercial possibilities fairly dawn upon fortunate holders of the stock.

Again, as insurance was a novelty, the unappreciative held aloof on the theory that ways good enough for their grandfathers were good enough for them. In every thing the mind was much less receptive of new ideas then than now. The pioneers did a great deal of missionary work in uprooting prejudice and making converts to the doctrine that insurance is both a privilege and a duty.

In planting agencies the board did not begin near home, or in large cities, but in small and remote towns. In 1811 Ebenezer F. Norton, of Canandaigua, N. Y., was commissioned to take insurance and countersign policies. In June, 1814, Ephraim Kingsbury was appointed at Haverhill, Mass., and, in February, 1816, Hooker and Brewster, at Middlebury, Vt., with authority to insure "houses, furniture, stores, merchandise and barns only," they to retain fifty cents on each policy. October, 1819, Hooker Leavitt was appointed for Greenfield, Mass., and, in addition to the charge for policies, was allowed five per cent. on premiums received. In 1820, James S. Seymour was appointed at Auburn, N. Y., and Samuel Cowls at Cleveland, Ohio.

For ten years the company was, apparently, experimenting with the agency system. In 1821 it entered upon a much more vigorous policy, appointing Anson G. Phelps at New York city, George Wales at Boston, Roger S. Skinner at New Haven, and others elsewhere. Thenceforth the net-work was rapidly extended. The question of entering a town ceased to be a matter of grave deliberation, and was followed by the question, Who is the best man to represent us? In July, 1822, the board voted that the agents at New Haven, Canandaigua and Middlebury "be allowed ten per cent. commission on all premiums received by them exceeding one thousand dollars for any one year, commencing the current year." Other contracts continued at five per cent., and numbers were afterwards made at the same rate.

Rigid ideas then prevailed respecting the use of corporate funds except for strictly corporate purposes. Still, the rule was now and then broken. November 17, 1818, the board voted to five persons gratuities amounting to sixty dollars, "in consideration of their active, laudable and successful exertions in extinguishing the fire in this city on the evening of the 2nd November inst." November 30, 1819, they voted that twenty dollars be paid by the company towards procuring a watch for the city. The watch, developed later into the police system, was at first supported by voluntary contributions, though its duties and powers were defined by the common council.

In June, 1822, the board ratified the contract entered into by Roger S. Skinner, agent at New Haven, with a committee of the New Haven Fire Insurance Company, to indemnify it against all loss and damage by fire in consequence of any outstanding policy. They also directed the president and secretary to execute a bond in the penal sum of $150,000 for the faithful execution of the contract.

Secretary Mitchell received an annual salary of $300, with an allowance of $30 for rent, the business of the company being transacted in his private office, till 1813, when it was raised to $330 from January. The next year it was again raised to $360, and by 1824 it had mounted upward to $460, with an allowance of $55 for office rent and stationery, but this was high water-mark, for in 1830 it was cut down to $450, in 1831 to $300, and in 1832 to $200.

He had no assistance at the desk till February, 1829, when Lewis Bliss was appointed clerk. The star of the clerk waxed as that of the secretary waned, for within three months he was sent to Georgia to adjust losses occurring in the Augusta and Savannah agencies, with authority to draw drafts on the company, payable sixty days from time of proof. His salary, too, beginning at $500, was increased to $600 in 1832, and to $800 in 1835.

President Terry received no salary till May 31, 1823, when $100 was voted him for services during the previous six months. It continued at the rate of $200 per annum till May, 1835, when for the previous half year he was voted an additional hundred. No salaries were fixed in advance, but were voted semi-annually, for work already performed.

Not a loss occurred the first year, and for the next three they amounted, all told, to $421.84 only. Again, from April, 1820, to November, 1823, they amounted to but $66.25. The year ended November, 1827, proved over five times as disastrous as the worst that preceded, the losses reaching $37,567.67, but this was a season of happiness compared with 1829, when they rose to $89,469.59.

For the twenty years ended April, 1830, total income was $241,297.29, made up of premiums $219,640.97, and net interest $21,656.32. Disbursements, on the other hand, reached $327,818.47, made up of losses, $175,926.65; expenses, $29,791.91; and dividends, $122,100. At this time the capital was impaired $42,907.14. May 5, 1829, the board designated Eliphalet Terry and David Watkinson a committee to effect a loan at the Hartford Bank for an amount not exceeding $60,000, and to pledge as security the stock of the company in the bank and the stock notes for the third installment. At this juncture the shareholders, over and above the securities in the treasury, were liable for about fifteen per cent. on their stock notes, barely to wipe out the deficiency. Against this minus quantity, owners, endowed with a faculty for seeing the bright side, might put as an offset the good-will and established business of the company.

All our early insurance companies made the deadly mistake of dividing profits in periods of prosperity, reserving little or nothing to meet the drains of adversity. Only two or three survived the wounds inflicted by the policy. These were saved in several crises by the heroism of the directors, who, by guaranties, threw their private fortunes into the breach.

Growing dissatisfaction came to a head in 1835, when the official connection of General Terry and Mr. Mitchell with the company was brought to an end. General Nathaniel Terry was born at Enfield, Conn., January 30, 1768; graduated at Yale College in 1786; studied law; moved to Hartford, and was long a leading figure in the state. He represented the town twelve sessions in the General Assembly; was judge of the county court, 1807-9; member of the Fifteenth Congress; of the Constitutional Convention of 1818, and mayor of the city, 1824-31. He was president of the Hartford Bank, 1819-1828. He married, in 1798, Catharine, daughter of Gen. Jeremiah Wadsworth, of whom a sketch has been given. General Terry commanded the governor's foot-guard from 1802 to 1813. Six feet and four inches tall, erect and imperious, he appeared in uniform the born soldier. On parade or in debate he was at home. In business, however, he was much less successful. He died at New Haven, June 14, 1844. Gen. Alfred H. Terry, captor of Fort Fisher, was a grandson.

Walter Mitchell is represented as somewhat heavy in person and intellect. At first parties desiring insurance were compelled to seek the broker. Competition soon changed the relations of the parties to the contract, but Mr. Mitchell did not drop with alacrity into new ways. It is said of him that he was averse to doing to-day what could conveniently be put off till to-morrow.

In June, 1835, Eliphalet Terry became president, James Bolles secretary, and in July, C. C. Lyman, assistant secretary. Mr. Lyman held the place forty-three years, refusing all offers of promotion. Six months of remarkable prosperity followed the installation of the new management, and, in December, a supper was given to celebrate the coming dividend, which, however, was doomed to disappear in smoke, for the next day came news of a great fire in New York city. The losses of the company reached $84,973.34, but the crisis was met with a courage that turned a calamity into a blessing, bringing at once a large, permanent and profitable enlargement to the volume of its business. Mr. Terry, having pledged his own property to the Hartford Bank as security for drafts to be drawn, with Mr. Bolles, started in a sleigh, with the mercury below zero, to grapple in person with the issue. On arriving in the city, they found most of the insurance companies bankrupt, and a state of despondency bordering on panic. Property-owners outside of the burned district felt that they were no longer protected, while the actual sufferers looked for small dividends on their policies. Mr. Terry announced that he would pay in full all losses of the Hartford, and take new insurance. The promise—the first sign of cheer in the gloom—was fulfilled to the letter. Business poured in at highly remunerative rates, and the deep gap in its assets was soon refilled. Premiums rose from $19,260.15 for six months ended April, 1835, to $97,841.75 for the corresponding term the next year. The day of small things had passed. Thenceforth, both for good and for ill, the annual operations of the company have been expressed in large and ever-swelling figures.

Dividends were omitted from November, 1829, till November, 1841, inclusive, and again from April, 1846, to April, 1853, inclusive.

Between July 19, 1845, and May 18, 1849, fires occurred at New York city, St. John's, N. F., Nantucket, Albany, and St. Louis, which cost the Hartford $69,691.30, $84,014.75, $54,521.65, $57,637.43, and $58,676.83, respectively, making a total of $324,577.96, in addition to ordinary losses. St. John's was burned, June 9, 1846. Mr. Bolles hastened thither and made settlements by giving the notes of the company. Landing from the steamer at Boston on the way home, he was informed of the fire in Nantucket, and there repeated the dreary routine. Meanwhile notes given for unpaid installments on stock no longer sufficed to uphold the credit of the company. To avert bankruptcy directors freely indorsed its paper. Some signed their names expecting that the necessity of meeting the obligation would ultimately fall upon them personally. Yet in the absence of sustaining faith such was the *esprit de corps* that they took the risk. The earnestness of a few moved the mass.

In 1850, when the fiery epoch already mentioned drew to a close, after deducting unpaid losses and claims, the company was able to muster $158,441.58 in assets, of which $87,000 consisted of stock notes. Among the investments the supporting column was four hundred and fifty-three shares of Hartford Bank stock, estimated at $49,589.75. On the other hand, one hundred and twenty shares of Connecticut River Company stock, valued at $12,000, and ninety-five shares of Hartford, Providence and Fishkill Railroad, valued at $9,500, were made to carry a much heavier load than they could rightfully bear.

At the annual meeting, in 1849, Eliphalet Terry declined a re-election on account of ill health, and Hezekiah Huntington was made president. Born at Enfield, December 25, 1776, Mr. Terry came to Hartford at the age of nineteen. At the death of his employer he succeeded to the business, and taking into partnership his brother Roderick, built up the house of E. & R. Terry, the leading Hartford firm in the West India trade, and one of the largest wholesale grocery houses in the Connecticut Valley. Their store was located at the corner of North Main street and Albany avenue. He died July 8, 1849.

By an act amending the charter passed in 1853, the company was authorized to increase the capital to an amount not exceeding $300,000, and to change the shares from $50 to $100 each. Both amendments were accepted. The amendment of 1857 authorized an increase to $1,000,000, and the amendment of 1865 to $3,000,000. At a special meeting, held February 2, 1854, the stockholders voted unanimously to raise the capital to $300,000. Subscribers for the additional shares agreed to pay sixty per cent. in cash, or by notes, dated March 1, 1854, payable in one year with interest, and the other forty per cent. in the regulation stock-notes, which had not yet fallen into discredit. Still the prosperity of the company was such that these were rapidly extinguished. July 14, 1857, profits in the treasury were capitalized to the extent of $200,000, making the capital $500,000, which by the same process was lifted to a round million in June, 1864.

A long period of exemption from notable disasters was followed in swift succession by fires at Augusta, Maine, September 16, 1865; at Portland, July 4, 1866, and at Vicksburg, December 24, 1866, involving losses of $57,022.16, $151,288.31, and $55,077.55 respectively. But the company was now much better prepared to withstand the strain, and even after the extraordinary payments at Portland and Vicksburg, was able to add over $200,000 to its assets from the business of 1866.

After an incumbency of fifteen years Mr. Huntington retired in 1864. He was born October 28, 1795, at Suffield, Conn., whence the family moved to Hartford in

1813. Alone and in partnership with his brother, Frank J. Huntington, he published various works, including the Greek text-books of Prof. Sophocles, at a time when this was one of the leading activities of the city. He died February 20, 1865. His father, also named Hezekiah, moved from Tolland to Suffield. In 1806 Mr. Jefferson appointed him United States Attorney for Connecticut, and he filled the office till 1829.

T. C. Allyn succeeded Mr. Huntington. His term was short, for in May, 1867, he resigned and went to New York city, where he formed a partnership with Ezra White, who had long been local agent of the company. The firm also managed the American branch of the North British and Mercantile Insurance Company of London and Edinburgh.

The company had grown to such proportions that the directors now, for the first time, went outside of the city to seek a president, and the choice fell upon George L. Chase, assistant general agent of the western department. Mr. Chase engaged in insurance at the age of nineteen, and in early manhood broadened his experience by serving as assistant superintendent and superintendent of the Central Ohio Railroad, re-entering the insurance field in 1860. Although born in Massachusetts, Mr. Chase had acquired a liking for western ways, and hence, with some hesitation, accepted the place in 1867. His previous connection had made him familiar with the affairs of the company, and besides he brought to the new position a close acquaintance with the men and methods of a great and growing region.

From the middle of the century the Hartford pushed westward and southward with great vigor, having the headquarters of a new department at Columbus, Ohio, under charge of Demas Adams, appointed in 1852, and later of David Alexander, appointed in October, 1854. When the Rebellion cut off relations with the South the western office was transferred to Chicago, where G. F. Bissell succeeded Alexander in 1863, and at the end of the war the loss of receipts from the Southern states had nearly been made good by extensions in the Northwest.

With the increase of population further subdivisions became expedient. In 1871 the Pacific Coast department was organized, and in 1889 the Metropolitan, made up of parts of New York state, Long Island and New Jersey.

The advent of Mr. Chase marks the beginning of a more aggressive era, and figures afford the most trustworthy measure of results. At the end of December, 1867, the assets of the company were $2,026,220.79; liabilities: capital, $1,000,000; unpaid losses, $167,350.23; unpaid dividends, $144; reinsurance reserve at an average of fifty per cent. of unexpired premiums, $831,975.87; total, $1,999,476.10, leaving a net surplus of $26,744.69.

The income for the year reached $1,673,582.69, of which the main sources were premiums, $1,559,040.09, and dividends and interest $102,688.07.

The new administration attempted nothing sensational or revolutionary, but simply crowded the established policy with more vigor. It aimed to have an agency at every settlement in the United States and Canada, where income bid fair to exceed outgo, thus reinforcing the streams from large cities by contributions from many rivulets. Its age, reputation and resources attracted everywhere agents of the highest character and business of the best quality.

A season of long, unbroken sunshine was cruelly interrupted by the Chicago fire of October, 1871, coming like a hurricane on a still summer day. In a few hours property valued at $150,000,000 was destroyed, and while the embers were still hot, it was known at the home office that the losses of the Hartford would reach nearly $2,000,000. So many companies were broken by the catastrophe that a flood of securities must fall upon the market, depressing prices and rendering the fulfillment of contracts still more difficult. In times of gloom the managers always turned to the Hartford Bank as an unfailing refuge. To an appeal for help the bank now replied that it would aid to the full extent of its resources. The courage of both— the one struggling for existence and the other not less for the honor of the city than to save an old comrade—seems almost a matter of course, as realities fade in the distance, but then amid the wreckage lifted the actors out of the world of commonplace into the realm of the heroic. The Connecticut Mutual Life also loaned the company half a million. The Hartford settled every loss in full, paying out $1,968,-225. A bare million—a sum insufficient to meet the requirements of the re-insurance fund—was left in the treasury. By a vote of the directors the capital was reduced to $500,000, and at once increased to $1,000,000 by fresh subscriptions, the rights to subscribe commanding a premium of $85 a share in the darkest days of the disaster. Thirteen months later, November 9, 1872, it incurred losses amounting to $485,356 at the Boston fire, but met the drain out of current receipts.

The Hartford Fire owned a block of stock in the Ocean National Bank of New York city, which, in December, 1871, passed into the hands of Theodore M. Davis as receiver. It had already been looted by burglars and badly burned by the patronage of William M. Tweed and his associates. January 19, 1872, the receiver issued a printed circular in which the excess of resources over all liabilities, including the amount due depositors, was estimated at $587,313.02. He stated that with good management and good luck the assets ought to yield a much larger sum. The only cloud then apparent on the horizon grew out of the suits for the recovery of the value of certain United States bonds, left in the bank for safe-keeping and carried off by burglars in 1869. In the event that those cases were decided adversely, he thought the above surplus might be diminished by $200,000. The bank won these suits, but before the trial, by way of caution to the stockholders not to sacrifice their interests, in a circular dated July 1, 1873, the receiver virtually promised a dividend of thirty-four (34) per cent. to stockholders, after discharging all obligations to depositors.

July 1, 1875, the receiver reported the assets remaining in his hands, "uncollected and not charged off as worthless," at $1,302,511.81. He also held the Portage Lake Canal Company debt, amounting with interest to $560,000, and expressed the conviction that this debt was secure and would ultimately be collected. At the same time the total obligations of the bank were given as $390,395.63 only.

Affairs drifted along for eighteen months more, when the shareholders were rudely awakened from dreams of prospective dividends by a printed notice, dated January 25, 1877, announcing that an assessment of forty (40) per cent. had been levied upon them to pay off the creditors. The receiver, with his customary disposition to make things pleasant, intimated that the comptroller of the currency was at the same time reserving for the stockholders assets which would ultimately yield a large sum, but which could be sold then only at heavy sacrifice. He declared it to be a part of the plan to collect upon these as soon as possible and to apply the proceeds to their benefit.

The circular awakened no small degree of astonishment and wrath in Eastern Connecticut, where for some reason the bank shares had been a favorite investment. A promised dividend of nearly sixty per cent. had dwindled to thirty-four, only to be transmuted further on into an assessment of forty. A call was sent out to interested parties to meet at the office of the Hartford Fire. Representative men came together from several counties to consider the matter.

Mr. Chase advocated the most vigorous and aggressive resistance to the demand until the facts of the receivership could be unearthed and laid bare. He took the position that on the ground of sound public policy it was just as much the duty of the executive officers of insurance companies and savings banks to resist unjust or fraudulent claims as to pay such as were just. He urged that all unite in employing the best talent to trace the assets from the vaults of the bank into the pockets whither they had disappeared, and if necessary to assault the comptroller of the currency in his stronghold to learn why through thick and thin he upheld an appointee who by his own circulars was convicted of playing high-handed tricks with his trust.

The earnest appeal of Mr. Chase brought several to the support of the plan, but the times discouraged heroic action. Just then the country was suffering the severest strain of the long depression that began with the panic of 1873. The air, charged with timidity and distrust, overpowered resolution. All appreciated the smokiness of the record as developed in the successive circulars of the receiver, but the majority saw no hopeful method of redress. The assessments were paid with much the same feelings that the belated traveler on the lonely moor surrenders his purse at the muzzle of the pistol.

Nearly a quarter of a century has passed since the comptroller of the currency and his appointee took charge of assets estimated to exceed all liabilities by over half a million of dollars. That large sum has vanished. The bottomless pit has swallowed four hundred thousand more, wrung by arbitrary orders from shareholders, not a few of them widows and orphans. Out of all the property not a cent has been paid to the owners of residuary interests.

Perhaps undue space has been given to this episode. The general adoption of the course advocated in this instance by Mr. Chase would go far to prevent such scandals and, where failures have occurred, to secure a just distribution of the salvage.

During Walter Mitchell's connection with the company the business was carried on in his law office on the site now occupied by the *Courant* building. In 1835, its rooms were moved one door eastward. In 1854, the company took quarters on Main street, north of Pratt, and with one more change in the interim removed to its own building, at the corner of Pearl and Trumbull, in 1870. The structure built of Quincy granite, having a frontage of sixty and a depth of one hundred feet, and rising four stories above the basement, served its purposes for twenty-six years. To meet the needs of a business that has grown far more rapidly than either officers or directors deemed possible a quarter of a century ago, the company in 1896-7 built an addition forty-four by seventy-two feet, six stories high, with a front also of Quincy granite. The old part was raised one story and both are surmounted by a continuous fire-proof roof, supported by steel beams and girders. By the removal of the division-wall the first floor is thrown into a single room, sixty-four by seventy feet. Here the main clerical work of the company is performed under the eyes of the officers. The new part is fire-proof, and the security of the old has been greatly increased. In the rear of the office, besides a large room for private consultations, is an additional fire-proof vault, sixteen by twenty-four and seventeen feet high, for the storage of books and valuable documents. The upper floors are rented for offices and bachelor apartments.

Out of profits a stock dividend of twenty-five per cent. was declared in 1877, raising the capital to $1,250,000. At that point it has since remained, all gains going to swell the surplus. Thus far the officers, supported by a conservative directory, have stubbornly resisted all attempts to increase the stock-liability.

The successors of James G. Bolles in the secretaryship have been Charles Taylor,

THE HARTFORD FIRE INSURANCE COMPANY.

1850-2; A. F. Wilmarth, 1852 (for six months); Caleb B. Bowers, 1853-July 1, 1858; Timothy C. Allyn, August 5, 1858-June 2, 1864; George M. Coit, June 2, 1864-February 1, 1870; John D. Browne, February 1, 1870-November 1, 1880; Charles B. Whiting, November 20, 1880-June 1, 1886; Philander C. Royce, since June 1, 1886.

Mr. Wilmarth was afterwards vice-president of the Home of New York. Mr. Bowers was president of the City and the Putnam, both of Hartford, and thence moved to New Haven. T. C. Allyn was promoted to the presidency. Mr. Coit left to represent the company in New York city, and later became assistant-manager of the Royal of Liverpool. Mr. Browne resigned to take the presidency of the Connecticut Fire, and Mr. Whiting to take the presidency of the Orient.

Christopher C. Lyman, appointed a clerk July 20, 1835, and assistant-secretary in 1840, filled the place till June 1, 1878, having charge of the bookkeeping department. After his death the position of assistant-secretary remained vacant till the appointment of Philander C. Royce, June 23, 1881. Mr. Royce was born of New England parentage in Plainfield, Ill., in 1838; graduated at Knox College in 1860; taught till 1866, when he entered the insurance field, first as local and later as special agent; served in the western department of the Hartford Fire Insurance Company, from May, 1872, till August, 1876; thence as secretary of the Girard Fire and Marine of Philadelphia, till in 1881 he returned to the Hartford Fire, where he has since remained, having been made secretary in 1886.

Thomas Turnbull succeeded Mr. Royce as assistant-secretary, June 11, 1886. Born in Scotland in 1834, and richly endowed with the sturdy qualities of the Scotch character, he came to America in 1852, and engaged in the wholesale tea trade in Philadelphia and New York. He was special agent of the Niagara Fire from 1869 till 1876, when he became general agent of the Hartford Fire in New York state, holding the position till 1886, when he was called, as above, to the home office.

Charles E. Chase, son of the president, born at Dubuque, Ia., March 29, 1857, having graduated at the Hartford High School in 1876, the next year entered the service of the company, and for efficiency was made second assistant-secretary July 1, 1890.

Cofran & Bissell manage the western department from Chicago, H. K. Belden the Pacific department from San Francisco, and Young & Hodges the Metropolitan department from New York city.

On the first of January, 1897, the gross assets of the company were $10,004,-697.55, and the net surplus, after deducting reserve for reinsurance and all unsettled claims, $3,264,392.15.

The small capital and large surplus of the Hartford give it an enormous advantage in the struggle for existence. Income from assets alone suffices to pay dividends that ought to satisfy the most exacting shareholder. All the profits from the business in seasons of general prosperity can, if needful, be added to the reserves to meet the drains which recur at irregular intervals, but with unerring certainty.

THE NEW HAVEN FIRE INSURANCE COMPANY.

The New Haven Fire Insurance Company, with a nominal capital of $100,000, was incorporated in 1813. Presidents were: Isaac Tomlinson, 1813; Charles Denison, 1818; Simeon Baldwin, 1820. Secretaries: John H. Lynde, 1813; William Connor, 1818; Roger S. Skinner, 1820. In 1822 Samuel Ward, Harvey Sanford and L. E. Wales were appointed a committee to negotiate a contract with the Hartford Fire Insurance Company to assume its outstanding risks. Mr. Skinner, the secretary, was also agent of the Hartford, and hence acted for both parties. The arrangement was completed in June, the Hartford giving a bond of indemnity in the penal sum of $150,000. The terms of the contract were not spread on the record, but the penalty of the bond probably equalled the entire amount at risk, since the sum paid for reinsurance made no perceptible addition to the current receipts of the Hartford. The charter was revoked the same year.

THE MIDDLETOWN FIRE INSURANCE COMPANY.

The Middletown Fire Insurance Company was incorporated in May, 1813, with a capital of $150,000, to be paid in the customary way. The first board of directors consisted of Elijah Hubbard, John R. Watkinson, Samuel Wetmore, Joseph W. Alsop, Josiah Williams, Daniel Rand, and Samuel Gill.

Elijah Hubbard was elected president, and Thomas Hubbard, secretary. Jonathan Barnes, Jr., soon succeeded Thomas Hubbard. The company ran along half a dozen years, making a feeble show of life, and then passed out of existence. Its outstanding risks were assumed, September 25, 1819, by the Ætna of Hartford, which executed a bond in the penal sum of $200,000 to save it harmless.

CHAPTER III.

INSURANCE IN CONNECTICUT—Continued.

THE ÆTNA INSURANCE COMPANY (HARTFORD).

WALTER MITCHELL, first secretary and factotum of the Hartford Fire, lived in Wethersfield, a village three or four miles south of the city. In the early days every resident desiring a policy had to seek him, and at hours to suit his convenience. The road over a clayey soil was frequently so bad that the trip to Wethersfield took more time than a trip to Springfield or New Haven does now. He had a way of closing his office at three or four o'clock in the afternoon, and on Saturdays much earlier. According to current tradition merchants, often inconvenienced by the daily habits of Mr. Mitchell, resolved to flank his position by forming a new company. Hence originated the conception of the Ætna.

The company was incorporated in May, 1819. The capital was placed at $150,000, with the privilege of increase to any further sum not exceeding $500,000. Subscribers were required to pay within thirty days after the first meeting of the corporation five per cent., within sixty days five per cent. more, and the remaining ninety per cent. either in mortgages on real estate, or indorsed promissory notes, approved by the president and directors and payable thirty days after demand. Each stockholder was entitled to one vote for every share up to fifty, and there his voting power came abruptly to an end. While both corporate and personal liability was limited to the investment, it was with the reservation that "for misconduct or fraud, the person guilty thereof shall be personally liable to said corporation, or to the insured, as the case may be."

At the first meeting of the stockholders held June 15, 1819, at Morgan's Coffee House, the following directors were chosen: Thomas K. Brace, Thomas Belden, Samuel Tudor, Jr., Henry Kilbourn, Eliphalet Averill, Henry Seymour, Griffin Stedman, Gaius Lyman, Judah Bliss, Caleb Pond, Nathaniel Bunce, Joseph Morgan, Jeremiah Brown, James M. Goodwin, Theodore Pease, Elisha Dodd, Charles Babcock.

At a meeting of the directors the same day Thomas K. Brace was chosen president, and Isaac Perkins, secretary. They voted to make the office of Mr. Perkins the office of the company also, and to keep its account at the Phœnix Bank. By-laws were adopted June 25th. These provided that the directors should be divided into four classes, taken in the order of appointment, each to be on duty one month, following in rotation. No money could be drawn from bank except on checks signed by the president and countersigned by the secretary. Directors were made *ex officio* surveyors for the company.

September 27, 1819, Mr. Brace resigned the presidency in consequence of pecuniary embarrassments, when Henry Leavitt Ellsworth, who had already been elected a director in the place of Theodore Pease, deceased, was chosen to fill the vacancy.

How modest were the beginnings of this great institution, appears from the balance sheet presenting its operations up to May 31, 1820. On the debit side the principal item is the dividend of six per cent., declared December 15, 1819, on the actual cash investment, making $900. From the organization till May 31, 1820, the total current expenses, including $225 for the salary of Mr. Perkins and rent, reached the sum of $451.82. During this period the receipts from all sources amounted to $3,646.42, and as no losses had occurred, the fiscal year closed with a profit balance of $2,294.60.

Mr. Ellsworth resigned the presidency March 6, 1821, when Thomas K. Brace, real father of the enterprise, whose embarrassments in the meantime had been removed, was re-elected.

Son of Chief Justice Oliver, and twin brother of Governor William W., Henry L. Ellsworth was born November 10, 1791; graduated at Yale in 1810; studied law, but subordinated professional practice to more active pursuits; erected several buildings in Hartford on Central Row; went to the frontier in 1832 as Indian Commissioner to the tribes in the southwest beyond Arkansas; was ten years at the head of the United States Patent Office in Washington, and then settled at Lafayette, Indiana, as United States Land Commissioner. He moved to Fair Haven, Connecticut, in 1856, and died there December 27, 1858. By will he left the bulk of a large estate to Yale College. A contest over the document ended in a compromise.

The first policy for $6000 was issued August 17, 1819, and is treasured among the choice possessions of the office. About a month later the Ætna contracted to assume all outstanding risks of the Middletown Fire Insurance Company, amounting as it seems to nearly $200,000. This is the first case of re-insurance of a company in the state, and is believed to be the first in the country.

In 1822 the board undertook to perform a similar act of grace for the New Haven Fire, then nearing the end, but Roger S. Skinner, its secretary, was also agent of the Hartford Fire, and diverted the contract to his principal.

Questions discussed and passed upon at early meetings of the directors often appear trivial, but none the less instructive because trivial, for they furnish data for measuring the length of the road from crude, tentative beginnings to the development of a highly educated profession. Matters of detail are now turned over to the experts, who fill the executive offices, and to their trained assistants. Then the vital parts of each policy, with the survey, were read to the board before delivery. Within eight months they wisely voted to take no new risk in excess of $10,000 without a unanimous vote in its favor, and in such cases nine were required to constitute a quorum. The next year an agent was authorized to write, not exceeding $17,000 on a single risk, and it is specially noted that nine directors were present and favored the exception. Evidently the original division into four classes had already fallen into disuse. To provide mental aliment for the wisdom that gathered around the table, the secretary was requested to procure for the use of the office, two newspapers, either semi- or tri-weekly, published one in New York and one in Boston, also a gazetteer and a big map. As a first essay to collect statistics the secretary was requested to register, in a suitable blank book, all losses by fire that might come to his knowledge, designating place, kind of property, etc., and for the service a reasonable compensation was promised in addition to salary. Thus the outlay for newspapers, aside from the gratification of *habitues*, was made to serve a permanent utility. Such incidents show the care bestowed upon minute details by the directors, and the vigilance with which they watched the expense account.

Until the formation of the Ætna, the few American companies in existence restricted their efforts almost entirely to the local business that could be conveniently secured by the executive officers. Very early the Ætna initiated a radical departure from the previous method, planting agencies cautiously at the more important centres of trade, and gradually extending the system till every desirable place in the country was occupied. April 2, 1822, the directors, by vote, requested the secretary "to journey on the seaboard of Massachusetts, New Hampshire and Maine, and from thence through the interior of the country home, and establish agencies at all places where he may think proper, and for his service he shall be allowed his expenses and two dollars per day." During the trip the *per diem* allowance took the place of salary. Again, in October, 1825, the president and secretary were authorized to employ a suitable person to travel through Pennsylvania, Ohio, Indiana, Illinois, Missouri and the states south for the purpose of establishing agencies.

A destructive fire, bringing heavy losses to the Ætna, occurred at Mobile, Ala., in the fall of 1827. Mr. Perkins was sent thither in November to settle claims and suspend the business of the agency. He was also empowered both to establish and suspend agencies at discretion on the journey. While at Mobile, although expected by the home office to pay by sight drafts, he invariably drew at thirty days. The process of adjustment proved somewhat tedious. Local business had been unsatisfactory. Mr. Perkins felt ill at ease, nursing exaggerated notions of southern carelessness in handling pistols and other implements suited to make life unpleasant for disagreeable strangers. He wished to avoid irritation and especially any outbreak of resentment. Hence, as he explained on reaching home, he intended to be well out of the way of harm in case losses elsewhere prevented the company from meeting the drafts and they went back protested.

The country was passing through a period of profound distress. One of the severest panics ever known struck England in 1825, suddenly ending an era of great apparent prosperity and riotous speculation.

From the intimacy of the business connections between the two countries our people, though in much sounder condition, were sucked into the whirlpool. Factories were idle, industries disorganized, trade sluggish, collections poor and bankruptcies frequent. Fires in 1827, as measured by the losses of insurance companies, were four-fold in excess of the normal ratio.

Perils so thickened around the Ætna that only the Roman courage of the directors saved it from destruction. A committee, appointed to devise ways and means to pay losses, made their report November 22, 1827, and recommended that the bank stocks, having a par value of $21,750, be sold, except $1,500 in the Eagle Bank of Providence; that all loans, amounting to $6,780, be collected as soon as it could be done without inconvenience to borrowers, and that agents be pressed to remit balances on hand. From the three sources it was thought that $30,000 could be raised in time to apply on outstanding losses. For the balance needed it was considered inexpedient to make an assessment on the stock notes. Accordingly they further recommended that loans be made at one or more of the city banks on paper endorsed by some of the directors, and that the board pledge themselves to save the endorsers harmless. By a unanimous vote the report was accepted and approved.

Thus the first dread crisis in the history of the Ætna was faced. From time to time other situations not less appalling have confronted the management. While the constituent members have changed, the spirit animating the body has never changed. Calamities sweeping away its assets and apparently leaving nothing but a shadow bereft of substance, have again and again been met with the same indomitable resolution and overcome.

Owing to the disorganized condition of business, the moral hazard was greatly increased. The Ætna appointed committees to confer with other offices which were undergoing like experiences, and, by mutual agreements, there followed before the end of the year a general raising of rates. Perhaps to-day this course would be stigmatized by a certain class of writers as a dangerous combination, but it saved the lives of such as survived.

After paying out the funds derived from the sale of stocks and the collection of loans, the company pledged to various banks stock-notes to the amount of $50,000 as security for loans. Before these were fully paid its condition had so improved that in June, 1830, the directors voted a dividend of two dollars per share.

Isaac Perkins retired in June, 1828. He practiced law in Hartford from 1805 till 1840, serving for two years as prosecuting officer for the county. For a while he was in partnership with Thomas C. Perkins, who became one of the most eminent lawyers in the state. For the first nine years the business of the company was transacted in the office of Mr. Perkins. His salary fluctuated, rising in 1823 and 1824 to the rate of $900 per annum, with an allowance of $100 additional for rent and firewood, and afterwards receding to $750. In lieu of salary he was voted four dollars per day while absent on the trip to Mobile, whence he reached home about the middle of March, 1828.

June 9, 1828, James M. Goodwin was appointed secretary, and served till May 1, 1837, when his resignation of April 24th took effect. June 8, 1837, Simeon L. Loomis, who for several years had been a faithful clerk in the office, was elected in place of Mr. Goodwin.

Dividends of $1 per share were paid with fair regularity from June, 1831, till December, 1834, when the rate was increased to $5. By May, 1836, the situation had so improved that the board voted a dividend of twenty-five per cent. to be applied on the stock-notes. Meanwhile the investment of funds was resumed, including a subscription for three hundred shares in the Hartford and New Haven Railroad in the year 1835.

Fire losses serve as quite an accurate gauge of general business conditions, rising with adversity and falling with prosperity. The panic of 1837 brought trouble to insurance offices, causing a large excess of outgo over income. With none of them was there a surplus seeking securities. To meet deficiences most were compelled to sell or borrow. The year 1839 opened favorably, but the panic of '37 had not yet spent its force. During the summer and fall heavy losses, occurring for the most part over a wide area, exhaustive more from frequency than magnitude, compelled the company to resort again to sales and loans.

At the request of the directors, and with full power to remove and appoint agents, settle accounts, collect dues, give discharges, and act otherwise for the benefit of the company, President Brace, in the summer of 1838, made a trip through New York, New Hampshire and the British dominions. His letters, by the way, addressed to Simeon L. Loomis, secretary, are still preserved in the archives of the company. The journey, which would now require a week, was then leisurely performed between the middle of June and the 1st of September.

The Ætna was the first company to issue a fire policy in Chicago, having, in 1834, appointed Gurdon S. Hubbard to represent it. The document was on exhibition in the historical library of that city till destroyed in the fire of 1871. Mr. Hubbard remained a trusted agent of the company till his retirement, after more than thirty years of faithful service.

No small part of the pioneer work was performed by the early director, who traveled west and south by stage and boat, long in advance of railways, establishing outposts at frontier towns which have since developed into populous cities. In this way, to a large extent, Cincinnati, Detroit, Chicago, Louisville, St. Louis, Memphis, Natchez, New Orleans, Mobile, and other places were reached, and the territory partially pre-empted. He went armed with ample powers, his instructions following in its essential features the commission given to Mr. Brace in 1838. In case of large fires the work now performed by the professional adjuster then fell to the director. As emergencies arose different members of the board were selected for special services at points near and far. Some became very expert in discriminating just from unjust claims, and in effecting settlements with all sorts and conditions of men.

During the period of infancy, while the company was fighting for existence, the economical scale of expenditures arranged for Secretary Perkins on his initiatory trip through New England was rigorously adhered to. Just twenty years later, in 1842, Joseph Morgan, one of the original directors, made an extensive circuit, taking in New Orleans and Chicago, and all the important intermediate towns. The journey, estimated at six thousand one hundred and four miles, occupied ten weeks, at an average expense, including fares and hotel bills, of $3.29 per day. During most of his long life Mr. Morgan kept a diary. The record, filling many volumes, is now in possession of his grandson, James J. Goodwin. Chicago then had four or five thousand inhabitants. St. Louis was six times as large. A notable incident of the trip was a detour to Ashland to visit Henry Clay. Mr. Morgan was called on oftener than either of his associates to do this kind of work. He was the father of Junius S. Morgan, the eminent London banker, and grandfather of J. Pierpont Morgan, whose more than royal power in financial circles has been used effectively to purify American railway management, and to rehabilitate great properties wrecked by incompetence and fraud. Three generations have been successively represented in the directory by Joseph, Junius S. and J. Pierpont Morgan. Mrs. James Goodwin, of Hartford, was a daughter. His descendants, both those who have remained at home and those who have found elsewhere broader fields, have bestowed upon the city munificent gifts, including nearly $300,000 for a free library and art gallery.

By an amendment to the charter secured in 1839, the company was empowered to issue policies against the hazards of inland navigation. The privilege was not exercised till the autumn of 1843, when the directors authorized agents at Apalachicola, Savannah, Macon, Columbus, Mobile, New Orleans, Natchez and Louisville, to take risks on cargoes on board of steamers and pole boats, but not on the boats themselves, nor on the cargoes loaded on "that species of craft called boxes, arks or broad-horns." A policy issued October 4, 1859, at the rate of one-half per cent., on fifteen negroes, valued at $16,000, bound from Glasgow, Mo., to Carrollton, Miss., is still preserved at the home office as a curiosity of inland insurance.

Affairs had so improved that in November, 1843, the board declared a dividend of 18 per cent.—eight in cash, and ten to be indorsed on the stock-notes.

The Ætna escaped the fire of December 16, 1835, in New York city—the first in the series of great American conflagrations—which destroyed property to the value of $15,000,000, and bankrupted twenty-three out of twenty-six local insurance companies. It entered the city the following year, having for agent Augustus G. Hazard, afterwards the organizer and president of the Hazard Powder Company, of Enfield. It was not so fortunate in the fire of 1845, which swept $6,000,000 of property from the business centre of the metropolis, and cost the Ætna $115,000. When the news reached Hartford, Mr. Brace called together the directors and told them that the calamity would probably exhaust the entire resources of the company. Going to the fire-proof, he took out and laid on the table the stocks and bonds representing its investments. Little was said, each member waiting for some one else to take the initiative. At length the silence was broken by the question: "Mr. Brace, what will you do?"

"Do?" replied he. "Go to New York and pay the losses if it takes every dollar there," pointing to the packages, "and my own fortune besides."

"Good, good," responded the others. "We will stand by you with our fortunes also."

Such an increase of premium-receipts followed, that in twelve months the Ætna was as strong in cash as before. In March, 1848, a dividend of twenty dollars a share, amounting to $50,000, was indorsed on the stock-notes, and the money invested in solid securities, some of which the company still holds. Hitherto, it had been forced again and again to part with favorite investments to pay losses, but here when about to enter upon the last half of the century, the somewhat periodical distresses due to smallness of resources passed away for good. In February, 1849, the board declared a dividend of twenty per cent., applicable only to the payment of the third and last installment upon the stock notes. By this operation these were finally extinguished.

Fifty thousand dollars were added to the original capital in December, 1822. The secretary was authorized to offer the new stock at an advance of $5.00 on a share, not *pro rata* to holders of record, but "in such number of shares and to such persons as in his opinion may be most for the interest of the company."

In 1846, in conformity with a vote passed the 30th of the previous December, $50,000 were added, one-half payable in cash or its equivalent, and one-half in the customary installment notes. In July, 1849, a third increase of $50,000 was voted, to be paid in cash or indorsed notes, running not more than eighteen months. Thus the company turned the middle of the century with a fully paid capital of $300,000.

January 1, 1849, the Ætna owned bonds and stocks valued at $269,550. Thirteen months later, with $50,000 of fresh capital in the treasury, its assets amounted to $456,327.46, and its liability for losses to $141,344. In the interim it disbursed $125,000 for a single fire in St. Louis.

But the season of storms which culminated at St. Louis, and sent many competitors to the bottom, convinced the public of the inherent staunchness of the Ætna, and by the prudent enterprise of its managers, even cruel reverses to the general interests of fire insurance, were made to bring to it large accessions of business and revenue.

The Protection, the third fire insurance company organized at Hartford, failed in 1854 through the continuous unprofitableness of its marine department, aggravated by the incurable injuries received at St. Louis in 1849. It had been the pioneer in occupying the small as well as the large towns of the West, but the gains from these sources were insufficient to offset the losses incurred at sea and on our inland waters. Here was a broad gap to be filled, and the Ætna lost no time in meeting the emergency, for it opened a branch office at Cincinnati in 1853 with the firm purpose of keeping step with civilization in progressive occupancy of the West. When a few months later the Protection yielded up the ghost a material share of the business dropped as ripened fruit into the lap of its rival. Soon a thousand agents were at work west of the Alleghenies, and in the ensuing period of exemption from large fires the company rolled up wealth with a rapidity never equalled before either in the United States or elsewhere. In 1854 the capital was increased from $300,000 to $500,000, one-half contributed by shareholders and the other half by a dividend from profits. The figures remained at this point but a short time, for in 1857 they were changed to an even million. In 1859, from the profits of two years, the owners were gladdened by a second stock dividend of half a million, which was followed in 1864 by another for $750,000. Evidently the figures, $2,250,000, offended the eyes of the directors, and accordingly after enduring the sight for two short years they raised the capitalization in 1866 by a stock dividend to the rounded, symmetrical and artistic sum of $3,000,000. Ambition to make the Ætna the largest fire insurance company in the country led the stockholders in 1881 by an issue of ten thousand new shares at par for cash to enlarge the capital to four millions, where it now stands.

In 1851 the company appointed its first traveling or special agent, A. F. Willmarth, who a few months later was made assistant secretary, but soon left. The position of assistant secretary, evidently created for Mr. Willmarth, remained vacant except during the brief incumbency of Jonathan Goodwin, Jr., appointed in 1863, till 1867, when it was permanently revived on the accession of William B. Clark to the official corps.

Thomas Kimberly Brace, through whose influence and exertions mainly the Ætna was brought into existence, warned by the infirmities of age, resigned the presidency in 1857, and died June 14, 1860, in his eighty-first year. Stephen Brace (Bracey), the emigrant ancestor, came from London and settled in Hartford. His grandson, Lieutenant Jonathan, moved to Harwinton in 1733; Jonathan, Jr., born in Harwinton, November 12, 1754, graduated at Yale College in 1779, studied law, acquired a large practice in Central Vermont, but returned to Connecticut, and after residing a while in Glastonbury took up his permanent abode in Hartford in 1794. He was in public life forty-two years, less from choice than from solicitation of his fellow-citizens.

Thomas K. Brace was born October 16, 1779, graduated at Yale College in 1801, and settling in Hartford built up the wholesale grocery house of T. K. Brace & Co. He was mayor of the city, 1840-43, and in the latter year consented to run for Congress on the Whig ticket, but was beaten by Col. Thomas H. Seymour. He was nominated for a subsequent term, but declined in favor of James Dixon, who was elected. Mr. Brace belonged to the safe and trusty order of men to whom others instinctively turn for guidance.

Edwin G. Ripley succeeded Mr. Brace August 4, 1857. A New Hampshire boy, Mr. Ripley emigrated to Hartford, where he learned the details of business in the establishment of T. K. Brace & Co. Later he became partner of his uncle, Philip Ripley, in the iron trade. He was elected secretary of the Ætna in June, 1853, and vice-president a year later. He died August 26, 1862. Quiet but forceful, his words were few, direct and convincing. He was one of the first to see the need of storing up reserves wherewith to meet the heavy drains of hard times, and to open book

FORMER PRESIDENTS ÆTNA INSURANCE COMPANY.

accounts with different classes of risks with a view to learn the average cost of carrying each.

On the 10th of September following Thomas A. Alexander was elected president and held the position till his death, March 29, 1866, although, broken in health by continuous labor, he had resigned the previous October. Mr. Alexander entered the service of the Ætna as a clerk in its New York agency in March, 1843. Upon the resignation of A. G. Hazard in July, 1845, he was promoted to fill the vacancy. He moved to Hartford in November, 1853, to take the secretaryship of the company. Having nearly reached the term of three-score years and ten he died at Bergen, N. J., greatly respected and lamented.

In April, 1852, Chillicothe, O., called for $115,000, and three months later Montreal took $105,000. For the next ten years the company enjoyed remarkable immunity from large losses, considering the extent and magnitude of its business. With the turn of the tide even the $163,000 required to settle the Portland claims in July, 1866, and the $120,000 sent to Vicksburg in January, 1867, did not perceptibly interrupt the upward flow of assets.

Strangely enough the phenomenal prosperity of the company provoked internal dissensions in regard to the disposition of profits. A party among the stockholders, strong in number and influence, strenuously resisted the policy of accumulating a reinsurance fund. Any deviation from the early practice of treating a premium as fully earned the instant it reached the treasury, was denounced as a "new-fangled" notion without justification in theory or fact. They demanded a distribution of all earnings either in cash or in new shares which the recipient could convert into cash. Reserves for reinsurance were not then required by law. Warned by the practices and consequent failure of the Protection, the managers of the Ætna, long in advance of legislative action, saw the fallacy of the reasoning and the danger of the method. They urged that over and above the capital an insurance company should have a fund large enough to reinsure outstanding risks. This view is now universally enforced by law and has become a truism of the trade, but early advocacy of the doctrine raised a tempest around the officers of the Ætna. Fortunately they were supported by the dominant directors and won the fight. The decision of that controversy played a large part in giving to Hartford its pre-eminence in underwriting.

A dealer, struck by the frequency of fires among his customers, asked Mr. Ripley if the company made money on paper-mills. He could not answer the question, but like Paul on the road to Damascus, saw a bright light. Several years in advance of competitors he began to arrange statistics in regard to relative hazards, and the task has been extended to cover every kind of risk. Upon the fulness and accuracy of the record must rest the claims of underwriting to a scientific basis, including the fairness with which the burden of losses is distributed by means of a justly graduated scale of premiums.

In 1853 the general agent of the Ætna at Cincinnati prepared the first blank proof of loss. In substantially the original form it has since come into universal use.

Not content with furnishing indemnity to an ever-widening circle of patrons, the Ætna initiated the work of educating the public in art by publishing the first chromo poster in 1855. The picture represented a steamer throwing a stream of water upon a burning block. How deep in human nature lay the hitherto dormant and unconscious appetite destined to be roused by the venture into omnivorous voracity, was quickly disclosed through the abundance of aliment supplied for its gratification.

The company was the first to introduce the use of outline charts in 1857. Out of this germ grew the Sanborn maps, now an essential part of the equipment of all large offices.

As far back as September, 1819, the Ætna issued a book of instructions for the use of its agents. It classifies risks, fixing the rate for each and excluding some as non-insurable. It insists upon correct surveys as serving to expose frauds, prevent lawsuits, and secure truthfulness. Buildings and fixtures must not be estimated above their worth in cash, and any proposal for more is of itself a cause of suspicion. The rule is not to be enforced against personal property, merchandise, etc., which is liable to vary in kind and quantity. The insured is entitled to no more than the value of the property proved to have been destroyed. The correctness of the rules laid down in this little book—believed to be the oldest of the kind in the country—has never been successfully assailed, though attempts have been made through valued policy laws and other schemes for the encouragement of robbery.

In April, 1866, Lucius J. Hendee was elected president and Jotham Goodnow, secretary. November 20, 1867, William B. Clark was appointed assistant secretary.

In 1835 the company bought of William H. Imlay, for $9,570, a lot on the north side of State street, and proceeded to erect the block now containing three stores, numbered 134–42. For its office it occupied No. 134 till the completion, in 1867, of its present home in the brown-stone building on Main street.

By the Chicago fire of 1871 the Ætna lost $3,782,000. To meet the impairment the capital was reduced one-half, and immediately refilled by cash payments of $1,500,000. Thirteen months afterward the Boston fire absorbed $1,635,067 more, and the inroad was made good by a further contribution of $1,000,000 from the shareholders, making $2,500,000 furnished by them in a year to maintain the technical solvency of the company. After deducting the losses at Chicago, over $2,600,000 of assets were left in the treasury exclusive of fresh contributions.

Mr. Hendee passed away September 4, 1888, aged seventy. He was born in Andover, Conn., July 13, 1818. He assisted his uncle, Abner Hendee, in his store in Hebron, from 1836 till 1852, when he succeeded to the business. Both uncle and nephew were faithful and trusted agents of the Ætna. While living in Hebron Lucius J. took deep interest in the political controversies that led up to the war, serving as State Senator in 1856, and as State Treasurer three terms, 1858–61. July 3, 1861, he was elected secretary of the Ætna, and in April, 1866, president, in both cases succeeding Mr. Alexander. Under his administration the great reverses at Chicago and Boston were met. After paying nearly $5,500,000 to the sufferers from those two fires alone, the company came out of the ordeal stauncher and with higher credit than ever before. Sincere and upright, genial and gentle, Mr. Hendee was beloved by his associates both in office and out.

September 26, 1888, Jotham Goodnow was elected president; William B. Clark, vice-president; Captain Andrew C. Bayne, secretary; and James F. Dudley and William H. King, assistant-secretaries.

Mr. Goodnow died suddenly, November 19, 1892, at the age of seventy-one. He came from Fall River to Hartford in 1856, was bookkeeper in the Hartford Bank till 1864, when he went to Rockville as cashier of the First National Bank. Soon after he accepted the cashiership of the City Bank of New Haven, and in 1866 the secretaryship of the Ætna. His most impressive characteristic was unswerving devotion to what he believed to be right. He detested evil-doing and fraud under all forms and guises. Love of right sometimes made him appear unduly intolerant of wrong. He served in the common council, not because the position was agreeable, but from a desire to promote the public welfare. The positions he held best indicate the estimate placed by others upon his capacity.

THE ÆTNA INSURANCE COMPANY OF HARTFORD.

Erastus J. Bassett, adjuster for the Ætna since 1862, and widely known for his skill in the profession, died July 27, 1891, at the age of seventy-one. Andrew C. Bayne followed, October 12, 1893. Although born in Scotland, he entered the military service of the United States at the outbreak of the Civil War, and was wounded five times, thrice seriously. He entered the regular army in 1866, and was retired in '71. Before his call to the home office, he had served the company as special agent, with headquarters at Albany.

November 30, 1892, William B. Clark was elected president; and, December 7th, A. C. Bayne, vice-president; James F. Dudley, secretary; and William H. King and E. O. Weeks, assistant-secretaries.

The death of Captain Bayne brought further changes in the official corps. James F. Dudley became vice-president; William H. King, secretary; and E. O. Weeks and F. W. Jenness, assistant-secretaries. All these gentlemen are veterans in the service of the company. Seth King, father of William H., was enrolled in 1838, and for ten years did all the clerical work in the office. His son followed in 1862, and his grandson, F. E. King, in 1893.

President Clark was born in Hartford, June 29, 1841. His father, A. N. Clark, was manager and part-owner of the *Courant* during and after the war. The son, after serving a short time on the newspaper, in 1857 entered the office of the Phœnix Fire, of which he became secretary in 1863. In 1867 he resigned to take the assistant-secretaryship of the Ætna. On the death of Mr. Goodnow, the office of vice-president, created in 1853 for Edwin G. Ripley, and after his promotion allowed to remain vacant, except when filled for a brief interval in 1862–3 by Henry Z. Pratt, was revived for Mr. Clark. Although still in the prime of life, in term of service he is the oldest insurance official in the city, and even from early manhood has been through the country recognized as one of the most competent men in the profession. He has served as an alderman, and on the board of water commissioners, and as a director is connected with several financial and benevolent institutions of the city.

James F. Dudley, vice-president, was born in Hampden, Me., February 1, 1841. graduated at Bowdoin College, taught awhile, for several years conducted a local insurance office at Bangor, Me.; in 1874 became special agent for Pennsylvania for the North British and Mercantile Insurance Company; in 1876 took the special agency for the Ætna for the same territory, and later for New York; in 1885 returned to the North British, acting as assistant manager in New York city when recalled to the Ætna in 1888.

William H. King, secretary, both by inheritance and association, seems to be almost an integral part of the Ætna. His father was connected with the company over forty-four years. William H., born July 4, 1840, after a short term of service during the war, entered the office of the Ætna in 1862, becoming second assistant secretary in 1888, first assistant secretary in 1892, and secretary in 1893. Declining attractive offers to go elsewhere, he has remained steadfast in attachment to the institution to which his life-work has been devoted.

Egbert O. Weeks, assistant secretary, was born of New England parentage in Pennsylvania, October 28, 1847. Beginning his work in insurance with the Wyoming Company of Wilkes-Barre, Pa., he later became special agent of the Lancashire, and of the Liverpool and London and Globe. In May, 1883, he entered the service of the Ætna with office at Wilkes-Barre. In 1889 he moved to Philadelphia, taking supervision of Pennsylvania, Delaware, Maryland, West Virginia and the District of Columbia. He was one of the founders of the Underwriters' Association of the middle department, serving almost continuously upon its Executive Committee, and as president one term. He was called to the home office in December, 1892.

F. C. Bennett, of Cincinnati, is general agent of the western branch; William H. Wyman, of Omaha, of the northwestern; Boardman & Spencer, of San Francisco, of the Pacific.

January 1, 1897, the Ætna had gross assets of $11,431,184.21. After providing for all liabilities, actual and contingent, its capital of $4,000,000 is reinforced by a net surplus of $3,849,988.05.

THE PROTECTION INSURANCE COMPANY.

Of all the early insurance companies of Connecticut, none began under such favorable conditions as the Protection, of Hartford. It was incorporated in 1825. The capital was to be not less than $150,000, with the privilege of increase at pleasure to any further sum not exceeding $500,000. Ten per cent. was required at the time of subscription, and the remaining ninety per cent. within thirty days was to be paid in notes secured by mortgage on real estate, or by approved indorsements and payable thirty days after demand. Each stockholder was entitled to one vote for every share up to one hundred, and at that limit his voting power ceased. The corporation was authorized to make both marine and fire insurance. By an amendment passed the next year the clause authorizing marine insurance was extended to the hazards of inland navigation. All stockholders in the Hartford Insurance Company had the special privilege of taking as many shares in the Protection as they held in the Hartford, provided the privilege was exercised at the opening of the books in June, 1825. The old company was forbidden to make any further insurance from the time when its successor went into operation.

It will be seen that in direct line of descent the Protection inherited the traditions and good will of the first generation of underwriters in Hartford. Back in 1795, Jeremiah Wadsworth, John Caldwell, Sanford and Wadsworth, Elias Shipman and John Morgan formed a copartnership "for the purpose of underwriting on vessels, stock, merchandise, etc., by the firm of the Hartford and New Haven Insurance Company." The year before some of the same parties, and probably all of them except Shipman, issued policies as the Hartford Fire Insurance Company. The combination did not last long. Having acquired an appetite for the business, Shipman organized a corporation under his own management at New Haven in 1797. The partnership of Sanford and Wadsworth was dissolved in January, 1798, and soon afterwards Sanford moved from the city. Beginning in 1799 with Ezekiel Williams as manager, John Caldwell and John Morgan, in association with others issued hundreds of marine policies, till, in 1803-4, the business was taken up by the Hartford Insurance Company, which, in turn, was merged in the Protection in 1825, the last secretary of the Hartford becoming its first president.

Books for subscription were opened June 13, 1825, at the office of the Hartford Insurance Company. The shares were quickly taken, and on the 22d of the same month the stockholders elected the following board of directors: Solomon Porter, Jeremiah Brown, William W. Ellsworth, Merick W. Chapin, James B. Hosmer, Nathan Morgan, Henry Hudson, Roderick Terry, Edward Watkinson, James H. Wells and Charles S. Phelps. On the same day the board elected William Wolcott Ellsworth president, and Thomas Clap Perkins, secretary.

William W., son of Chief Justice Oliver Ellsworth, was born November 10, 1791; graduated at Yale College in 1810; studied law; was elected three times to Congress, but resigned before the close of his third term; beginning in 1838, was four times elected governor of Connecticut, and later judge of the Supreme Court and of the Supreme Court of Errors, where he served till retired by law, at the age of seventy. He died January 15, 1868.

Thomas Clap Perkins, secretary till 1837, was born at Hartford, July 30, 1798; graduated at Yale College in 1818, standing second in his class, and practiced law in Hartford, where he rose to such eminence that he was employed on one side or the other of nearly every important case that came before the courts. He declined an appointment to the bench of the Supreme Court of the state, preferring private practice to judicial honors. He died October 11, 1870.

Fortunate in lineage and its first executive officers, the company was equally fortunate in meeting the man who built up its agency system at the West. Ephraim Robins, a merchant, well educated, tall and attractive in person, elegant in manners, systematic, conscientious, powerful with the pen and generally versatile in accomplishments, at the age of forty-one saw his property vanish in the cyclone of 1825. Amid widespread ruin his eye fell upon a notice in a Hartford newspaper of the formation of the Protection Insurance Company. Having lost by the perils of inland navigation, his vision, further sharpened by mental pain, saw at once the utility and beneficence of the scheme. With his own experience as a text to preach from he felt that he had a call to go forth into the world to save others from the ruin that had overtaken himself.

Son of Ephraim Robins, Sr., of Hartford, Conn., in 1797, at the age of thirteen, he entered the employ of Harrison, Wilby & Co., of Boston, importers of English queensware. Later he established a business in New York city, which he transferred to Cincinnati in 1820.

When the possibilities of the West as a field for insurance flashed upon him he hurried to Hartford, on the way working out the details of his scheme. Seeking Mr. Perkins he presented the advantages certain, as he argued, to accrue to the company from the establishment of a branch agency at Cincinnati, in the heart of a new and growing region, with the power of appointment, removal and supervision in the hands of a competent general manager.

Both the secretary and the directors were convinced. Mr. Robins was accordingly made general agent and put in charge of the western department. Returning to Cincinnati September 1, 1825, he rented for an office the vacant banking house of the Miami Exporting Company. Selecting John P. Foote, a well and widely known resident, he sent him out through Ohio and other states to select in important towns the best available men for agents. These carefully instructed and trained, within a few years, numbered two hundred and fifty, and from their general character gave a high standing to the company.

The office in Cincinnati, furnished with the leading newspapers of the day and warmed in winter by hickory logs burning in a broad open fire-place, was also a sort of club room for the local chiefs of the Whig Party. It was frequented by General William H. Harrison, Bellamy Storer, Judge Burnet, Isaac G. Burnet, Daniel Drake, Alphonso Taft, Nicholas Longworth and many others who met to talk over public affairs.

In a business way the office became a normal school in which fire insurance in progressive and systematized form was taught to employees and agents.

Mr. Robins died in 1846, having in the twenty years taken three millions in premiums, of which ten per cent. on an average went to the company in profits.

Meanwhile changes occurred in the management. Mr. Ellsworth retired in 1836. Subsequent presidents were David F. Robinson, 1836–9; Hezekiah King, 1839–40; Eliphalet Averill, 1840–1; Daniel W. Clark, 1841–54. Secretaries were Thomas C. Perkins, 1826–37; James L. Goodwin, 1837–40; William Conner, 1840–54.

As the Protection was the pioneer in organizing the agency system on a comprehensive scale, so it was the first to employ a special agent for the exclusive work of travel, supervision and adjustment. In this capacity Mark Howard entered the service of the company in 1846. Railways were then few. Mr. Howard traveled east and west, north and south, from Maine to Louisiana, mostly by canal, stage and steamboat.

The three Hartford companies then in existence suffered bitterly by the St. Louis fire of 1849. The losses of the Protection exceeded $130,000, and coming as a climax in a season of woeful disasters led the management to debate the question of giving up the fight for life without further struggle. Mr. Howard denounced the proposal and volunteered to go in person to settle the claims, although cholera was raging in the city. He found the streets deserted. Thousands had fled and scores were dying daily. Undaunted he walked into the pestilence. Adjusting and paying in full all claims against his own company and the Ætna, he added much to the general confidence already felt in Hartford underwriters.

Correct theories of fire insurance, so far as a line of effort so uncertain and variable can claim a scientific basis, have been developed slowly and enforced by countless failures. During the first half of the century companies lived from hand to mouth. When affairs ran cheerfully, current profits were scattered in dividends. Premiums at the instant of receipt were assumed to be fully earned. A few years of continuous prosperity always saw the birth of a lot of weaklings that lived just long enough to give a bad name to the business. To meet competition rates dropped to levels that barely yielded living returns under the most favorable conditions. No preparations were made for impending evils. Yet panics, followed by stagnation and an enormous increase of the "moral hazard," succeed periods of hope and boom as wave chases wave. Institutions had not then learned the imperative need of piling up reserves in good times to meet the drains that bad times will surely bring. Consequently the history of fire insurance during the first six decades of the century is mostly a history of wreck and ruin. Those that survived the stage of ignorance pulled through by virtue of the personal faith and courage of managers.

W. B. Robins succeeded his father in 1846, continuing in charge of the department till the company suspended. Before the close four hundred agents reported to him. During the eight years he took two millions in premiums, with a fair average of profit. As St. Louis reported directly to the home office the adverse balance arising from the fire of 1849 was not charged against him.

Measured by the standard of local contemporaries the Protection exceeded the average in mistakes. Exhaustive dividends were declared as a matter of course whenever there was an apparent surplus. The management clung to losing lines. They insured whaling ships after the industry was clearly doomed. They sought the coasting trade despite continuous disaster.

A reported interview between President Clark and Mark Howard exposes the distress of the treasury.

"Have you made money on distilleries?" asked Mr. Howard. "No," replied Mr. Clark, "we are far behind on them."

"Have you made money on paper-mills?" "No. On paper-mills the balance is heavily against us."

"How is it with wholesale drug stores?" "Oh, on them we have lost right along."

"Well, Mr. President, are you still insuring distilleries, paper-mills and wholesale drug stores?" "Yes, we are. *We must have the premiums.*"

Mr. Howard saw the drift of affairs too clearly not to forecast the inevitable.

Loyal to the company, he at first remonstrated against the continuance of ruinous methods, and when his warnings passed unheeded quietly withdrew.

In 1845 the capital was increased to $200,000, and in 1849 to the nominal sum of $300,000, but grounded on the figures $291,800, and there held fast. During the last years one-half was represented by stock-notes and one-half by cash. Final statements to state authorities were strained to make as fair a showing as a certain vague traditional regard for truth would permit. At last, on the 7th of September, 1854, amid heart-burnings and reproaches, aggravated by calls to pay the stock-notes lodged in banks as security for loans, the suspension of the company was formally announced.

The collapse of the Protection, by directing attention to both the strong and the weak features of its policy, taught lessons that were not lost. Other Hartford companies profited, not only by taking on a large share of its business, but by accessions from its disbanding ranks of bright, energetic, well-trained agents. In the fall of 1853, J. B. Bennett abandoned the sinking ship, and under contract with the Ætna took full charge of its western business, with headquarters in Cincinnati. Young, magnetic, and overflowing with mental resources, he pushed the work with unprecedented vigor. In the next seventeen years the branch, through a thousand subordinate agents, handled seventeen millions of premiums, of which over three and one-half millions accrued to the home office in profits. F. C. Bennett, brother of J. B., and also a graduate of the Protection, has, since 1871, had charge of the business of the Ætna in the Central West. Another graduate, H. M. Magill, a versatile and accomplished underwriter, has long been general agent of the Phœnix, of Hartford, managing from Cincinnati, its department made up of southern and western states. Mark Howard organized the Merchants', and after the Chicago fire, the National. The list might be extended to include notices of W. H. Wyman, J. W. G. Simrall, Samuel E. Mack, J. C. Mitchell, J. C. Davies, and others of high repute in the upbuilding of insurance interests in America.

CHAPTER IV.

INSURANCE IN CONNECTICUT—Continued.

SECURITY INSURANCE COMPANY (NEW HAVEN).

THIS company was chartered in 1841 as the Mutual Security, with the view of doing business on both the stock and mutual plans. The latter feature was abandoned in 1843. For a long time the paid capital remained $50,000. In 1872 it was increased to $100,000, and in '75 to $200,000. It fortunately escaped the great fires of Chicago and Boston. From 1841 till 1872 the Security did mainly an ocean marine business, confining its fire risks to New Haven and vicinity. It then made a radical change of policy, reducing its marine risks to a small volume, and extending the fire business till it now has about one thousand agencies, covering nearly all of the Eastern and Western states. Having paid in losses $6,425,107, and dividends averaging over 8 per cent. annually for fifty-six years, it had, January 1, 1897, capital, $200,000; assets, $755,666; and net surplus, $123,257.

Presidents in succession have been Joseph N. Clark, Theron Towner, Justus Harrison, William Lewis, Willis Bristol, John S. Griffing, Charles Peterson and Charles S. Leete.

H. Mason succeeded Philip S. Galpin as secretary and manager in 1871, and has held the position since.

The company has been a favorite in New Haven, having from time to time in its directorate many of her most prominent business men.

THE CITY FIRE (HARTFORD).

The company that came at last to be known as the "City Fire," of Hartford, was long in getting a start and a name. Chartered in 1847 as the Connecticut Mutual Fire, with the view of applying the mutual principle to the insurance of property in cities, it soon learned that this was not the kind of protection which merchants and town residents desired. By an amendment secured in 1851, the corporation was authorized to raise a guaranty capital of not less than $50,000, nor over $100,000. It began at the full limit. Ten per cent. was paid in cash, and 90 per cent. secured by stock-notes. In 1853 the name was changed to the Hartford City Fire Insurance Company, but as the "Old Hartford" protested vigorously against such enroachment upon its vested rights, the word Hartford was dropped the following year.

The company did not organize for work prior to 1853. Leverett Brainard, who has since in many ways been actively identified with the industries and institutions of Hartford, moved thither to take the secretaryship, Ralph Gillett becoming president. A careful policy was followed by uniform prosperity till, with few mistakes to regret, it was suddenly destroyed by the Chicago fire of 1871. The capital was increased to $150,000 in 1856, and two years later to $250,000, where it afterwards remained. For 1870 its premiums reached $346,560. On the 1st of January, 1871, it had gross assets of $554,287, and a net surplus of $69,163.

Mr. Brainard resigned January 1, 1858, to enter the partnership of Case, Lockwood & Co., which has long been one of the leading printing and book-binding houses in New England. He was succeeded by C. C. Waite, who left in 1862, and is better known in hotel than in insurance circles. William E. Baker was secretary 1862-4, and George W. Lester, 1864-71.

Presidents were Ralph Gillett, H. D. Condict, C. B. Bowers, W. E. Baker and C. T. Webster.

THE BRIDGEPORT FIRE AND MARINE INSURANCE COMPANY.

This company was incorporated in 1850, but did not organize until 1854. It began with a capital of $100,000, ten per cent. paid in cash and ninety per cent. in the customary stock-notes. No shareholder was permitted to vote on over sixty shares at annual or special meetings. Besides the ordinary fire risks it was authorized to insure against perils of the seas and of inland navigation. In 1856 the capital was increased to $300,000, and in 1857 the name was changed to the Bridgeport Insurance Company. At the close of 1857 the company claimed to have assets valued at $367,000, with liabilities present and prospective of $70,000. At this juncture the comptroller of New York refused to renew its license to do business in that state, not on account of the slight technical impairment of the capital, but because its securities were of doubtful character. On the assurance of the officers that its affairs were in sound condition, the comptroller finally consented to recall his adverse decision on the understanding that an agent of his own selection should be permitted to make a full examination of its affairs. Early in February he appointed Samuel B. Ruggles.

Nathaniel Green, acting president of the company, on the 17th of March submitted to Mr. Ruggles his sworn statement that Joseph Richardson, an original director of the company and still a director, had in 1857 given to the company bonds of sound corporations amounting to $98,000, in exchange for $26,000 of its own stock, and $150,000 in the stock of the Hudson County Paint Manufacturing Company, and that the transfer was absolute and unconditional. To the affidavit Richardson appended his certificate setting forth that the statements were correct.

Mr. Ruggles left Bridgeport apparently satisfied. A few days later Richardson, trembling for the safety of his securities, turned up in Albany for the purpose of denying the truth contained in the affidavit and certificate. He alleged that he could not read writing and had been deceived by Green. With this new light the commissioner reported, April 20, 1858, that the company did not possess the amount of capital, $150,000, required by the statute, unimpaired to the extent of twenty-five per cent., and that in his opinion its affairs were in an emphatically unsound condition. From the evidence submitted by Mr. Ruggles the comptroller was convinced that nearly all the assets of the company of much real value were not in fact the property of the institution. He accordingly revoked the certificate given conditionally a few months before.

In 1857 the company was excluded from Massachusetts, the commissioners explicitly cautioning the public against making any further engagements with it.

Driven from two important states, and discredited elsewhere, it went into insolvency May 27, 1858. Philo C. Calhoun was appointed trustee.

Presidents were P. M. Thorp, H. W. Chatfield, Thomas E. Courteney and Nathaniel Green. Secretaries: J. H. Washburn and Timothy Hough.

THE CITY INSURANCE COMPANY OF NEW HAVEN

was incorporated in 1850, with a capital of $100,000. Before proceeding to business, the subscribers were required to pay in ten per cent., to deposit securities for forty per cent., and to give personal security for the balance. At first the company was empowered to issue policies against loss by fire and inland navigation, but in 1855 marine risks of every kind were expressly prohibited. Wells Southworth was the first president, and Henry L. Cannon, secretary. For a number of years they made money, but about the time the war ended the tide had turned and the managers reasoned that their interests would be best served by retiring from the field. Having decided on this course, they closed the affairs of the company, paying in full all claims and 140 per cent. on the cash investment to stockholders.

For nearly ten years the charter lay dormant. In 1874 it was purchased by James M. Mason, E. J. Mason and H. Mason, and the company was revived under the presidency of James M. Mason. The subscribers paid in the capital, as required by the original act, $50,000 in cash and in pledges of securities, and $50,000 in stock-notes. It confined its operations to the home field, and, after a trial of two years, again retired from business without loss of principal to the parties who risked their money to repeat the experiment.

THE CONNECTICUT FIRE INSURANCE COMPANY (HARTFORD).

This institution was organized in June, 1850, with a capital of $200,000, of which ten per cent. was paid in cash, and ninety per cent. in stock-notes. On the 29th of the month the stockholders elected as directors Joseph Trumbull, Benjamin W. Greene, James B. Hosmer, David F. Robinson, Julius Catlin, Harvey Seymour, Edwin D. Morgan, James Dixon, Edmund G. Howe, Tertius Wadsworth, Timothy

M. Allen, John L. Bunce and Edson Fessenden. The same day Benjamin W. Greene was elected president, and, July 4th, John B. Eldredge was appointed secretary.

By a policy deliberately adopted and consistently pursued, the management restricted the operations of the company to non-hazardous risks, subordinating ambition for large receipts to desire for safety. For similar reasons, agencies were planted with caution, and chiefly in towns with well-equipped fire departments. By the end of June, 1855, total dividends in cash amounted to $10.50 per share, while $15.00 per share had been endorsed on the stock-notes. At this time the directors voted to raise the cash capital to $100,000 by calling for an instalment of twenty-five per cent., payable on or before July 28th. Thenceforward it became the settled policy of the company to extinguish the stock-notes by the application of net earnings, which were devoted exclusively to that end. On the 16th day of July, 1859, the task was accomplished, and the shares became fully paid, sixty-five per cent. having been contributed from profits. At the end of the year assets in round numbers amounted to $231,000; liabilities, including re-insurance reserve, to $32,600; gross premiums for 1859, to $78,000; and gross income, to $90,000.

At the end of the first decade the company had made enough on a small but carefully conducted business, to virtually pay ninety per cent. in instalments on the stock. It had sixty-three agents, a surplus of about $4,000, and a premium income of less than $80,000.

In October, 1865, Benjamin W. Greene resigned, and Mr. Eldredge was elected president. Mr. Greene had been an active director in the Protection, and had earnestly but vainly protested against the policy which ended in its destruction. He was born in 1801 at Uxbridge, Mass. At the age of fourteen he moved to Windsor, Vt., and thence to Hartford, where he had a saddle and harness factory on Pratt street, with James B. Hosmer for a silent partner. Warned by the fate of the Protection, he studiously shunned its errors. Of his conservatism it was facetiously said that if he insured a load of pig iron in a ten-acre lot, he would lie awake nights fearing it would take fire from spontaneous combustion. He died soon after his resignation.

Martin Bennett, who, fresh from college, entered the service of the company as general agent and adjuster in August, 1860, was elected secretary, October 23, 1865. Two years later, in December, 1867, Charles R. Burt was made assistant secretary.

In 1871, after twenty years of continuous prosperity, the company was brought to the brink of destruction by the Chicago fire. Its losses far exceeded its assets. Payment in full was out of the question. Two courses only lay before it, either to go into bankruptcy and give up all, including good will and a well-established business, or to compromise with the policy-holders in that city. Amid the confusion and jar of conflicting interests a committee of seven had been selected to represent the sufferers. They were men of such character and standing that their decision was accepted as final. To them were presented the proposals of the companies that had anything to offer between complete surrender and payment in full. M. Bennett, Jr., its secretary, made a determined effort to secure a settlement for the Connecticut and succeeded. The facts were a matter of record. Official returns showed assets and liabilities on the first of January. Nine months of ordinary business could not greatly change the figures. So far as the local situation was concerned, the committee had a list of the policies, and of the loss under each. If the company went on, it must carry all the risks on its books, and pay in full subsequent losses. Two apparent elements of uncertainty entered into the question: the effect on prices of the large outpour of securities from companies forced into insolvency, and the fatality of existing risks.

CONNECTICUT FIRE INSURANCE COMPANY.

INSURANCE IN CONNECTICUT.

Mr. Bennett believed that the company could pay thirty-five per cent. and go on. The committee, after a careful examination, concluded that the proposal was fair to all parties and accordingly endorsed it. Policy-holders accepted the decision as equitable, the money was paid, and thus the Connecticut was enabled to save both its charter and its plant.

During the next few months general conditions greatly favored the insurance interest. The absorption of securities by newly-formed companies, and by the fresh capital put into those that survived, held up prices beyond expectation and thus added to the salvage. On account of higher rates and diminished facilities the insured carried an increased percentage of risks, and hence used greater care in guarding against fire. For a time premiums rose above and losses fell below the average. From both causes the Connecticut derived unforeseen benefits from its settlement.

Underwriters were taught by the hard lesson, that the day of small companies had gone to return no more, and accordingly, after the removal of the *débris*, the Connecticut reorganized with a fully paid capital of $500,000. A year later, the Boston conflagration called for $132,580, but within a few weeks the premium income more than repaired the loss. January 28, 1873, Mr. Eldredge resigned the presidency. The same day Martin Bennett was elected to fill the vacancy, and Charles R. Burt was made secretary. On the 28th of the following June, James H. Brewster was elected assistant secretary.

Mr. Eldredge remained an active member of the directory till his death in June, 1882. In early life he was connected with the press, having edited the *Connecticut Sentinel*, in New London, and the *Springfield Whig*. In 1835 he established in Hartford the *Patriot and Democrat*, which was later merged in the *State Eagle* and under that name expired in 1842. He was appointed marshal for the state in 1840, and after retiring from office engaged in the boot and shoe trade. During life he gave to various charities with a liberal hand and left a large estate.

In November, 1876, the company voted to increase the capital to $1,000,000. An extra dividend of $20 per share was voted in December to apply on the new stock, and the remaining eighty per cent. was paid in cash. On January 1, 1877, its statement showed a net surplus of over eighteen per cent. on the enlarged capital.

After twenty years of continuous and faithful service Mr. Bennett resigned the presidency October 11, 1880, to take the general management for the United States of the Lion and Scottish Union. Mr. Brewster also resigned the same day. On the 16th J. D. Browne was elected president. February 1, 1881, L. W. Clark, late president of the Meriden Insurance Company, was elected assistant secretary.

Born at Plainfield, Conn., August 26, 1836, at the age of twenty-one Mr. Browne moved to Minneapolis, where with youthful ardor he engaged in business. He was selected to take the electoral vote of Minnesota to Washington in the fall of 1860. During the administration of President Lincoln he was chief clerk in the office of the surveyor-general of public lands at St. Paul. In 1865 Mr. Browne returned to the East, becoming general agent and adjuster for the Hartford Fire Insurance Company in 1867. Three years later he was elected secretary of the company, and held the position till called to the presidency of the Connecticut.

The home office of the Connecticut, completed in 1885, is one of the most notable structures in the city, combining beauty and utility to a degree rarely attained. The location at the corner of Prospect and Grove streets, within a block of City Hall Square on the north, and Main street on the west, is central, quiet, and in every way desirable. It is built of brick, brown stone and terra cotta, after the

Byzantine style of architecture, fifty-eight by one hundred and twenty feet, two stories in height, with an hexagonal tower of three stories, every part of which is utilized. The general office, forty by forty-five, with ceiling twenty feet high, lighted and ventilated on three sides, is not only admirably adapted to the present requirements of the business, but will answer equally well, when its magnitude shall have expanded four or five fold. Directly in the rear of this is placed the vault, twenty feet square on the floor, and twenty-two feet high, so arranged with galleries and light stair-cases as to afford a maximum of available and easily accessible space. Underneath is a second vault of equal length and breadth, which will ultimately be needed for storage purposes. The vestibule, the rooms of the directors and president, and the large clerical room, all finished in hard woods, are models of quiet elegance. The company occupy the entire building, and all the supplies of a large insurance company can be prepared for shipment within its walls. Built upon land advantageously purchased at a time when the cost of material and labor was low, the enterprise has proved profitable in giving every desirable convenience at the equivalent of a small rental.

Since the date of reorganization in 1871, the history of the Connecticut is the record of uninterrupted progress, which, though bare of dramatic incidents, is of a kind to bring contentment to patrons and solid satisfaction to shareholders. The books show gross assets of $1,483,480.02, $2,347,692.99 and $3,300,017.88 on the 1st of January for the years 1880, 1890 and 1897 respectively; and at the same dates a net surplus of $209,662.34, $522,254.96 and $668,331.50, and for the years preceding the above dates premiums of $399,348.07, $1,069,531,04 and $1,724,851.53.

For twelve years prior to January 1, 1897, all dividends were paid exclusively out of income from assets, and a balance of over $325,000 from this source alone was added to the general fund for the protection of policy-holders.

Charles R. Burt, secretary, has been identified with the company from boyhood, having, after an active connection with the local agency for several years, entered the office as clerk in 1865, at the age of twenty. In December, 1867, he was made assistant secretary, and in January, 1873, secretary. Though still in the prime of manhood, he is a patriarch among local underwriters, very few surviving who were active in the business when he joined the ranks.

L. Walter Clark, born in Cornwall, Conn., entered the insurance field in 1865, as special agent for the Home of New Haven. Shortly before the Chicago fire of 1871 he took the vice-presidency of the Enterprise of Philadelphia, which went down through losses incurred by that calamity. After a brief term as special agent with the Springfield Fire and Marine, he accepted the presidency of the Meriden, but resigned in 1881 to enter the Connecticut.

Abram Williams, a man of mature judgment, who had been at the head of the western department from the time of its formation, died at Chicago in January, 1897.

Robert Dickson manages the Pacific department, from San Francisco. The business of the Atlantic and Gulf states, inclusive of Ohio, is managed from the home office.

THE PHŒNIX FIRE INSURANCE COMPANY (HARTFORD).

In 1853 the late Henry Kellogg was bookkeeper of the Connecticut Mutual Life. On the death of its Boston agent, he applied for the vacant place, believing that he had fairly earned promotion. To his chagrin, the situation was given to another, whose record for the company was yet to be made. By way of explanation, he was told that he could not be spared from the position he then held. Sensitive, ambitious, and conscious of capacity, he concluded that if his services were so valuable to others, the time had come to make them more valuable to himself. On a survey of the field, he felt that a new fire insurance company in Hartford could be made a success—possibly a striking success. Friends caught his enthusiasm, and promised their aid. Thus encouraged, he selected the corporators of the Phœnix, drew the charter, and saw it safely through the legislature.

By the terms of the charter the capital was placed at not less than $100,000, with the privilege of increase to any sum not exceeding $300,000. Books were opened by the corporators June 21, 1854, and stock to the amount of $100,000, the limit agreed upon, was subscribed at once. The same day the subscribers elected the following directors: Chester Adams, Erastus Smith, Nathan M. Waterman, John A. Butler, William Faxon, Samuel B. Beresford, Elisha T. Smith, James C. Walkley, Lyman Stockbridge, Edwin T. Pease, Joseph Merriman, Nathaniel H. Morgan and Ralph Cheney.

Before adjournment the stockholders voted to increase the capital to $200,000. One week later, June 28th, the books were reopened and the additional shares eagerly taken. There were then one hundred and three separate subscriptions.

Mr. Kellogg took the secretaryship with the view of making the development of the enterprise the work of his life. As a matter of convenience Nathaniel H. Morgan consented to act as president temporarily till a man possessing the requisite technical knowledge and other needed qualities could be found. Mr. Morgan, the fourteenth of seventeen children, was born June 8, 1805, in Salem, then a part of Colchester, whence the family moved to Lebanon in 1814. Having settled in Hartford, as merchant, captain in the coasting trade, a trusted servant of the town in different offices, a student of genealogy and local history, he filled a long life with a great variety of useful work. Through his efforts the Halls of Record were built at the corner of Pearl and Trumbull streets.

At the time of subscription $10 per share were paid in cash, and soon after the remaining ninety per cent. was secured by stock-notes. At the end of the first year, or more exactly June 27, 1855, Simeon L. Loomis was elected president. From the Ætna he had gone to New York city to organize the Home Insurance Company, but gladly accepted the invitation to return to Hartford. Messrs. Loomis and Kellogg, working in complete harmony, mapped out the policy which the company has since pursued without deviation or faltering. On the failure of the Protection in September, 1854, the Phœnix secured some of its best men at the West and a fair share of its business. Strengthened by the profits of the first year the president and secretary determined not to confine operations to our cities or older settlements, but to occupy as fully as possible the long fringes of our frontiers. The Phœnix took the lead in planting agencies up and down the Pacific coast. Till then merchants and others even hundreds of miles distant were compelled to procure insurance through their correspondents in San Francisco. The brothers R. H. and H. M. Magill were specially active in pre-empting territory on both sides of the Rocky Mountains.

Unlike its elder brothers, the Hartford and Ætna, the Phœnix did not pass through a prolonged period of infancy, but by a few stalwart bounds leaped into the strength and responsibilities of manhood. On the 15th of June, 1855, a dividend of $20,000 was endorsed on the stock-notes, and six months later a second of equal amount was similarly applied.

But the exigencies of the situation did not permit the delay required to pay the stock-notes out of profits even at the rate of ten per cent. semi-annually. Numerous failures among fire insurance companies gave rise in various quarters to more stringent legislation, and several of the states passed laws permitting only those whose capitals were fully paid in cash to do business within their borders. Accordingly, on the 25th of February, 1856, the directors voted to call in the remaining seventy per cent., and by the 28th of March the money was all in the treasury.

Having obtained legislative permission, the capital was increased to $400,000, in June, 1859, one-half contributed from profits and one-half called in cash. It was again increased in 1864 to $600,000 by an issue of new shares at par.

Mr. Loomis passed away August 23, 1863, beloved by his associates and highly respected by the community. He was a skillful underwriter, versed in the intricacies of the profession, cautious yet bold, careful in forming plans, but vigorous in pushing them. He was an admirable correspondent, and if occasion required could discipline an agent so gently and dexterously that the victim often took the lesson with pleasure as well as profit.

August 27, 1863, Mr. Kellogg was elected president and William B. Clark secretary. In 1867 Mr. Clark went to the Ætna, and was succeeded, December 1st, by D. W. C. Skilton. The same day George H. Burdick was elected assistant secretary. Asa W. Jillson was made vice-president in April, 1864.

In 1871 the Phœnix had accumulated over $1,900,000 of solid assets, which enabled it to pay in full at Chicago losses, under two hundred and eighty policies, amounting to $937,219.23. At the request of President Kellogg, Marshall Jewell, a large stockholder and a director, happening to be in Detroit at the time, hurried thither to look after the interests of the company. A feeling of despair pervaded the city. Thousands of homeless people were encamped on the outskirts, without money, without hope, and almost without clothing and food. In a calamity so unlooked for and so overwhelming, and hence so far removed from the hazards contemplated in the business of underwriting, the sufferers believed their policies to be nearly or quite worthless. Press dispatches, laden with painful rumors, deepened the despondency.

On the morning of October 13th Governor Jewell stood on the banks of the river overlooking three thousand flame-swept acres from which a mighty city had vanished. Around was a surging, sullen, half-crazed, despairing crowd, which seemed to feel that even the foundations of the earth were crumbling with the destruction of their fortunes. Aware that the Phœnix had both the means and the will to meet every claim, Governor Jewell, not less prompt to act than quick to see, lost no time in making known the purpose of the company. Mounted on a dry-goods box with a smile in itself a benediction, he announced that the Phœnix would pay all losses in full, and offered to draw his check on the spot for any claim approved by H. M. Magill, general agent of the western department. Shortly policy No. 10,752, for $10,000, was presented by Isaac C. Day, when, as director, Mr. Jewell drew on the company for the full amount, less interest for two months—the term allowed for payment.

Though the remarks of Governor Jewell contained no suggestion of oratorical display, no other speech ever delivered in the Lake City compressed into a few words so much cheer and helpfulness, or changed so quickly and effectively the temper of the people. The draft bears date October 13, 1871. Immediately the *Tribune* dropped from its window a hugh placard, announcing that the Phœnix, of Hartford, had begun to pay its losses in full. As the news spread from one to another, the multitude cheered, and cried, and laughed by turns. From overburdened hearts the vapors began to roll away, as even then clouds of smoke were drifting from the scene, and, as if her baptismal name had been selected in anticipation of the event, both company and city rose from the ashes stronger than before.

THE PHOENIX INSURANCE COMPANY.

The 8th and 9th of October, 1871, are also memorable in insurance annals on account of the simultaneous forest fires in Michigan and Wisconsin, which drew from the coffers of the Phœnix $50,176.73, making the total losses for the two days $987,395.96, or one hundred and sixty-four per cent. on its capital stock. After meeting without delay these extraordinary demands, the company had nearly a million of assets left, but to repair the reserves required by law, the capital was reduced December 1, one-half, to $300,000, and immediately restored through subscription of stockholders. Although the Boston fire, November 10, 1872, called for $385,956.18 more, the burden was met without assistance from the shareholders.

January 1, 1876, the company had gross assets of over $1,900,000 and a net surplus of $385,000. Six months later the capital was raised to a million, an extra dividend of fifteen per cent., or $90,000, having been applied toward payment of the new issue. In 1881 it was made two millions by cash subscriptions.

The company was organized in a rear room of the office of Wm. H. Imlay, on the second floor of "Union Hall," afterwards demolished to make place for the building of the Connecticut Mutual Life. For a few months the same room was used for an office, till in December quarters were taken at No. 275 Main street, on the second floor. In December, 1862, the office was moved to "Hill's Block," No. 333 Main street. To secure the facilities required for a rapidly growing business the company decided to build, and in November, 1873, moved into the ample quarters which it owns as well as occupies.

From enfeebled health Mr. Jillson resigned in August, 1888, and died April 21, 1893. Born in Boston in April, 1823, he spent most of his early life in Willimantic, Conn., the Jillson family having been largely the pioneers in building up the manufactures of that thriving borough. For fifteen years from 1847 he was agent for the Connecticut Mutual Life, and for two years agent of the Hartford Fire.

For the same cause Mr. Kellogg also practically retired from all active participation in the affairs of the company in August, 1888, but remained honorary president till his death, January 21, 1891. He was born of sea-faring stock at East Hartford, September 9, 1820. In early life he was clerk on the Vanderbilt steamboats. In 1849 he entered the office of the Connecticut Mutual Life. From 1854 his energies were devoted to the company which he founded and ardently loved. Active in organizing the National Board of Underwriters, he always sacredly observed every express and implied obligation which membership involved. In the conduct of the Phœnix there was never the slightest discrepancy between profession and practice. When Mr. Kellogg subscribed to an agreement it was with the intention of keeping it both in letter and in spirit. Independent himself, he liked independence in others, and was pleased to have his own views combatted by an intelligent adversary. Acting the part of a public-spirited citizen he was connected with various enterprises, having held among other places the presidency of the Hartford Trust Company.

D. W. C. Skilton was elected vice-president and acting president August 1, 1888, and retained the secretaryship till September 11th, when George H. Burdick was promoted to that position. Born at Plymouth Hollow, Conn., January 11, 1839, Mr. Skilton came to Hartford in 1855, and after a probation of six years in the dry-goods trade entered the office of the Hartford Fire, October 24, 1861. In August, 1862, he enlisted, was appointed second lieutenant, and at the expiration of the term of service was mustered out as first lieutenant, when he returned to his former place which had been retained for him. Of the National Board of Underwriters, Mr. Skilton was three years secretary; seven, vice-president; and three, president.

Mr. Skilton has always been a firm believer in the efficacy of organized effort and hence has cheerfully given much time and thought to the upbuilding of the National association. He entered it so early and has maintained the connection so closely that nearly every representative whom in those days he was wont to meet has passed away, and present members, though no younger than himself, regard him as a veteran. He was selected by the New York City Association of Underwriters to represent the Connecticut companies on the committee which prepared the standard policy for fire insurance. By many states this form has been adopted and made obligatory.

J. H. Mitchell was elected second vice-president September 11, 1888, and vice-president February 2, 1891; Charles E. Galacar, assistant secretary March 10, 1888, and second vice-president February 2, 1891; John B. Knox, assistant secretary October 1, 1891.

Up to January 1, 1897, the Phœnix had received for premiums $65,137,672.81 and paid in losses $39,739,174.81, or by decades:

PREMIUMS.		LOSSES PAID.
First year,	$39,053.74	$12,745.29
Tenth year,	463,419.28	285,614.06
Twentieth year,	1,512,710.02	760,255.95
Thirtieth year,	2,038,470.52	1,290,204.81
Fortieth year,	3,507,580.82	2,206,976.70

Assets at the end of the first, tenth, twentieth, thirtieth and fortieth years were $212,896.61, $925,902.97, $1,852,894.12, $4,316,957.91, $5,588,058.07 respectively, and January 1, 1897, $5,320,265.42, with a net surplus, $730,511,57.

George Harrison Burdick, born at Granville, N. Y., December 17, 1841, after a partial course at college, at the age of nineteen entered the office of the Phœnix, where, as clerk, assistant secretary and secretary, he spent the remaining years of his life. He died suddenly at Heidelberg, Germany, July 2, 1896, having left home about a month before.

Mr. Galacar resigned in the fall of 1896 to take the vice-presidency of the Springfield Fire and Marine. Officers, January 1, 1897, were D. W. C. Skilton, president; J. H. Mitchell, vice-president; Edward Milligan, secretary, and John B. Knox, assistant secretary.

Capt. J. H. Mitchell was born in Venango county, Penna.; served in the late war; shared in several battles, including Chancellorsville and Gettysburg; was afterwards a merchant; entered the insurance business about a quarter of a century ago, first as local and later as special agent of the Niagara; joined the special corps of the Phœnix in 1884, and came to the home office, as above described.

Edward Milligan, born at Haddonfield, N. J., June 1, 1862, began work while a boy as clerk in the local insurance agency of Kremer & Durban, of Philadelphia; was later surveyor of the Ætna, of Hartford, in the same city; in November, 1888, became special of the Phœnix for the middle department, and was elected secretary in September, 1896.

John B. Knox, born in Hartford, April 30, 1857, after one year in the local insurance agency of W. F. Rice & Co., entered the office of the Phœnix September 15, 1873, and having been clerk, adjuster and special agent for Western New England, was elected assistant secretary September 24, 1891.

The Phœnix has three departments. H. M. Magill conducts the Western from Cincinnati; A. E. Magill the Pacific, from San Francisco; and Smith & Tately, the Canadian from Montreal.

THE STATE FIRE INSURANCE COMPANY OF NEW HAVEN.

The above company was incorporated in 1855. The capital stock was fixed at not less than $100,000, with the privilege of increase to any sum not exceeding $200,000. Subscribers were required to pay an installment of ten per cent. at the time of subscribing, and within sixty days thereafter to secure the payment of the remaining ninety per cent. either by mortgages of real estate or by endorsed promissory notes, payable within ninety days after demand, by order of the directors. The board was also empowered, at discretion, to require payment in cash on the ninety per cent. thus secured.

For about two years the charter was unused. In the summer of 1857 the company came before the public by opening an office in New Haven. Nothing in its records throws any light upon the time, place, or manner of organization. It started with a nominal capital of $150,000, all held by New York parties. This was made up of mortgages, of a character to be described hereafter, to the extent of $102,500, and of endorsed promissory notes amounting to $47,500. Thus far not a dollar in cash had found its way into the treasury of the concern, yet certificates for full paid stock were issued to the manipulators.

In November, 1857, the directors voted to increase the capital to $200,000, and appointed a committee to attend to the matter, which reported on the 8th of February following, that the additional capital was all received and in possession of the company.

Meanwhile, at a meeting of the directors held January 5, 1858, a committee, of which Benjamin Noyes was the active spirit, was appointed to dispose of fresh stock to the extent of $47,500, to take the place of a like amount embraced in the original output, and represented in the assets by promissory notes. Through some understanding with the New York parties, their certificates were returned in exchange for their personal obligations. Noyes presented the prospects of the enterprise in such a rosy light that sundry persons were induced to come into it in a somewhat vague and shadowy way. Under the proposed arrangement new subscribers were to draw double income—dividends on the insurance stock issued to them and also on the collaterals of which they still retained ownership, though apparently turning them into the treasury in payment of their subscriptions.

On the 1st of April, 1858, a single share of stock each was issued without consideration, to eleven citizens of New Haven to qualify them to act as directors. Most of the gentlemen singled out for the distinction were not notified by the officers, and perhaps some first heard of it when threatened with suits. Early in 1858 the company advertised for business in the local papers and in printed circulars.

Having at length started upon its short but stormy career the company applied for a license to do business in Massachusetts, which was granted April 9, 1860.

Its financial statement was presented to the commissioners by Mr. Augustus O. Brewster, the first incumbent of the newly created office, and a relative of a leading director. On a capital of $200,000 the gross assets were set down at $250,795, and the net surplus at $8,081. The list of securities looked irreproachable, including among the items bank and railway stocks and bonds exceeding $75,000, issued by institutions of well-known strength. Loans on mortgages of real estate reached $138,100, and were said by Mr. Brewster to be on city property in New Haven and New York. With childlike confidence in human nature he had, without due inquiry, accepted as true the representations made by Benjamin Noyes, both a director and a kinsman. The statement was sworn to before a notary by John B.

Robertson, president, and G. Farnham Stevens, secretary. Of the twenty directors, seventeen resided in New Haven, several of whom were obviously selected, not to share in knowlege or conduct of the business, but to impart to it by reflected light an air of respectability.

The statement for November 1, 1860, seemed to indicate marked improvement during the interval in the condition of the company, gross assets having increased to $278,411.92, and the net surplus to $24,313.26.

In June, 1861, Secretary Stevens suddenly disappeared from New Haven. The news did not reach the office of the insurance commissioner in Boston, through the loudness of the local outcry, but came several weeks later in letters from claimants, unable to collect losses under policies of the company. Mr. Elizur Wright, then commissioner for Massachusetts, lost no time in hurrying to the home office in New Haven. He was there told by the managing directors that heavy losses in New York had absorbed the most available of the assets. He learned, too, that the $138,100 of mortgages did not rest on city property, but on vast tracts of wild lands in northern New York. Collaterals deposited to secure notes of stockholders to the amount of $30,000 were said to have disappeared with the lost secretary. With regard to other securities, Mr. Wright was assured that they were kept in bank and were all right. Promise was also made that the notes given by shareholders should be collected at once, and that the company would soon settle in full all claims in Massachusetts.

Hoodwinked, as Mr. Brewster had been before him, Mr. Wright proceeded on to New York city with his suspicions completely allayed. On the return trip, as it was a warm summer day, he decided to take the afternoon boat to New Haven. Here, by mere accident, he happened to overhear the conversation of a little group of fellow-passengers seated near. The line of talk ran along the shady side of things, and they seemed particularly amused at the success of a "job" put up to tide the "State Fire" over a crisis in its affairs. A prophetic perception of the true situation dawned upon him. Visiting the local corporations whose stocks the insurance company had professed to own, he learned that at least $50,000 of the list which had been included in the sworn statements as assets never belonged to the company, having been hired for show occasions, and to swear by. Four per cent., or $2,000 a year, were paid to the lenders. In most cases certificates were made directly to the company to heighten the deception. The banks were told that the shares were wanted as a "temporary guaranty," or "preferred stock"—phrases not unpleasant to the ear, and helping to hide the enormity of the cheat behind a veil of mystery.

Detesting fraud and falsehood in every form, Mr. Wright was specially incensed at the deception practiced upon him as commissioner. He not only denounced the officers as rascals—a position which few were inclined to dispute—but also jumped to the conclusion that all the directors must have known about the crookedness, and hence were little less guilty. Accordingly he laid the facts before Hon. E. K. Foster, state's attorney for the county, asking that the officers be prosecuted criminally. He also employed counsel to enter civil suits against the directors for the losses and unearned premiums due to citizens of Massachusetts.

On the 15th of November, 1861, Mr. Foster reported that he was not altogether satisfied that criminal proceedings could be instituted successfully, though there was enough "to justify action," should it be thought advisable to proceed at any time. A few weeks later he wrote to the commissioner thus:

NEW HAVEN, December 9, 1861.

DEAR SIR,—An examination of our law by no means satisfies me that I can successfully prosecute the officers of the State Fire Insurance Company; and, indeed, it determines my mind quite otherwise except as to the secretary, Farnham Stevens, who has gone to parts unknown. The reason for this conclusion I will state to you the first time I meet you.

Respectfully yours,
E. K. FOSTER.

For several years the commissioner continued to press the several suits. He placed the case against the directors in the hands of Tilton E. Doolittle, Esq., and the following letters will indicate the drift of affairs:

OFFICE OF INSURANCE COMMISSIONERS, BOSTON, January 13, 1863.
TILTON E. DOOLITTLE, ESQ., New Haven, Conn.:

DEAR SIR,—Will you be so good as to inform me by letter what progress has been made in the suit I authorized you to bring against the directors of the State Fire Insurance Company, and what obstacles, if any, stand in its way? I am as desirous as ever to know whether there is law in Connecticut to hold those gentlemen to the oaths, words and figures by which they got business in Massachusetts, and the suit shall not fail through any failure on my part.

Very respectfully yours,
ELIZUR WRIGHT.

In his reply, dated January 16, Mr. Doolittle wrote that the case would be tried at the first jury term of court, either in March or October, and that no obstacle stood in the way.

Nearly two years later, however, having submitted terms for the compromise of a Massachusetts case, which were not accepted, December 28, 1864, he wrote as follows:

"The most weighty reason in my mind, if not the most obvious one, why we should not get a verdict is the high standing and political influence of the defendants. While I do not doubt the law, I have but little faith that a jury will ever agree upon a verdict against these defendants. You may say that they ought to, and all that sort of thing, but the mischief of it is, that the jury have the power and they won't."

Mr. Doolittle's conclusions were certainly correct. Several of the directors were men of very high character. Their names were used without their consent, unless consent is implied from failure to repudiate the connection by public notice. They knew nothing of the affairs of the concern, nor would the managers under any circumstances have disclosed to them its guilty secrets. If the contention of the commissioner prevailed, that directors of companies should be held pecuniarily responsible for the correctness of statements sworn to by executive officers, in a case like this a person for simply neglecting to read advertisements in newspapers, or for failure to inspect the literature put forth to win business, might find himself exposed to heavy penalties.

Benjamin Noyes was elected secretary August 20, 1861. On the 2nd of November following, the company made a voluntary assignment for the benefit of creditors, and Frederick W. Northrop was subsequently appointed trustee in insolvency. As a test case he brought suit against Cornelius S. Bushnell, a director, for the balance due on a stock-note, and obtained judgment for the amount. It was shown that Bushnell was elected without his knowledge or consent. It was not shown that he had taken any part in the direction of the company. The court held that as he had not promptly resigned the position and repudiated the contract into which he had been entrapped, but permitted his name to remain for two years before the public as one of the directors, and had thus contributed to win for the company public trust and confidence, he could not set up as a defense against creditors a previous compromise and settlement with Benjamin Noyes, although the latter had been authorized by the board to settle claims and execute instruments of release. Mr. Bushnell, after the decision, paid the judgment in full. Others, not directors, were then sued on their stock-notes, and paid more or less to get out of the scrape.

The mortgages on lands in northern New York, that constituted over one-half of the capital, proved worse than worthless, for when sold in foreclosure the proceeds were insufficient to pay the costs.

When the appraisers of the insolvent estate returned to the court in January, 1862, a sworn inventory of assets, the $278,411.92 of November 1, 1860, had dwindled to a beggarly $83.49.

The document is a curiosity in the literature of insurance. Falstaff's half-penny worth of bread to an "intolerable deal of sack" would pass for solid diet when compared with the assumption of several millions of risks on assets of $83.49 invested as shown.

"*To the Probate Court for the District of New Haven.*

Estate of State Fire Insurance Company of New Haven in said district insolvent debtor.

The subscribers appointed appraisers on said estate, having been legally sworn, have appraised all of said estate, both real and personal, according to its value, and have assisted in making a true and perfect inventory thereof as follows, viz.:

6 arm chairs $6.00, 1 spittoon .25, 1 pail .05, 1 pair of tongs .10	$ 6.40
1 wash stand .50, 1 basket .25, 1 card rack .50	1.25
1 envelope rack .62, one twine box .13, 1 Post Office box .25	1.00
Two tin boxes $1.00, wetting machine .25, one small press .50	1.75
Old paper $1.00, blank books $2.00, one stove and pipe $10.00	13.00
One map of United States $2.50, one map of Connecticut $2.00	4.50
One map of New Haven $2.50, one office desk and fixtures $10	12.50
One long counter and standing desk $25.00, pens .25	25.25
Lot of writing paper $1.00, one picture, basin and tumblers .37	1.37
Duster .05, postage scales .75, gas fixtures and shades $8.75	9.55
Lot of curtains and fixtures $2.00, three portfolios .87	2.87
Paper clasps .50, lot of envelopes $1.00, one ink stand $1.00	2.50
One broom .05, step ladder $1.50	1.55
	$83.49

WILLIS BRISTOL, } Appraisers.
ALFRED DAGGETT, }

F. W. NORTHROP, Trustee.

Received, sworn to and accepted January 17, 1862.

LUZON B. MORRIS,
Judge."

The thought of the projectors is easily divined. If small companies elsewhere, with a small percentage of the nominal capital paid in cash, had attained conspicuous success, why could not their venture, without any cash whatever, meet with similar good fortune? Fraud and perjury certainly did not stand in the way. Had luck been different, the weakness of the beginnings might never have been suspected by the public. But losses in excess of premiums killed the experiment in the bud.

CHAPTER V.

INSURANCE IN CONNECTICUT—Continued.

THE MERCHANTS' AND THE NATIONAL (HARTFORD).

ALTHOUGH distinct, the above corporations are so closely identified in the line of succession, that an account of both can best be given in a continuous story. The Merchants' was chartered in 1857, with a capital to be fixed at pleasure between the extreme limits of $200,000 and $500,000.

In the act the old formula was pursued of requiring a cash payment of 10 per cent., and permitting the other 90 per cent. to be secured by stock notes. A book for subscriptions was opened July 2, 1857. Such was the eagerness of the public to take a hand in the venture, that five thousand five hundred and sixteen shares ($551,600) were at once applied for. Two days later the corporators met and scaled the subscriptions to two thousand shares ($200,000). On the 7th the following board of directors was elected: Mark Howard, Samuel Woodruff, James Bolter, Ebenezer Roberts, Guy R. Phelps, Timothy Sheldon, James P. Foster, W. H. D. Callender, Sidney A. White, Charles T. Hillyer, Elijah H. Owen, Homer Blanchard, Richard D. Hubbard, Matthew M. Merriman and William L. Collins. The same day Mark Howard was elected president, and E. Thomas Lobdell secretary.

Mr. Howard, traveling agent of the Protection till he gave up the position after striving earnestly but in vain to reform its methods, had been a close observer of the mistakes that led to its downfall. He adopted and pursued a widely different policy. While energy was put forth in planting agencies and soliciting business, care was everywhere taken to confine risks to the less hazardous classes of property. Mr. Howard impressed upon his associates the theory that better results in the long run were likely to follow from carefully-selected lines than from a great volume of premiums.

The Merchants' was the first company in Connecticut to repudiate the custom of building on a foundation of stock notes—a privilege long embraced in every charter granted by the Legislature. Within five weeks after organization, the directors voted a cash installment of 40 per cent. Similar calls followed at convenient intervals till the shares were fully paid.

For a long period the record tells a story of uniform prosperity enlivened by no dramatic incident. Directors almost ceased to attend meetings. It was even hard to get a quorum to vote dividends, which were paid at the rate of 5, 6 and 8 per cent. semi-annually, till July, 1869, when the rate was raised to 10, or 20 per cent. a year.

Mr. Lobdell died in November, 1870, and was succeeded, January 23, 1871, by James Nichols, general agent of the company.

At the annual meeting in July, 1871, assets were reported to be $580,270.71. Shares brought $250. Viewed in the light of experience, the position of the Merchants' was supposed to be impregnable.

In October came the Chicago fire, with losses of $1,075,643—over five times the amount of its capital, and nearly half a million in excess of its entire assets. Payment in full was clearly impossible. The Merchants' held a number of mortgages on propetry in the burned district, which not only lessened available resources, but increased the difficulty of effecting settlements. Probably the best thing for all parties would have been a compromise. All but a small majority of the sufferers were entirely willing to accept the terms offered by the company—terms which would have justified the managers in calling in fresh capital, and thus saving it from destruction. A few held off, hoping by obstinacy to secure larger dividends than their more considerate neighbors. Mr. Howard, with the strong support of Mr. Nichols, took the ground that all should be treated precisely alike. Both had promised parties who signed the compromise that, whether it succeeded or failed, they should receive as much as any other creditor. With them, rising above every consideration of expediency, a promise was sacred and inviolable. Thwarted in their efforts to secure unanimous consent to the terms of settlement by the attitude of a mere handful of policy-holders, the directors, without a dissenting voice, voted to distribute the entire assets of the company *pro rata* among creditors. Everything down to the smallest article of office furniture was sold, and the proceeds thus applied. Those who had already signed full releases received a small additional dividend. But a company of stainless record and brilliant promise was forced out of existence.

An act had been passed in 1869 incorporating the National Fire Insurance Company, but at the time of the Chicago fire no steps had been taken toward making use of the franchise. It was now decided to continue the business of the Merchants' through an entirely new company organized under this charter. Accordingly, books were opened November 14, 1871, and when closed November 20th, six thousand and eighty shares had been applied for. General William B. Franklin, James G. Batterson and Richard D. Hubbard, corporators, named in the charter to receive subscriptions, scaled the allotments down to a total of two thousand.

At the first meeting of stockholders, held November 27th, it was voted to increase the capital from $200,000 to $500,000 and the following board of directors was elected, *viz.:* Mark Howard, E. H. Owen, Richard D. Hubbard, J. P. Foster, E. N. Welch, James Bolter, Ebenezer Roberts, William B. Franklin, Homer Blanchard, Wareham Griswold, J. F. Judd, D. F. Seymour, Frank Cheney, Harrison B. Freeman, William S. Pierson, Timothy Sheldon and William H. Lee.

The same day Mark Howard was elected president and James Nichols secretary. Our familiar acquaintance, the stock note, played no part in the organization of the National, the entire capital having been paid in cash.

During the first eleven months of business the National increased its assets to $623,000. Then followed the Boston fire with losses of $161,000. To meet the emergency the capital was reduced to $350,000, and at once restored to the former figures by subscriptions of the shareholders. From that day on its success and growth have been uninterrupted. In 1878 the contribution for Boston was in part returned in a stock dividend of $100,000 from net profits, and in July, 1881, the capital was further increased to $1,000,000 by cash subscriptions.

President Howard died January 24, 1887. He was born in Loose, county of Kent, England, May 27, 1817, and came to America with his father and one brother in 1831. The three proceeded to Ann Arbor in the territory of Michigan, where four weeks later the father died. When seventeen years old Mark established a Whig paper at Ann Arbor. While still a minor he was appointed clerk of one of the branches of the legislature and held the place for two terms. As local agent for the Protection Insurance Company he exhibited such admirable qualities that in 1846 he was made its special agent with broad powers of supervision and appointment. It is claimed that he was the first person in the United States to be employed exclusively in the

MARK HOWARD,
President 1871-87

JAMES NICHOLS,
President.

E. G. RICHARDS,
Vice President and Secretary.

B. R. STILLMAN,
Assistant Secretary.

NATIONAL FIRE INSURANCE COMPANY OF HARTFORD.

field. He now made his residence in Hartford, but traveled up and down our frontiers from the lakes to the Gulf of Mexico by stage and steamer. In the story of the Protection we have told of his visit to St. Louis in the height of the cholera epidemic of 1849, and of his heroism in facing perils from which old residents fled in panic. That one act brought untold credit and business to Hartford insurance interests.

The instruction book which he prepared for the Protection about 1848 marks an epoch in the literature of the science. Speaking of it Charles B. Whiting, president of the Orient, says:—

"It was much the most elaborate of any before issued and is the basis for all our modern books. Here appear for the first time the definitions of insurance terms. It treats of the 'Moral Hazard,' the 'Local and Internal Hazard,' and gives full instruction for the inspection of risks. Here also appear standards for the rating of a large number of risks ; forms of policy for a great many hazards, and for the first time the three-quarter value clause. This book was the greatest contribution to insurance literature that had been issued up to that time, and very far in advance of any of the others. The definitions are those in vogue to-day, and there has been but little if any improvement on the forms there put forth. Subsequent books are but an enlargement of this. The text for them all is found within its covers."

He was appointed by President Lincoln first internal revenue collector for Connecticut. He was so fair that appeals were seldom taken from his rulings, several of which became incorporated in the system.

Mr. Howard was a man of lofty ideals. The inspiration of high aims lifted him out of the atmosphere of the common place. Wherever the battle for principle raged hardest he was sure to be found taking blows if need be, but giving sturdy ones in return.

James Nichols, long and intimately associated with Mr. Howard, was elected president February 9, 1887. He was born December 25, 1830, at Weston, Conn. Admitted to the bar in 1854, he settled a year or two later in Hartford, having been made assistant clerk of the Superior Court of the county. In 1861, when the district embraced seven towns, he was elected judge of probate, a position for which he was peculiarly fitted. Attracted by business connections into the field of insurance, he became adjuster and special agent of the Merchants' in 1867, and three years later its secretary. Anxious as the executive officers were to save the charter of the company after the Chicago fire, both agreed that the end must be reached if at all by treating the strong and the weak precisely alike. Hints from rich claimants eager for an undue share fell upon deaf ears. The result has been told. Mr. Howard was so exhausted by the vexations and labors in which both equally shared that he fell ill and went abroad to find rest. He was still in Europe at the time of the Boston fire, in October, 1872. Mr. Nichols was then in charge, and the gap made in the assets was filled under his direction. Differing in temperaments, Mr. Howard and his chosen lieutenants were alike in inflexible adherence to do what they believed to be right.

In April, 1887, Ellis G. Richards, of Boston, an experienced underwriter, was elected secretary. In March, 1891, Benjamin R. Stillman was elected assistant secretary.

In January, 1888, the National reinsured the Washington Fire and Marine Insurance Company of Boston on all their business throughout the United States, except in Connecticut, New York, Pennsylvania, New Jersey, Delaware, and Maryland ; established a western department at Chicago, and reorganized and enlarged the Pacific department, with headquarters at San Francisco. The transaction added to the company a large amount of good business, guarantying a large and permanent increase of premium receipts.

In the fall of 1893 at a cost of nearly $200,000 the company completed its handsome home office upon the corner of Pearl and Lewis streets. It has a frontage of seventy-one with a depth of one hundred and thirty-four feet, and comprises a main building, forty-nine by seventy-one feet, three stories high, and a large wing in the rear, flanked on the Lewis street side by a two-story annex. The building is of fireproof construction with floors of iron beams and tile arches and with stairways and roof of iron.

During the life of President Howard the growth of the National was slow. His successor, supported by able assistants, has pursued a much more aggressive policy with eminently satisfactory results. Net premium receipts increased from $521,960 in 1886, to $2,254,240 in 1896, with an average loss ratio for the period of 52.4; the reinsurance reserve from $341,677 to $1,806,990; the gross assets from $1,958,506 to $4,120,260. During 1896 net surplus increased $324,382 to $1,037,580. Meanwhile annual dividends have never fallen below ten per cent., and have always been paid exclusively out of income from assets.

Ellis Gray Richards, vice-president and secretary, born at Worcester, Mass., December 16, 1848, left school for business at the age of seventeen, and at twenty-one was head bookkeeper for a large iron manufacturing establishment. The concern was so disabled by the panic of 1873, that the next year he took a clerkship in the Boston office of the Commercial Union Assurance Company. Within a few months he was made secretary and surveyor of the Worcester County Board of Underwriters, and in May, 1877, special agent of the Royal and the Pennsylvania for service in New England. In May, 1881, he accepted a similar position in the same field with enlarged responsibilities from the Queen Insurance Company, taking an active part two years later in organizing the New England Insurance Exchange. In the changes that followed the death of president Howard, he accepted the secretaryship of the National in April, 1887, and was elected vice-president in December, 1896.

Benjamin Rhodes Stillman, assistant secretary, born at Adams, N. Y., March 31, 1852, after preparing for Hamilton College, changed his plans and entered the office of Mollison & Hastings, merchants, millers and insurance agents, where soon his time was wholly devoted to the last-named branch. Later he served at the home office of the Watertown Fire and the Sun, till appointed general agent of the Springfield Fire and Marine in 1884, with which he remained six years, resigning in 1890 to take the secretaryship of the Safety Car Heating and Lighting Company of New York City. He came to the National as assistant secretary in 1891.

Fred. S. James supervises the western department from Chicago, and George D. Dornin the Pacific, from San Francisco.

THE CHARTER OAK FIRE AND MARINE INSURANCE COMPANY.

The Charter Oak Fire and Marine Insurance Company, of Hartford, was organized with a capital of $300,000, July 16, 1856. Ralph Gillett was elected president and Joseph H. Sprague, secretary. During the war the capital was in a state of chronic impairment. In August, 1866, the commissioner of New York revoked its certificate to do business in that state because the impairment exceeded twenty per cent. To restore technical solvency the capital was reduced to $150,000. At the time of its destruction by the Chicago fire its surplus was nominal. Presidents were Ralph Gillett, B. Hudson, *pro tem*, and Joseph H. Sprague; secretaries, Joseph H. Sprague, Julius M Sexton, James Goodwin and George Nevers.

THE HOME INSURANCE COMPANY OF NEW HAVEN

Was organized in 1859 on a capital of $150,000, which was increased in February, 1860, to $200,000. D. R. Satterlee was elected president and Charles Wilson secretary. For the first two years it did both a fire and marine business, but after January 15, 1862, risks were confined to fire and inland navigation. Progress was slow during the war. At the beginning of 1862 its statement showed an impairment of over $44,000. The capital was increased to $500,000 in April, 1864, and in January, 1866, to $1,000,000, of which $350,000 were contributed in cash and $150,000 in a stock dividend. Losses were so heavy during the year that the directors laid an assessment of fifteen per cent., thus replacing the scrip with cash. During the twelve months the price of the shares fell from $180 to $100. Although the impairment continued the company paid dividends at the rate of about ten per cent. per annum from the start till near the end. With almost a thousand agents in the field it pushed for business with zeal untempered by discretion.

An official examination of the Home in June, 1870, showed that at least one-half of the capital was extinguished. It was now reduced to $500,000, and important changes were made in the management. But old wounds were severe, its investments in bad shape, and heavy losses continued. Early the next year it went into liquidation, and General S. E. Merwin was appointed trustee. The wreck proved unexpectedly disastrous, the stockholders getting nothing and the creditors very little. Payment of unjustifiable dividends had caused the shares to be sought as an investment, so that the failure caused much local distress.

Benjamin Noyes, first insurance commissioner of Connecticut, whose experience as dominant director of the State Fire, and as manager of a life company, that under a succession of names went from bad to worse till death closed its career, gave him good opportunities to study from the inside the effects of abnormal methods, in his last report wrote thus of the Home. Wrath that such things should occur at his own door puts a twist into the words through which his feelings find utterance.

"There never was a more reckless business conceived of than may be made out of fire insurance, and when we think of the case of the 'Home' at our own door, we blush for its management, while we strongly endorse the integrity of its stockholders and directors, not that the latter did wisely, or that they were influenced by good counsel as manager, for the result shows they were made to believe by an officer of the company that unearned premiums were profits realized, and that borrowing and returning was an every-day affair, especially, when after receipts seemingly justified the return.

"The rocks which dashed the 'Home,' of New Haven in pieces are all within the soundings we have been taking for the fraternity in former reports, and the only difference which marks the case of this company is its rapidity. After they had doubled their capital twice, doubled their agencies and quadrupled their risks on many classes of property, the business became too large to control, and the losses followed too rapidly to make them known to the directors; as a matter of course confusion and uncertainty soon involved the company in such a dense cloud that the directors, in a state of alarm, ended the matter, as they supposed, by placing the property in the hands of a trustee, to be closed up, for the benefit of the creditors, with no prospect of saving much, if anything, for the stockholders."

THE NORTH AMERICAN FIRE INSURANCE COMPANY OF HARTFORD.

This company was organized in 1857, on a capital of $300,000, of which the charter required ten per cent. to be paid in cash, while allowing the remaining ninety per cent. to rest on stock notes. However, as one state after another fell into line in refusing longer to recognize the stock note as an asset, it soon vanished. Except in 1862, the company paid dividends without interruption, and for the last three years before its downfall at Chicago, at the rate of twelve per cent. per annum. In fact, the company was so depleted by dividends that it seldom had a surplus. Presidents were: James G. Bolles, 1857; A. F. Hastings, 1860; James G. Bolles, 1866; W. C. Hastings, 1868. Secretaries: J. A. Wallace, 1857; W. C. Hastings, 1860; J. B. Pierce, 1868.

THE NEW ENGLAND FIRE AND MARINE INSURANCE COMPANY OF HARTFORD.

This company, with a capital of $200,000, was organized in 1858. Nathan M. Waterman was elected president, and George D. Jewett, secretary. In 1863 Mr. Jewett became president and Robert A. Johnson, secretary. From the start the company struggled against adverse conditions and wound up in 1866.

THE NORWALK MARINE AND FIRE INSURANCE COMPANY.

This company was chartered in 1858, and began business in 1860, on a paid capital of $50,000. About six years ago a controlling interest in the stock was bought by the London and Lancashire Insurance Company of Liverpool, England, and the organization has since been utilized in the conduct of its American business. The capital was subsequently increased to $200,000.

THE THAMES FIRE INSURANCE COMPANY OF NORWICH.

This company was organized in 1859. It began with a capital of $113,700, which was increased in 1864 to $200,000. It went out of business in 1866, and having settled all claims, paid back to the stockholders about fifty per cent. of the face value of the shares. Amos W. Prentice was president. Secretaries were: O. P. Rice, 1859; B. B. Whittemore, 1864.

THE UNION FIRE INSURANCE COMPANY OF HARTFORD.

This company was formed in 1859, but soon after the beginning of the war retired from the field and returned the capital to the shareholders. Presidents were: J. W. Danforth and Ralph Gillett.

THE PUTNAM FIRE INSURANCE COMPANY OF HARTFORD.

This company was organized September 1, 1864, on a capital of $300,000. Caleb B. Bowers was elected president, Daniel Buck, secretary, and in October William N. Bowers was added to the official corps as vice-president. After a hot fight the Bowers *regime* was overthrown at the annual election in June, 1865, when Samuel Woodruff, of Woodruff & Beach, boilermakers and machinists—a firm of national reputation during the war—was made president. That residence in Hartford presumptively qualified a person to run an insurance company had become a current superstition. First and last the delusion cost investors and other victims of misplaced confidence a great deal of money. From the start the venture ran behind, and though the pace now and then slackened, the drift was never long reversed. The secretary had no taste for the economies which successful companies in their early days have found indispensable. The president had been willingly lured into a variety of outside schemes. Promoters looked to him for cash. Meanwhile war-contracts had dried up. He borrowed large sums from the company which it was inconvenient to pay. A small over-issue of stock, due to carelessness, as his friends claimed, added to the confusion. Mr. Buck was succeeded by S. G. Parsons in 1868. The next year Mr. Woodruff was forced to retire. In his valedictory he attributed the misfortunes of the enterprise to the mismanagement of the first secretary.

George M. Welch followed as *ad interim* president from January 3rd till August 18, 1870, when Robert E. Day was elected. On probing its wounds the capital was found to be impaired over thirty-three per cent. It was now reduced to $300,000, and then raised by cash payments to $400,000. While the new management was striving to correct past errors the company was destroyed by the great Chicago fire, its losses amounting to $1,206,000.

THE QUINNIPIAC INSURANCE COMPANY OF NEW HAVEN,

Chartered in 1869, was organized with a capital of $100,000. J. D. Dewell was elected president, and George S. Lester secretary. In 1871 the company voluntarily retired, paying in full all claims and returning its capital to shareholders.

ORIENT INSURANCE COMPANY (HARTFORD).

Although the charter of the Orient was granted by the legislature of Connecticut in May, 1867, the company did not organize until November 23, 1871, being the lineal successor of the City Fire Insurance Company, which, with most of its contemporaries was blotted out of existence in the holocaust at Chicago. By the terms of the charter, a capital of $2,000,000 was authorized with the privilege of doing business on a minimum of $500,000. In view of the enormous drafts upon the resources of Hartford required to pay the losses at Chicago, the corporators thought best to begin with half a million, and to increase as the growth of business might demand.

The first directors were David Gallup, Newton Case, George M. Bartholomew, Charles T. Webster, William Boardman, Daniel Phillips, Augustus S. Jerome, Fred R. Foster, John W. Danforth, Selden C. Preston, James G. Batterson, Thomas T. Fisher, Joseph S. Woodruff, Leverett Brainard, Charles J. Cole, William H. Bulkeley, Knight D. Cheney, George S. Lincoln, Samuel F. Jones, James Campbell and George M. Pullman. The first officers were, Charles T. Webster, president; Selden C. Preston, vice president, and George W. Lester, secretary; these gentlemen having held similar positions in the City Fire, whose agency system the Orient proceeded to adopt.

January 1, 1872, the first policies were written, and a handsome business was assured from the outset. Ten months later came the Boston fire, which took $164,000 from the Orient, a heavy blow to befall a small company at the beginning of its career. However, it met every obligation by sight drafts, paying all losses in full.

To preserve technical solvency the capital was now reduced to $350,000. In January, 1875, an extra dividend of $50,000 in cash was declared and simultaneously turned back into the treasury so as to raise the capital to $400,000. The process was repeated in January, 1876, and in January, 1877, when out of earnings the capital was fully restored to its original figures. Those were good days for insurance interests, for the ruin of many companies by the Chicago and Boston fires stopped for a time destructive competition.

S. C. Preston succeeded Mr. Webster in May, 1874, and held the place till 1883. In 1881 the capital was raised by cash subscriptions to $1,000,000. John W. Brooks, a banker of Torrington, who had just completed a term of three years as insurance commissioner of Connecticut, held the presidency from 1883 till May, 1886, when he was followed by Charles B. Whiting.

Mr. Whiting was born of New England parentage at Greenbush, N. Y., September 3, 1828. After passing, both at the east and the west, through rather more than the usual variety of experiences that befall adventurous young men, he returned from the banks of the Mississippi to New York city in 1866, and permanently entered the field of insurance. From October, of that year, till May, 1870, he was secretary of the National Board of Fire Underwriters. Thence he faithfully served the

Home of New York city for ten years, till forced by broken health to seek rest. After recovery and a brief connection with the Springfield Fire and Marine, he came to Hartford in October, 1881, as secretary of the Hartford, and held the place till elected president of the Orient. Mr. Whiting is also a racy and entertaining writer. He has delivered a number of addresses. One, essentially historical, delivered at Niagara Falls, June 9, 1885, has been of great service in the preparation of these papers.

Like mercury in a thermometer the prosperity of insurance interests rises in good times and drops (often to zero) in seasons of adversity. The panic of April, 1893, with its long sequence of failures and disorder, so increased the loss ratio from fires that in the height of the trouble veteran underwriters stood aghast at sight of the ruins. To add to the strain, the assets of companies fell heavily in market value to that extent diminishing their resources. At the time of the outbreak the net surplus of the Orient was too small to carry the company through without impairment. Hence, in December, 1893, the stockholders voted to reduce the capital to $500,000.

January 1, 1897, gross assets amounted to $2,215,470.20, and net surplus to $562,165.37, the last item having increased $243,769.54 since January 1, 1894. These wide and rapid fluctuations illustrate the vagaries of fire insurance. Statistics cease to guide when the moral hazard breaks loose.

Secretaries have been George W. Lester, 1872-February, 1886; George B. Bodwell, February, 1886-June, 1888; James U. Taintor, June 1, 1888-. Assistant secretaries, George B. Bodwell, October, 1885; Howard W. Cook, June 1, 1888.

James U. Taintor, secretary, was born October 23, 1844, in Pomfret Conn., whence the family moved to Colchester in 1848; graduated at Yale College in 1866; was assistant clerk of the Connecticut House of Representatives in 1866, clerk in 1867, and clerk of the Senate in 1868; for a short time in 1869 belonged to an insurance firm in Meriden; in July of the same year became a special agent of the Phœnix Fire, of Hartford; and in June, 1888, secretary of the Orient.

Howard W. Cook, born in Hartford August 19, 1858, left the high school in his junior year to enter the Orient, where, having served faithfully and intelligently through lower grades, he was made assistant secretary in 1888.

B. W. French manages the western department from Chicago; Trezevant & Cochran, the southwestern from Dallas, Texas; and W. J. Callingham the Pacific from San Francisco.

THE MERIDEN INSURANCE COMPANY,

Incorporated in 1868, was organized early in 1872, with a capital of $200,000. Jedediah Wilcox was elected president, and E. B. Cowles, secretary. A few months later the Boston fire drew $36,000 from its assets. While supervising the settlement of claims in that city, the vice-president, L. W. Clark, just about filled the gap with fresh premiums. In 1878 the capital was increased to $300,000, but it was again reduced to $200,000 in December, 1881, when its business outside of New England was reinsured in the German-American and Niagara, of New York. In January, 1892, the company reinsured its risks and retired altogether, not from necessity, but because the stockholders saw that the advantages held by powerful rivals would ultimately force small concerns out of existence.

In round numbers, during twenty years, the company took $2,488,000 in premiums, paid $1,500,000 in losses, and $280,000 in dividends.

L. W. Clark was president from 1874 to 1881, when he became assistant secretary of the Connecticut, and was succeeded by A. Chamberlin. E. B. Cowles continued secretary throughout. He then became assistant manager for New England of the Royal Insurance Company, with headquarters at Boston.

THE ATLAS INSURANCE COMPANY,

Successor of the Charter Oak, was chartered in 1872, and began business in July, 1873, on a capital of $200,000. In August, 1877, the management ceased taking new business, but carried existing risks till they ran off. In June, 1879, the stockholders voted to reduce the capital to $100,000 and resume business. An examination in November, 1881, disclosed an impairment of over twenty-five per cent. in the capital, when the commissioner successfully petitioned the court to restrain the company from the further prosecution of business. Joseph H. Sprague was president, and Edward B. Huntington and George S. Merritt, secretaries.

MANAGEMENT OF FOREIGN COMPANIES.

In 1880 the Scottish Union and National Insurance Company, of Edinburgh, and the Lion Fire, of London, having decided to enter the United States, sent committees hither to select a general manager. After examining the field they tendered the place, entirely without solicitation on his part, to Martin Bennett, of Hartford. His position at the head of the Connecticut Fire was eminently agreeable, but the offer came in such form as to be irresistible. The record and presence of Mr. Bennett determined the decision of the committees, and results have shown the wisdom of their choice. Graduating at Brown University as a civil engineer in 1860, he entered the office of the Connecticut Fire August 14th, was elected secretary October 23, 1865, and president January 28, 1873. After the Chicago fire he presented the case of his company with such captivating candor that every creditor assented to terms of settlement that saved its charter.

October 11, 1880, Mr. Bennett resigned the presidency of the Connecticut to enter upon his new duties. Instead of going to New York or elsewhere he established the American headquarters of the two foreign companies in Hartford. The venture has been remarkably successful. A net remittance to this country by the Scottish Union of $839,695 had grown January 1, 1897, to $3,681,118.60, nearly all invested in the United States. During the period its receipts in this country were $12,549,454.87; losses and expenses, $10,615,318, all calculated on a net basis.

Mr. Bennett has been president of the Hartford Local Board and of the National Board of Underwriters. He is a forceful and witty writer, and has often been called to read addresses at important meetings.

James H. Brewster, assistant manager, was born at Coventry, Conn., December 24, 1845. In the Connecticut Fire Insurance Company and in his present position he had on the 25th of February, 1897, been associated with Mr. Bennett thirty years continuously.

CHAPTER VI.

INSURANCE IN CONNECTICUT—Continued.

EARLY forty mutual fire insurance companies, from time to time, have been chartered by the General Assembly of Connecticut. January 1, 1897, seventeen were in existence. Their names, dates of incorporation and gross assets, less premium notes, were as follows:

Name.	When incorporated.	Gross assets, less premium notes, January 1, 1896.
Mutual Assurance of Norwich	1795	$ 13,256.29
Windham County Mutual	1826	47,342.38
Tolland County Mutual	1828	67,656.40
Hartford County Mutual	1831	575,500.00
Litchfield Mutual	1833	97,704.99
Middlesex Mutual Assurance	1836	720,225.55
New London County Mutual	1840	121,806.46
Danbury Mutual	1850	29,570.17
Farmers' Mutual	1853	229.85
Farmington Valley Mutual	1854	5,710.85
Madison Mutual	1855	8,498.41
Greenwich Mutual	1855	6,915.44
Harwinton Mutual	1856	197.30
Washington Mutual	1862	101.10
State Mutual	1867	30,786.46
Rockville Mutual	1868	8,073.32
Patrons' Mutual	1888	1,266.10

The needs, which brought into being the oldest of the Mutuals, have been briefly stated in the account already given of the Mutual Assurance of Norwich. A few words with regard to three or four of the larger companies will perhaps give a sufficiently clear idea of the manner of growth.

Upon petition of Vine Robinson, and fifty-five others, the Windham County Mutual was incorporated in May, 1826, and organized the following June. It was allowed to insure only houses and other buildings. The insured paid a small percentage of the premium in cash, and the rest in a note liable to assessment in case of losses by fire.

Only three assessments have ever been laid: the first in 1829, yielding $653; the second in 1830, yielding $607.41; and the third in 1831, yielding $498.64. In 1871 the company was authorized to dispense with premium notes. Policies were made a lien on buildings and lands.

The position of president was at first honorary, but the directors made a radical departure in June, 1837, when they voted him an annual salary of $9. Revolutions, it is said, never go backward. In 1842 the directors voted to allow themselves $1 each for attendance at meetings. As they resided in all parts of the county, and were compelled to drive from six or eight to twenty-five miles over hilly roads, they claimed that the pay was not excessive. A charge of seventy-five cents for new policies, and of fifty for renewals, which made up the entire compensation of the secretary, was voted in 1839, and proved such a mine of wealth that in 1845 he paid $40 for the contract for the year. The first statement to be found bears date October 1, 1851, when the company had in cash and in the hands of agents $190.05, and in interest-bearing notes $1018.

Presidents have been: Vine Robinson, 1826–43; Asael Hammond, 1843–49; Armin Bolles, 1849–56; Aaron H. Storrs, 1856–78; John Gallup, 1878–9; David Greenslit, 1879.

The positions of secretary and treasurer have been filled by the same persons, except from 1848 till 1856, and again since 1892. Executive functions have been lodged mostly in the office of the secretary. Secretaries have been: Adams White, 1826–48; B. Wheaton, 1848–9; Edwin S. Chase, 1849–56; Aug. F. Fisher, 1856–7; John Palmer, 1857–92; James C. Palmer, 1892.

John Palmer was connected with the company thirty-six years, and during the time its assets grew from $2,016 in 1856, to $51,160 in 1892.

THE HARTFORD COUNTY MUTUAL

was incorporated in May, 1831, for the purpose of insuring houses and other buildings in the county of Hartford without the limits of the city of Hartford. At the first meeting held in the State House September 19th, David Grant was elected president, and Elisha Phelps, secretary. After a few weeks Mr. Phelps resigned and was succeeded by Charles Shepard.

The "premium note" was perhaps the most characteristic feature in the early history of the Mutuals. Upon ordinary detached risks the company required a note equal to two (2) per cent. of the face of the policy and ten per cent. of the first year's premium in cash. On buildings more exposed the rates were higher.

The following year the company was authorized to insure property outside the limits of the county, and to charge the premium in a gross sum instead of rating the same by the year, the lien remaining the same.

In 1835 the cash payment on effecting insurance was raised to three and one-third per cent. of the premium charge. The system with occasional variations in the rates continued till 1889, when the premium note was discarded and the whole business put on a purely cash basis.

The Hartford County began modestly, and after disbursing $12 in losses, and $179 in contingent expenses, had a surplus of $12 at the end of the first twelve months. For the next eleven years the business grew slowly, and at each annual meeting the books showed a small balance on the credit side of the ledger. In 1842, however, came a turn in the tide. Losses mounted up to $3,269.14, and at the close of the fiscal year, in December, the directors were confronted with a deficit of $362.11. Matters seemingly trivial have often proved to be pivots on which the fate not only of nations, but of civilization itself, has turned. So in a small way of this deficit. It provoked earnest thought and much discussion. Some advocated an assessment. Mr. Shepard took ground in favor of borrowing the money and raising the cash rates to a remunerative basis. Already the theory which prevailed at the outset, and which in many changeful forms has been revived and discarded since, had proved its insufficiency. The sensible views of the secretary were approved, and a note for the arrearages, presumably indorsed by the officers, was discounted at the Hartford Bank. From current receipts the obligation was soon discharged, and the company has never been compelled by reverses to pass through a similar experience since.

Not till 1853 was the company permitted to insure buildings within the city limits of Hartford. On the morning after the great Chicago fire, residents of the city did not know whether the policies on their property issued by stock companies were worthless or not. Of the solvency of the Hartford County Mutual they were certain, for it did no business beyond the boundaries of Connecticut. Many came in at that time to take advantage of the protection it offered, and have since remained upon its books.

From 1835 to 1844 policies were renewed on the payment of a fee of twenty-five cents to the secretary, with no further cost to the insured. Meanwhile new members paid their initiatory premium.

The company takes only the safer class of risks, as dwellings and farm buildings with their contents. It does not insure churches, school-houses, stores or factories. Its business has always been confined to the state of Connecticut.

Presidents have been David Grant, 1831-38; Daniel St. John, 1838-44; Charles Shepard, 1844-67; D. D. Erving, 1867-73; Julius Catlin, 1873-4; Walter H. Havens, 1874-6; James B. Shultas, 1876-80; William E. Sugden, 1880.

Secretaries, Elisha Phelps, one month in 1831; Charles Shepard, October, 1831-44; R. A. Erving, 1844-53; D. D. Erving, 1853-67; William A. Erving, 1867-.

R. A. Erving resigned to accept the position of secretary of legation under Ex-Governor Thomas H. Seymour, then recently appointed minister to the court of St. Petersburg. Having spent a number of years in Russia, he was lost with the steamer Pacific on the voyage home. The secretary has always been the executive officer.

THE MIDDLESEX MUTUAL ASSURANCE COMPANY.

Not the oldest but the largest of the mutual fire companies of the state in business and assets, is the Middlesex Mutual Assurance Company of Middletown, chartered in May, 1836, and organized June 13th of the same year. Richard Hubbard was elected president, and John L. Smith, secretary and treasurer. During the first year four hundred and sixty-seven policies were written. At the annual meeting in June, 1838, William Woodward was elected secretary, and Samuel Cooper treasurer. It was voted to move the office from the store of John L. Smith to that of E. Hunt & Co. In 1865 it was moved to a room under the Universalist church, and was again transferred to permanent quarters in the new building of the company the next year.

At first a small cash premium was required from the insured to meet current expenses and ordinary losses, and a promissory note to be held in reserve for emergencies. In 1859 the premium note system was abandoned. By a charter amendment policies gave the company a lien on the buildings insured and on the land.

In June, 1886, the assets having increased to $530,174.77, a still further innovation was made. The directors voted to cancel and release the lien reserved on all policies outstanding at the close of business, June 30, 1886, and to reserve no lien aside from the cash premium, in policies issued on or after July 1, 1886.

Presidents have been Richard Hubbard, 1836-9; Samuel Cooper, 1839-54; William S. Camp, 1856-66; William D. Willard, 1866-67; William R. Galpin, 1867-79; Elijah Ackley, 1879-83; John N. Camp (temporary) October, 1883-June, 1884; 1884, O. Vincent Coffin. Besides holding many positions of trust the present incumbent, Mr. Coffin, was mayor of Middletown for two terms, was elected to the State Senate in 1887 and 1889, and Governor of Connecticut in 1894.

Secretaries have been John L. Smith, 1836-38; William Woodward, 1838-49; Stephen Taylor, 1849-56; William Woodward, 1856-66; John W. Hoyt, 1866-67; H. F. Boardman, 1867-82; C. W. Harris, 1882-.

THE NEW LONDON COUNTY MUTUAL.

Organized July 1, 1840, has won a secure position. Presidents have been Joseph Backus, 1840-44; Joel W. White, 1844 (March till October); John G. Huntington, 1844-61; Elijah A. Bill, 1861-68; E. F. Parker, 1868-95; Charles J. Winters, January, 1895-.

Secretaries, J. DeWitt, 1840-7; John H. DeWitt, 1847-54; John L. Devotion, 1854-75; C. J. Fillmore, 1875-78; William Roath, 1878-85; J. F. Williams, 1885-.

THE STATE MUTUAL OF HARTFORD.

Though nearly the youngest on the list, has gained sufficient strength to guarantee its permanence. September 2, 1867, Ralph Gillett was chosen president, and Isaac Cross, Jr., secretary and treasurer. There was no change in the management till the death of Mr. Gillett April 17, 1894, when Mr. Cross was made president, and Franklin A. Morley, secretary. A loss of $4,000 on policy No. 61 insuring one of the best dwellings in Windsor occurred June 29, 1869. The assets of the company were insufficient to meet the call, but the officers made up the deficiency out of their private funds and paid the claim within a week. It pursues a conservative course, issuing no policy for over $2,000.

Ralph Gillett, born in Gilead, Conn., October 24, 1811, moved from Ellington to Hartford in 1849, and was one of the first to start in this city of insurance a general insurance agency. He was first president of both the City and Charter Oak Fire Insurance Companies and of the Union in 1860.

CHAPTER VII.

INSURANCE IN CONNECTICUT—Continued.

LIFE INSURANCE.*

IT may be said that the successful development of life insurance in Connecticut has been confined to Hartford. Companies started elsewhere on the plan of accumulating sufficient reserves to meet every claim at maturity, have ended in failure. Within a few years some fraternities have adopted the plan of contributing a fixed sum to the families of deceased members, and several bodies have been chartered with authority to pay losses by assessments on survivors. Such schemes may apparently flourish for a while, but they lack the features that insure permanence. Life insurance proper has come to be a matter of science and equity. Its methods have been evolved so as to conform to laws of average which are almost as exact in operation as the laws of physics.

Dr. Pinckney W. Ellsworth and James L. Howard were the first to call the attention of the people of Hartford, at least, in an effective way, to the subject. Dr. Ellsworth was agent of the International, of London, England. Mr. Howard, in February, 1846, took out policy No. 1079, in the Mutual Benefit of New Jersey, and at the same time accepted the local agency of the company. Joseph Lord came up from New York city to initiate him in the theory and practice of canvassing. Mr. Howard started off with a boom, presenting the subject not only in private interviews, but in public addresses. Guy R. Phelps was so impressed with the merits of the system that he took a policy in the Mutual Benefit. Elisha B. Pratt became an early convert. Other men of prominence quickly followed. All at once the novelty became the talk of the town.

---

* In this sketch of life insurance in Connecticut, no account is given of the operations of assessment companies or of fraternal or benevolent associations.

It was a new subject, and the vigorous presentation of the affirmative side provoked a good deal of curious opposition. Some good people argued that the scheme was irreligious in substituting reliance upon human instrumentalities for trust in Providence. Elder Swan, a revivalist famous for rough eloquence, and for the lurid colors in which he painted the terrors of the law, in a sermon at an annual state convention, resolved to crush the pernicious novelty at a blow. Rising to a climax in denunciation, he said: "Suppose that Jesus, on His way to the Jordan, had met John among the foothills, and to the question, 'Whither goest thou?' John had answered: 'Behold, all these years have I trusted in the God of Israel, and have been sorely pressed by many troubles. Wist thou not that I go up to Jerusalem to get my life insured?' Would the church, my hearers, have outlived the few and feeble days of infancy had treachery so foul been permitted to occur and to pass unrebuked? If lack of faith was a sin then, it is a sin now. Avoid the snares of a perverse generation, and say to the tempter, 'Get thee behind me, Satan.'"

Prejudice yielded before enlightened discussion. The act condemned by the good elder as a sin is now classed with the duties.

THE CONNECTICUT MUTUAL LIFE INSURANCE COMPANY (HARTFORD).

Discussion of the merits of life insurance in private counting-rooms would have continued indefinitely in many towns without suggesting the thought of forming a company to enter upon the work. Not so in Hartford. For a full half century the city had been engaged in fire and marine underwriting. Abilities of a high order had been attracted to the field. Carrying on operations over a wide area, coming in contact with many minds, and trying to generalize laws from accumulating stores of fact, managers not only acquired a fondness for the business, but unconsciously found it an efficient instrument for sharpening the wits. At this juncture, too, it was beginning to pass out of the empirical stage. Principles now recognized as fundamental were discussed pro and con in the offices of the Hartford, the Ætna, and the Protection. The first two saw the light and lived. The third passed on in the old way and died.

Early in 1846 James L. Howard took thirty applications for policies in the Mutual Benefit in two months. Very quickly the familiar arguments in favor of life insurance penetrated the community. It was like the fall of a stream of sparks on tinder. Long habit had developed in the city an instinct for underwriting which seized at once upon the advantages to be gained by entering the field promptly. A charter incorporating The Connecticut Mutual Life Insurance Company was drawn up and passed by the General Assembly at the May session in 1846.

The document carefully guards the rights of all parties. In case of loans on real estate it requires double security on unencumbered property, and in loans on state stocks and bank stocks a margin of twenty-five per cent. As a rule managers do not seek to have their freedom limited by sharp restrictions, for it is only in seasons of panic and disaster that the wisdom of iron-bound rules becomes manifest. The corporation was impowered to insure husbands for the exclusive benefit of wives and children, free from all claims originating on the side of the husband, provided the annual premium did not exceed $100 (raised to $150 in 1848), unless paid from the private property of the wife. This was at a time when the law regarded husband and wife as one, and that "one" the husband. It was allowed to take from the insured notes for the premium in part or for the whole at discretion, and in case just claims at any time exceeded the cash on hand to lay assessments on the notes *pro rata*. At the beginning of each year the company was required to make an estimate of profits and of the true state of affairs for the previous year, to charge each member with a proportionate share of losses and expenses, and to credit him with a proportionate share of profits. Other provisions were made for carrying out the system of distribution in a way that then seemed equitable.

The corporators met first July 16, 1846, at the Eagle Hotel, and adjourned from time to time till July 29th, when the company was organized by choice of the following directors, viz.: Thomas K. Brace, Robert Buell, David S. Dodge, Guy R. Phelps, Elisha B. Pratt, Edson Fessenden, James A. Ayrault, Eliphalet A. Bulkeley, Lorenzo B. Goodman, Nathaniel H. Morgan, Nathan M. Waterman, and Henry L. Miller.

August 11th Eliphalet A. Bulkeley was chosen president; Guy R. Phelps, secretary; and David S. Dodge, physician. Elisha B. Pratt was subsequently elected vice-president.

The board met frequently, but for several months made little progress. As the scheme was purely mutual they saw that heavy losses in the infancy of the association might crush out its life by the weight of assessments. For bridging the danger, and thus opening a sure road to permanence, they decided, as permitted by the charter, to raise a guaranty fund of $50,000. It was to be made up of well-secured notes, given in advance for premiums, one-half payable five and the other half ten years from date. In case of asssessments the makers were to be reimbursed from premiums earned immediately afterwards. The company paid for the credit six per cent. annually. Except for losses and assessments previously incurred the notes became void at the end of their respective terms, and were to be then surrendered. Death of the maker operated as a cancellation for future liability. A like rule applied to the guarantor. Provision was made for substituting new obligations in place of those withdrawn by cancellation or failure.

The plan was approved December 1st, and, at a meeting on the 7th, the entire amount was apportioned to nineteen subscribers, in sums ranging from $4,000 to $1,000 each. On the 11th of the same month the board voted that policies might be issued to approved parties, as applications had already been received to the amount of $100,000. Meanwhile suitable forms and literature had been prepared and printed and tables of premiums adopted. At the annual meeting, in January, 1847, James Goodwin and William T. Hooker took the places of Messrs. Phelps and Goodman in the directory. The work of appointing agents and procuring risks was pushed with vigor, not over $5,000 at first being taken on a single life.

The first Finance Committee to which the by-laws intrusted the care and investment of funds, consisted of Messrs. Bulkeley, Goodwin and Hooker.

January 6, 1848, James Goodwin was elected president, and James A. Ayrault was appointed actuary, other officers remaining as before.

Applications for insurance were all submitted to the full board of directors. These came in such volume, however, that in January, 1848, the board authorized the officers to issue policies upon unexceptionable applications presented during the recess of the board, upon obtaining the approval of three members, of whom the medical examiner must be one.

The following March Isaac Toucey, afterwards governor, United States senator and secretary of the navy, was appointed first legal counsellor.

The first serious dissension arose over the rigid economy shown by the executive officers in making allowances to agents. It was a fixed rule to pay no bills incurred by them for furniture, fixtures, stationery, etc., unless appropriations had been specifically asked and been approved by the board. All literature emanated from the home office. Agents were invited to send in any matter which they desired to see in type, and were told that if approved it would be duly incorporated and supplied to them gratuitously. They were required, however, to foot printing and other bills if incurred without authority.

N. D. Morgan, agent in New York city, grew restive and resentful under the restrictions imposed upon him. Elisha B. Pratt, in charge at Boston, was also dissatisfied. In anticipation of the election to be held in February, 1849, they made a determined effort to capture the company, with the avowed purpose of introducing a more liberal and expansive policy. But the garrison holding the fort was not asleep. December 16th a vote was passed to notify Mr. Morgan that his term of service would expire on the 19th, three days later. A powerful minority in the board sympathized with the malcontents. On the first day of the new year Messrs. Brace, Hooker, Miller and Dodge resigned from the directory, and after a decorous delay their resignations were accepted. Mr. Pratt had retired the previous September, and the following September he gave up the agency at Boston.

The election was hotly contested. Of the twenty-four hundred and one votes cast James Goodwin received twenty-three hundred and ninety-seven. The rest of the successful ticket was elected by majorities of about two hundred. The new board consisted of James Goodwin, William W. Ellsworth, Ebenezer Flower, Edmund G. Howe, George Sumner, Zephaniah Preston, Edwin Tiffany, Samuel Woodruff, Simeon L. Loomis, Mason Gross, William E. Dodge, of New York, and John W. Sullivan, of Boston. Messrs. Dodge and Sullivan declined to serve, when Henry Z. Pratt, of New York, and William T. Hooker were chosen to fill the vacancies. A brief war of circulars was followed by a long calm.

In the partial reorganization that ensued Ebenezer Flower, sea captain, coal merchant and afterwards mayor, was elected vice-president. Dr. George Sumner succeeded Dr. David S. Dodge as physician. The position of actuary was abolished. The business had so grown that the board now authorized the employment of a bookkeeper, clerk and office-boy.

The statement for the year ended January 31, 1850, showed that over six hundred more policies were issued during the twelve months than during the entire previous existence of the company. The number of clerks had increased to four. The annual election passed without a ripple.

The guarantee notes were retired at maturity in 1851 and 1856 respectively, having by their mere presence in the treasury fulfilled their purpose without assessment of any kind.

Till the outbreak of the war growth was more solid than showy. At that time the company had about three and one-third millions of dollars in assets and about twenty-five millions at risk. It had already won the confidence of the public and had in the field many devoted and enthusiastic workers. In one western city after another it secured correspondents of high character and ability to act as loan agents. As the transactions were eminently profitable to both lenders and borrowers the arrangement brought a large clientage, and by aiding the development of the country continually broadened the field of operations. Not less popular than its enterprise in offering loans were its unique provisions for guarding the interests of women and children.

The premium note, too, proved an unexcelled device for canvassing purposes. Under this system fifty per cent. of the first four premiums was payable in a note, bearing six per cent. interest, which was made a policy lien and was deducted from the death claim by the terms of the contract. Limited to the first four years, the method made it easy to take large amounts of insurance at small cost. These were extinguished by dividends with a rapidity dependent on rates of interest. Counted at their face they reached a maximum of $11,859,974 in 1870, and had fallen to $1,065,427.28 at the beginning of 1897. The officers have always regarded the notes as an excellent asset. These were unsatisfactory, however, to claimants who wanted the face of their claims in cash. This was one reason for giving up the system.

In 1863 an acrid controversy arose between William Barnes, superintendent of the insurance department of New York, and Secretary Phelps, with regard to an assumed failure to report as a liability dividends to policy-holders provisionally declared by the directors. The superintendent went so far as to threaten, unless his demands were complied with, to decline to renew the certificate of the company allowing it to issue new policies in that state. The subject matter of dispute is of far less interest than the defiant, almost contemptuous, attitude maintained throughout by Mr. Phelps. He asked no favors, courted the fullest inquiry and met insinuations with scorn.

A few years later a successor of Mr. Barnes, in wanton disregard of decency, let loose upon the life companies of New York a swarm of bummers under pretense of examining their condition. For alleged investigations these foragers presented enormous bills, which were paid without audible protest. It was notorious that most of the men commissioned to go on the raid had little fitness for any work outside of political chicanery. In short, the scheme began and ended in blackmail pure and simple. Why did the victims submit in silence to imposition and robbery? The question has been often asked, but never answered "officially."

We may infer from the letters of Mr. Phelps, and from the fearlessness uniformly shown since then in dealing with frauds of every name and nature, that an expedition fitted out at Albany to assault the treasury of the Connecticut Mutual would have met there a very different reception.

Till 1869 the company returned to each member, without regard to the age of his policy, a uniform percentage of the premium, thus discriminating in favor of newcomers. Meanwhile, keen minds penetrating to the core the mathematical intricacies of the subject, detected the inequalities of existing methods of distribution. In 1869, the contribution plan devised by Shepard Homans, then actuary of the Mutual Life of New York, was adopted. Under it each one theoretically receives in dividends or return premiums, from year to year, precisely the share that his payments entitle him to. In view of the difficulty of combining mutuality with strength in the early stages of the attempt, the system has been accepted by competent critics as a close approach to perfect equity, and has been everywhere adopted in this country.

In early days by the terms of the contract failure to pay premiums universally forfeited the policy. Not a few companies reckoned largely upon this source of revenue. Many persons were thus subjected to great hardships, from which through change of fortune they could not escape. In 1864 the Connecticut Mutual voluntarily changed the form of its contracts so as to give members the full value of past premiums in paid-up insurance, where they found it inconvenient to continue.

When business rebounded after the first shock of war the fruitfulness of wise seed-sowing became clear. An issue of one thousand, two hundred and seventy-five policies in 1859—the highest record up to that time—fell to nine hundred and fifty-nine in 1860, but increased to five thousand and ninety, in 1863; to eight thousand and forty-five in 1864; and to fourteen thousand, one hundred and fifty-one, high water mark, in 1867. Meanwhile, assets had increased to over twenty-two and a half millions. The amount written in 1867 reached $45,647,191.

Hartford did not escape the speculative mania that followed the outpour of paper-money during the war. Suburban farms were bought at high figures and on charts laid out in building lots. Prices soared. Others caught the frenzy. More land was bought to be sold to new-comers whom heated imaginations saw thronging toward the city. By and by the balloon wavered in its upward flight. Something must be done. Money was sorely needed to sustain the weight. One after another asked loans from the Connecticut Mutual. Was it not the duty, they asked, of a Hartford institution controlling many millions, to uphold Hartford interests? Supported by the directory Major Goodwin promptly and peremptorily declined. He met insistent appeals by showing how the folly must inevitably end.

For the speculators the situation was desperate. Quietly and secretly they formed plans for the capture of the company. In July, 1867, they procured the passage by the legislature of an act less than three lines long, repealing section 376 of the revised statutes, and thus changing the mode of electing directors. Simultaneously they scoured the country for proxies. The plot was discovered only a few days before the annual election, but happily in time to frustrate it. In view of the relative claims and rights of the two parties it now seems incredible that the attempt so nearly succeeded. Separate communities and the country have suffered untold evils from heedless legislation pushed through to promote private interests.

Dr. Phelps was secretary till 1866, and president thence till his death in 1869. Born at Simsbury, Conn., he graduated at the Yale Medical School in 1825, and after a few years of practice in different places, opened a popular drug store in Hartford. During his long connection with the Connecticut Mutual, he aimed to make the company strong and rich.

Except during the brief incumbency of Dr. Phelps, Major James Goodwin was president from January, 1848, till his death, March 15, 1878. Born March 2, 1803, he early exhibited great aptitude for the management of large affairs, having while still a minor become owner of the main line of mail stages running east from Hartford. In association with others he extended his interests till most of the lines centering in the city were included. He quickly foresaw the supersedure of the stage by the railway, and changed his investments accordingly. He was largely interested also in fire insurance, banking, and manufactures, and on all these varied lines of effort his counsels were highly valued. Local benevolent and educational institutions, too, profited from his guidance and gifts. He married, in 1832, Lucy, daughter of Joseph Morgan and sister of Junius S. Morgan, long a leading banker of London. For thirty years Major Goodwin largely directed the financial policy of the Connecticut Mutual in the matter of loans and investments. To his sagacity it is greatly indebted for the strong position which it won early and has easily maintained. He knew personally, and accurately measured the leading financiers of both the East and the West, and was thus enabled often on short notice to make large and advantageous purchases.

For the most part the executive officers of the company have served till death closed their labors. Woodbridge S. Olmstead succeeded Mr. Phelps as secretary in 1866, and died in 1871. Colonel Jacob L. Greene, for whom the office of assistant secretary was created in 1870, succeeded Mr. Olmstead in 1871 and was elected president in '78. John M. Taylor was assistant secretary, '72–'78; secretary, '78–'84, and has been vice-president since '84. Later secretaries have been, William G. Abbot, '84–'89, and Edward M. Bunce, '89– ; assistant secretaries, Daniel H. Wells, William G. Abbot, and John D. Parker. Since March, 1881, Mr. Wells has also been actuary, and his work as such is held in high regard. After Mr. Flower, Edmund G. Howe

JACOB L. GREENE,
President.

GUY R. PHELPS,
President 1866

JOHN M. TAYLOR,
Vice-President

JAMES GOODWIN,
President

EDWARD M. BUNCE,
Secretary

GEORGE R. SHEPHERD,

DANIEL H. WELLS,
Actuary.

THE CONNECTICUT MUTUAL LIFE INSURANCE COMPANY.

was vice-president, '51-'57; Zephaniah Preston, '57-'77; Edward B. Watkinson, '78-'84. Mr. Watkinson also, as chairman of the committee on building, supervised the construction of the home office.

Colonel Greene was born at Waterford, Me., August 9, 1837, studied at Michigan University, and began the practice of law. Soon after came the war, with its loud calls for young men. At the age of twenty-four he enlisted in the Seventh Michigan infantry, and except when on a sick bed or in southern prisons, served in the Union army till one year after federal authority was fully restored. In 1863 he was appointed assistant adjutant-general on the staff of General Custer, and in 1865, chief of staff to the same commander. April, 1866, he was mustered out with the full rank of major and the brevet rank of lieutenant-colonel, bestowed for distinguished gallantry. Colonel Greene then took an agency for the Berkshire Life Insurance Company of Pittsfield, Mass., and was soon invited to join the office staff as assistant secretary. For a quarter of a century he has served the Connecticut Mutual. Colonel Greene takes an active interest and occasionally an aggressive part in public affairs, always, in seasons both of calm and contention, on the side of sound morals, clean politics, and good government. His pen has enforced the use of correct methods in life insurance, and has mercilessly laid bare the injustice of alluring but deceptive devices for entrapping the unwary. In March, 1896, he read a paper before the Hartford Board of Trade on "Our Currency Problems," of which over one hundred and ninety thousand copies were circulated, largely through the South and West. During the troubles that have sprung from tampering with the currency, he has been a stalwart leader in exposing the heresies wrapt up in the pretensions of fiat money.

Mr. Taylor was born of New England parentage at Cortland, N. Y., February 18, 1845, graduated with class and scholarship honors in 1867, at Williams College, and was admitted to the bar in 1870, when he opened an office in Pittsfield, Mass. Incidentally he was elected town clerk, clerk of the district court, and to other positions. He gave up a career at the bar to link his fortunes with the Connecticut Mutual, but the connection has been happy for both parties. Thorough legal training at the outset reinforced by familiarity with current legislation and court decisions affecting insurance, exact knowledge of principles and mastery of details, long ago made him a trusted and authoritative guide through the changeful complexities that continually arise. To the general management he has contributed his full store of thought and responsibility. Mr. Taylor has decided literary and critical ability as shown by his recent historical work, "Maximilian and Carlotta, a Story of Imperialism."

The Connecticut Mutual is peculiarly strong, not only in solid assets, but in a conservatism of policy, the wisdom of which will become more and more apparent with the lapse of time. Its premiums and reserves upon risks taken since April, 1882, are computed on the assumption that before the liabilities mature, safe investments cannot with certainty be depended upon to yield a yearly net income of over three per cent. instead of four per cent., the basis heretofore required in prudent legislation and estimates. When taken, the step, quite at variance with the prevalent tendency, provoked, in certain quarters, acrid criticism, but its justification came more quickly, perhaps, than its advocates foresaw. The discussion drew from able economists elaborate papers to prove that for a generation, at least, the annual rate of interest in the United States, except for short and transient intervals, could not fall below six per cent. The arguments were based upon the extent of our undeveloped and partially developed territory, the tireless energy of our people, and the enormous sum certain to be required both for the enlargement of old and the initiation of new enterprises. In reality, capital increases much more rapidly than the demand for it in safe investments. In a panic the rate may mount upward according to the necessities of the borrower. During the last decade, on the contrary, call loans on the best security have ranged for months at a time from one per cent. a year to a fraction above, while much of the time United States and some state bonds have yielded less than the assumption of the company requires. Nothing but a long and destructive war can arrest except temporarily the downward movement. In view of the further fact that life insurance contracts, in many instances, will run fifty or sixty years, and that every one kept in force must be provided for at the outset and ultimately be paid in full on penalty of bankruptcy, it is easy to see that all similar institutions, to meet remote obligations, must follow in practice, if not avowedly, the example first set by the Connecticut Mutual.

On the highly improbable assumption, that the destruction of capital in wasteful wars should restore, for a long period, former rates of interest, and thus postpone the necessity for revising the tables of cost, patrons of the company would reap the entire benefit in the way of larger dividends. In case the accumulation of wealth, with the attendant decrease of income, goes on without interruption, they are fully protected, and in case the natural order of economical development is suspended or temporarily reversed, they lose nothing by the changes introduced in preparation for the seemingly inevitable.

In 1871-2 several ambitious companies that had pushed their business at such an expense as to affect their dividends very unfavorably when compared with those of more conservative competitors, revived the "tontine" scheme under which insurers agreed to forego all dividends for ten to twenty years and pay full premiums.

Those who died during the term lost such surplus as had accumulated up to the time, and those who ceased to pay, no matter when, lost everything. It was represented that the forfeitures arising from the two sources would make a very large sum in addition to the face of the policy, to be divided among the select few who persevered till the end of the period.

The Connecticut Mutual, with unanswerable logic, pointed out the injustice of the scheme, taking the ground that as the surplus accrued from year to year it ought to be used to aid in keeping the policy in force, and in case of lapse, that the reserves were entitled to an eqivalent value of paid-up insurance. If the plan was carried out faithfully it simply meant the robbery of the many for the benefit of the few, and hence pushed a demoralizing speculation into sacred ground that should be kept free from such intrusion.

Even as a contrivance for enriching the fortunate at the expense of the unfortunate the devise has proved a failure, for as the policies are now falling due the holders are receiving less than forty per cent. of the profits which were promised by way of temptation. Where the balance has gone, raises another question yet to be answered "officially." Costly business blocks built by the companies in different quarters of the globe, that may excite the wonder of beholders, but for the most part yield scant returns on the outlay; large salaries to many employees; and, in short, a heavy ratio of expenses—indicate, in part, where the other sixty per cent. may be looked for.

Prior to January 1, 1897, the Connecticut Mutual had received:

For Premiums	$192,111,805.65
" Interest	76,438,281.19
" Rents	7,059,292.87
" Profit and loss	1,035,219.59
Total	$276,644,599.30

DISBURSED.

For Death claims and endowments	$102,683,616.37
" Dividends	55,966,763.64
" Surrendered policies	23,803,729.92
Total paid policy-holders	$182,454,109.93
Expenses	24,316,102.41
Taxes	8,892,715.35
Total	$215,662,927.69
Ledger assets, January 1, 1897	60,981,671.61
Net surplus	$7,153,297.04

The surplus would be over a million of dollars more if wholly computed on the legal standard of 4 per cent. On tables in use since April, 1882, the company has assumed 3 per cent. as the rate of interest on accumulations accruing after that date. In the management of the Connecticut Mutual, one is impressed by the thoroughness and equity with which principles are studied and applied.

Edward M. Bunce, secretary, was born in Hartford in 1841, educated at the Hartford Public High School, and on graduation was appointed clerk in the Phœnix Bank, where, having served under the state and national systems, as teller, assistant cashier and cashier, was elected a director in the Connecticut Mutual Life in 1878, and its secretary in 1889.

Daniel H. Wells was born at Riverhead, L. I., in 1845; graduated at the Yale Sheffield Scientific School in the class of 1867 with the degree of C. E., later receiving the degree of Ph.B., and remaining there as instructor in mathematics and engineering for seven years. In 1874 he became a clerk in the actuarial department of the Connecticut Mutual; was placed in charge in 1876 as second assistant secretary; was elected assistant secretary in 1878, and actuary of the company in 1881.

John D. Parker was born in Pittsfield, Mass., in 1850; educated in the Pittsfield High School; joined the clerical force of the Berkshire Life Insurance Company in 1866, and after five years' service there, was appointed clerk in the Connecticut Mutual Life Insurance Company in 1871; chosen second assistant secretary in 1889, and assistant secretary in March, 1890.

CHAPTER VIII.

INSURANCE IN CONNECTICUT—Continued.

THE AMERICAN MUTUAL LIFE INSURANCE COMPANY, AND THE AMERICAN NATIONAL LIFE AND TRUST COMPANY (NEW HAVEN).

THIS company was incorporated in 1847. Six commissioners were authorized to open books and receive applications for insurance to be effected, not to exceed $5,000 upon the life of any one person, and when the amount reached $100,000, to call a meeting at New Haven for the purpose of organizing and electing a board of trustees, every member to have one vote on each $500 applied for.

Benjamin Silliman, an honored professor in Yale College, was elected president, and Benjamin Noyes, secretary. Tables fixing the rates to be charged for insurance on lives generally assumed, in the earlier days of the business, that an income of at least 4½ per cent. per annum could be realized on the accumulations made up of premiums and interest. If through good investments higher rates were obtained, the excess was so much clear profit, either to be added to the reserves, or to be returned in dividends to the insured. As loanable funds increased, it was found that the estimate was too high. States like Massachusetts, New York and Connecticut long ago reduced the limit by law to 4 per cent., while far-seeing managers have for some time been recasting their tables on a still more conservative basis.

The American Mutual, however, started on the dangerous assumption that it could realize at least six per cent. on all funds in the treasury. On that theory it made contracts liable to run in some cases for half a century. Whenever, from any cause, the average rate of interest on the combined assets fell below six per cent., a loss arose that could only be charged against principal. In long periods the margin of two per cent. placed at compound interest produces quite astonishing results. On annual payments of $100, the difference amounts in twenty-five years to $1,484, and in fifty years to $14,898. The company, too, made up a table of mortality less conservative than those now in use. Low rates and the world-wide fame of the president gave the American Mutual a good start. In 1855 it claimed to have $4,960,450 insured by existing policies, although the following year the amount had fallen to $3,500,000. Its annual statements puzzled the newly-created insurance bureaus of Massachusetts and New York. The commissioners of Massachusetts, in the report of January, 1858, treat the valuation of $30,000 put on existing policies as "evidently guesswork and not deemed reliable." The next year its statement first came under the searching scrutiny of Elizur Wright, who brought to the office great technical knowledge, integrity and courage. From his eye vagueness could not hide absurdity in estimates. He failed to see how five millions at risk could be transferred to a reliable company for a "sum not exceeding $37,500," as claimed in the statement. To his mind the figures were given, "not as the result of any calculation or investigation, whatever, but of wholesale conjecture." Considering the age of the company and the amount at risk, he was inclined to believe that no other company would be justified in taking its risks for $162,212.98—the whole amount of its net assets. At the same time he suggests that there may be some peculiarity in its business to relieve it of suspicion. This much is conceded "out of regard to the venerable gentleman who has stood at its head, and whose name has been its chief tower of strength—a name dear to the whole world for his noble zeal and eloquence in the cause of science and humanity."

In 1862 the company was excluded from doing business in the state of New York, where it then had ten agents. For a long period Commissioner Wright dealt with it very tenderly out of regard for its distinguished president. He was at a loss to see how reports, hazy, indefinite and strained could be fathered by a gentleman trained to exact methods of science, and known to be scrupulously correct in every relation of life. He knew that no taint of mercenary motive could stain the character of one who had devoted splendid talents and incessant toil to the cause of truth and popular education. But at length the suspicion ripened into conviction "that men of science may misplace their confidence in the science of others," and he goes on to show that the calculations avowedly made by Benjamin Noyes for the sworn return deposited with the department, October 30, 1852, involve gross and palpable impossibilities.

Professor Silliman died in 1864. For a short term Willis Bristol held the presidency, and was succeeded by Mr. Noyes, who had held uncontrolled sway from the start. In 1865 an insurance department, with limited functions, was established in Connecticut. Benjamin Noyes was appointed first commissioner. He held the place till 1871, when the department was reorganized with much broader duties and powers. Thus the American Mutual enjoyed double services from the same person. The wisdom, however, of hiring an official to watch himself is yet to be proved. Although shut out from Massachusetts and New York, within the jurisdiction of Connecticut he could manipulate figures under authority of the commonwealth, applying methods and tests which were wholly his own. In his report to the legislature in 1867—the first embracing home institutions—he presented a table to prove inferentially that the American Mutual was by far the strongest of the eight life companies then doing business under charters from the state. But it is useless to waste words in refuting manifest absurdities.

In 1871 an act was worked through the General Assembly authorizing the company to lease land from Trinity Church, New Haven, and to erect thereon such building or buildings as should be deemed expedient. Under the permission thus granted much the larger part of its available assets was soon solidified in brick and mortar. It was carried on the books at $350,000, while the lease was claimed to add $50,000 more to the value of the property.

Mr. Noyes appreciated the commercial value of nominal connections with men of high character and wide reputation. The more engrossing their labors the better, for their other activities would then leave little leisure for prying into secrets of management. For his purposes Professor Silliman made an ideal figure-head. Too noble and truthful to suspect trickery and falsehood in an associate, and too busy with pursuits that delighted his heart to descend to the details of money-making, he was content to be an apparent leader in life insurance from a conviction that the work was essentially beneficent. From time to time excellent men were also placed on the board, but, so far as the company was concerned, they were expected to look wise and know nothing.

Rarely, by mistake, persons were selected who declined to be hypnotized. Prof. A. C. Twining, of Yale College, an influential trustee, dissatisfied with the loose methods and indefinite reports of the secretary, urged his associates to apply the curb. By a flank attack he was driven from the board. He also tried to procure a legislative inquiry, but was easily baffled by his wily adversary.

When Joseph G. Lamb resigned the agency at Norwich, Mr. Noyes engaged John L. Dennison to collect premiums on renewals in the town and its vicinity. In forwarding the receipts he added that policy-holders had from time to time received dividends in scrip representing surplus earnings, and asked him to collect all in that section and return the same to the home office with his next monthly statement. Mr. Dennison, from whose training the art of reaching ends by devious paths had been omitted, paid the holders the face value out of his collections and reported accordingly. Mr. Noyes was much displeased. He wrote, "I never intended you to pay the scrip-holders. The object was upon their return to me to consolidate the various pieces, and issue a form of obligation which would be of the same relative value to the holders at maturity." He also requested Mr. Dennison to forward the amount paid in cash in order properly to settle his account.

Mr. Dennison replied that the office had sent no blank to be filled, and given as a voucher to be held during the exchange, or even mentioned the proposed substitution. Hence he had but one way of obtaining the script, and that by paying for it. The explanation brought no answer. Mr. Noyes acted on the theory that to sophisticate the form of an obligation was the easiest way to get rid of it.

In 1870 several leading citizens of Norwich, policy-holders in the company, in a communication printed over their names in the *Advertiser*, made an outspoken attack on the management. Mr. Noyes hurried over to quiet the disturbance. Some of the interviews took a decidedly personal turn, and he was forced to listen to plain talk. At length they finally agreed, as perhaps the best way out of a bad fix, to sell their policies at fifty per cent. of the amount paid in to Dr. J. B. Robertson, vice-president of the company.

As the American Mutual Life had long rested under a cloud, various plans were considered by the managers for getting rid of the discredit without sacrificing the assets and business. In pursuance of the scheme they came before the legislature of Connecticut in 1866, and secured the passage of an act incorporating The American National Life Insurance Company. The capital stock was to be not less than $100,000, with the privilege of increase at the pleasure of the directors to $500,000. The subscribers were required to pay the amounts subscribed for, "in such installments as the directors shall order and direct." As subsequently construed, this provision was assumed to authorize the company to begin and continue business with no paid capital whatever. Similar latitude of phraseology runs through the entire document. Section 7 begins, "The capital stock and the accumulations of said company may be invested in mortgages upon real estate worth double the amount loaned," etc. In other words, the managers were permitted, if it suited their purposes, to invest in sundry classes of good securities, but the permission was not coupled with any obligation or penalty. The company was authorized to accept and execute any and all trusts that might be committed to it by any court, or person, or persons, whatsoever, and to "assume or to reinsure any risks involving the casualties of life, either separately or otherwise." The last clause, half hidden under the shadow of innocent privileges, embodied the essence of all that was sought for.

Section 6 allowed dividends to be paid "in cash or scrip, or in stock, or in new policies of insurance, or (to) be added to old ones. It was the original plan to draw from the treasury of the American Mutual Life the funds needed to pay for the capital stock of its offspring. At the next session of the General Assembly the charter of the old company was so amended as to authorize it to loan on vague and illusive conditions to the individual members of its board the amount required to pay for such shares in the new company as they might subscribe for. That Benjamin Noyes and his associates could obtain from successive legislatures the authority to handle without restriction trust funds of the most sacred character, is, perhaps, not so much an evidence of confidence in their integrity as of their adroitness in effecting combinations for political and other purposes.

A long period of gestation followed. In 1871 the corporate name was changed to "The American National Life and Trust Company." The following September stock subscriptions to the amount of $125,000 were entered on a sheet provided for the purpose, and an organization was consummated by electing as its officers the officers of the American Mutual Life. Benjamin Noyes, president, and Richard F. Lyon, secretary.

The larger part of the subscriptions were made in the name of sundry persons by B. Noyes, "attorney." A little in the same line was done by R. F. Lyon, "attorney." Willis Bristol, treasurer, in trust for the company, took one hundred and twenty shares, which were afterwards vacated by vote of the board. Then came another long and involuntary delay. The annual statement of the American Mutual Life for December, 1871, as made up in the home office, showed a deficiency of $18,678.84. Dr. George S. Miller, the first regular insurance commissioner of Connecticut, as directed by the Act of 1871, creating the office, notified the company to cease the issue of new policies and the payment of dividends till the impairment should be made good. Accordingly a "guaranty capital," so called, of $75,000 was subscribed to fill the gap in the early part of 1873. About the same time, as permitted by a special act passed in 1871, the state treasurer surrendered to the American National Life and Trust Company, the securities deposited with him by the American Mutual Life, in exchange for an equal amount substituted by the former.

As a part of the same transaction the new company assumed all the liabilities of the old one and took its entire assets, including the guaranty capital. In spite of many difficulties the transmigration was complete. A soul had so passed from one body to another that the closest observer from external appearances would never have suspected the fact. Nothing visible was changed except the title. Not only assets and liabilities, but the premises occupied, the management and atmosphere remained the same. After an examination of its condition in April, 1873, Commissioner Miller gave the company a license to issue policies and transact business.

As it was brought into being with the primary purpose of absorbing dead and dying institutions, it lost little time, after swallowing its parent, in hunting for the next meal. The following December it reinsured the risks of the National Life of New York, which had failed in October. The bargain was bad in every way, the buyer getting little and assuming much. Among the securities assigned were bonds to the amount of $100,000, deposited with the superintendent of insurance at Albany. It was to get hold of these that the trade was made. Here Mr. Noyes met unexpected difficulties. His manipulations as lobbyist in his own state had given him great confidence in his prowess. But he was now manœuvering on unfamiliar ground. The superintendent was deaf equally to demands and entreaties, successfully claiming that the bonds could not be used for any other purpose than the protection of policy-holders of the bankrupt company in that state. Aside from the deposit of $105,500 (including excess of price over par) retained by the superintendent, the concern had the December before only $18,208.97, made up of cash and accrued interest, available for the payment of losses. The balance out of a total of $760,034.87 of assumed assets consisted of premium notes, loans on policies in force and unpaid premiums. At the same time the liabilities reached $760,034.87. Had the New York superintendent given up the deposit, the contract of reinsurance would still seem an act of madness.

John W. Stedman, second insurance commissioner of Connecticut, served two terms, having been appointed by Gov. Charles R. Ingersoll and reappointed by Gov. Richard D. Hubbard. He entered upon the duties of the office in July, 1874. Complaints from the beneficiaries of deceased policy-holders in the American National Life and Trust, and from others, came with alarming frequency. Proof accumulated in his hands to indicate that the company was pursuing vigorously the system of freezing out old policy-holders and of compromising death claims on the hardest terms possible. Some, in ignorance, submitted, taking whatever they could get. Others directly or through friends, sent to the department for advice. Mr. Stedman felt that he would be criminally negligent if he allowed such practices to continue without inquiry or rebuke. Accordingly, beginning on the 20th of October, with the aid of several experts, he made an exhaustive examination of the condition of the company and a revaluation of the liabilities on all outstanding policies. The resulting statement showed its condition on the first day of October, 1874.

Putting upon the famous building erected on Chapel street a much higher estimate than was realized in the final settlement, he made the total assets $923,220.71, the liabilities $1,335,068.28, and the deficiency $411,847.57. Among the assets he included the bonds, now valued at $108,000, which were deposited with the superintendent at Albany and which never did or could come into the hands of the New Haven company. He disallowed the following items, and over them a fierce contest arose:

Capital stock unpaid	$84,700
Guarantee capital	75,000
Agencies balances	15,706
Virginia Coal Company stock	26,600
	$202.006

Section 28 of the act of 1871 provides that if on examination by the commissioner, the assets of any company chartered by this state to grant insurances or make contracts contingent upon lives, are less than its liabilities, the commissioner shall forthwith notify such company to cease the issue of new policies and the payment of dividends until the deficiency shall be supplied, or at his discretion he may apply to the local court of probate for an appointment of a trustee to take possession of the property for the benefit of the creditors.

Section 29 further provides that if the assets are less than three-fourths of the liabilities the commissioner shall without delay bring petition as above, and the court shall thereupon appoint a trustee. It also prescribes the further steps to be taken to accomplish the dissolution of the company.

As the deficiency exceeded twenty-five per cent., no discretion was allowed the commissioner. He therefore applied to the court of probate for the district of New Haven for the appointment of a trustee to take possession of the property and wind up the affairs of the company. At the first hearing the application was resisted on the ground that the law was unconstitutional. The plea was overruled and a trial ordered on the merits of the case. After some delay the hearing began January 18, 1875, before Judge Bradley of the Probate Court, assisted by Judge Phelps of the Superior Court, and closed March 19th. Various adjournments reduced the time actually consumed to twenty days. The court decided, April 12th, that the allegation in the petition that the assets were less than three-fourths of the liabilities was untrue, that the allegation that the assets were less than the liabilities was true, and that the deficiency was not such that the prayer should be granted. Accordingly the petition was dismissed, the court giving no hint of its opinion regarding the value of the property owned by the company, or of the amount of deficiency. Up to this point Henry B. Harrison, afterwards governor, prosecuted the case in behalf of the state. He was so astounded and shocked, however, at the outcome that he withdrew peremptorily from any further connection with it. He was succeeded by Simeon E. Baldwin, now on the bench of the Supreme Court of Connecticut, who with great ability and unfaltering persistence conducted the case to the end. Let us examine the situation in the light of the evidence.

The guaranty capital of $75,000 was an inheritance, as already narrated, from the American Mutual Life, and was made up in order that the process of absorption might proceed in apparent accordance with law. In a contract between the trustees of the company and the subscribers, dated March 15, 1873, it was agreed that the company should pay six per cent. per annum interest on the several subscriptions, that the fund should not be used or resorted to unless all the resources of the company were exhausted, that all income derived from the securities transferred from private hands to make up the amount, should, when collected by the treasurer, be paid to the owners, and that the securities themselves should be returned at the end of three years from the 15th day of December, 1872.

Less than $12,000 in marketable bonds were lodged with the company under the contract. The balance was made up mostly of mythical mortgages, Fair Haven Water Company stock, and town of Brighton, Ill., bonds. The use of the stuff drew from the treasury $4,500 annually, to which, in return, even the fractional $12,000 contributed not a cent of revenue. It is obvious that a fund thus constituted, whether good or bad, if allowed as an asset, should be charged also as a liability.

The amount of the regular capital stock is variously stated. In the report for 1873 it is put at $100,000, with the legend "actually paid up in cash." It matters little whether it is called less or more, for not a dollar had been paid on a single share. June 2, 1873, by vote of the directors a dividend of twenty-three per cent. was declared to be endorsed on the certificates, an assessment of like amount having been ordered at the same meeting. It appears from the testimony that several gentlemen credited on the books with the ownership of stock were entirely unaware of the bounties which had been showered upon them. On the original paper five hundred and forty shares were subscribed for sundry parties "by B. Noyes." From these blocks he seems to have made transfers freely without consulting either ostensible sellers or buyers.

C. S. Maltby testified that he never authorized B. Noyes to subscribe for fifty shares for him or to transfer or receive it. J. A. Bishop, of the Yale National Bank, testified that he did not authorize B. Noyes to make a subscription of fifty shares for him, that he had received no certificate for it, and did not authorize B. Noyes to transfer it to Samuel S. Noyes. Joseph A. Smith testified that he never authorized B. Noyes to transfer five shares to him. The mayor of the city, H. G. Lewis, swore that he owned none of the stock and had never authorized any transfer to him.

The dividend of twenty-three per cent., amounting to $25,300, was made on a nominal capital of $110,000, leaving $84,700 unpaid. It was declared out of the surplus created by the deposit of the guaranty capital already described. As nearly as existing conditions permit, Benjamin Noyes had succeeded in creating something out of nothing. These phantoms, too, he treated as realities with such apparent sincerity that men of considerable intelligence were deluded by the show. The other two items thrown out by the commissioner, agency balances and Virginia Coal Company stock, were about equally worthless.

Returning to assets allowed we find the commissioner too liberal by over $200,000. He included at a valuation of $108,000, the bonds conveyed by the National Life of New York, but never delivered because the superintendent at Albany kept them securely locked in his vault for the protection of the policy-holders of that state.

He estimated the building of the company at $269,822.50. By special permission of the general assembly this structure was erected on ground leased from Trinity Parish, New Haven, for sixty years from October 1, 1871, at an annual rental of $8,000 for the first ten years, $9,000 for the next ten, and for the rest of the term at six per cent. on the appraised value of the ground, the yearly rent to be never less than $9,000. At the hearing the witnesses produced by the commissioner estimated the value of the leasehold at from $100,000 to $125,000. The experts of Mr. Noyes thought much more highly of the investment ranging from $250,000 upward. Till the time of the hearing it had not yielded sufficient revenue to meet the ground-rent and current expenses.

After the finding of the court many officials would have abandoned further attempts to break up a combination so securely intrenched, and backed by such varied and powerful influences. Whatever disaster might come in the future, a commissioner unwilling to encounter trouble could hold up the record to show that he had fully complied with the law, and that further responsibility rested elsewhere. Not thus, however, with Mr. Stedman. He felt that his duty to husbands and fathers who for many years had paid premiums through trust in false promises, to widows and orphans threatened with robbery in the hour of bereavement, and to the state which had made him guardian of these special interests, demanded that he should press forward without faltering. Accordingly, on the 5th of May, 1875, he submitted a special report to the general assembly. After marshaling the facts he demonstrated by applying to the case the well-known principles of the science, that the company was hopelessly insolvent, that recovery was impossible, and that the longer it continued in business the more disastrous would be its unavoidable failure. He also quoted from his voluminous files to show how Noyes was working to frighten policy-holders into the surrender of claims at fractions of their face.

On the 24th of the month came a reply addressed to the general assembly and signed by thirteen directors. It throws little fresh light on the controversy. In answer to the charge that not a dollar had ever been paid on the capital stock it defends the course of the company on the grounds, 1st, that the charter authorizes it to go into operation upon subscribed capital; and, 2nd, "that the payment of the stock had not been called for by the directors, either in whole or in part, simply for the reason that no necessity had arisen for calling for its payment."

Evidently Mr. Noyes foresaw with far more penetrating vision than the legislature the use that could be made of the instrument.

July 14th the Senate passed a resolution unanimously recommended by the Committee on Insurance, to annul, on the first day of September, 1875, the charters of the American Mutual Life Insurance Company, and of the American National Life and Trust Company, unless the latter, on or before that day should supply the deficiency existing in its assets, and receive from the commissioner a certificate to that effect.

On the 20th of July the matter came up in the House, when two provisos appeared, the first offered by Lynde Harrison, of Guilford, in the interest of the managers, and the second by Elisha Johnson, of Hartford, who favored the naked resolution of the Senate. By the first it was provided that in case of disagreement between the commissioner and the company in regard to the sufficiency of the assets, upon the application of either, the chief justice of the state should designate one of the judges of the Superior Court to sit with him to try the issue, that their determination respecting the amount, value and sufficiency of the assets, should be conclusive, and that they should thereupon issue their certificate of the amount of the deficiency, if any, to be paid in, and if the company within thirty days made up the deficiency so found, the main resolution should become inoperative and void. The decision was required to be made and the certificate delivered before November 1, 1875.

By the second it was provided that in case of disagreement between the commissioner and the company as to the sufficiency of its assets, and the deficiency was not supplied on or before September 1, 1875, the commissioner should on that day take possession of all the assets, books and papers of the company, and hold them subject to the order of the chief justice, and to be disposed of as provided by law.

On the 21st the Senate voted to concur, and the bill, as amended, became law. Before the final vote in the house several sudden and radical conversions took place. The reasons for the changes were freely suggested in the debate. In his next annual report the commissioner, with a courage as breezy and refreshing as it is unusual, in drawing back a corner of the curtain, disclosed not hints and suspicions, but names and prices.

"And it should also be stated that two of the members of the House, Buswell Carter, of Plainville (holding a policy for $1,000 in the company), and George T. Steel, of Bristol (holding one for $2,000), speaking earnestly and with great apparent sincerity, as policy-holders, plead for leniency to the company, and induced the members to consent to the first House proviso. Up to within two hours of this action of theirs they had been vehement against the company, and against any change in the action of the Insurance Committee. Two days afterwards they surrendered their policies to the company and received their money value."

Stubs in the check-book of Noyes show that out of the funds of the company during the year 1875 and the early part of 1876, he paid over twenty-seven thousand dollars to lawyers, lobbyists and scribblers. Much of this was used around the capitol. Some of the money passed through hands notoriously corrupt. Some was accepted by men of high repute, who, for a price, consented to act as secret agents in aiding the continuance of one of the most detestable forms of fraud. Perhaps in open court it is proper to defend and to defend vigorously even the worst offenders. But when one, no matter how thickly veneered with respectability, takes a fee for prowling with hidden and unavowed designs around the halls of legislation in the interests of crime, it is fairly questionable whether the hireling is not more guilty than his employer.

As the company had not made good the deficiency, the commissioner, in compliance with law, prepared to take possession on the 1st of September. He was restrained by an injunction, issued August 31, by Judge Beardsley, of the Superior Court. This was dissolved on the 8th of September, but while it was in force the United States District Judge in New York city, upon the petition of local policy-holders, issued a restraining order, which was also dissolved after a hearing.

In pursuance of the special law passed to meet the case, a hearing before Chief Justice Park, assisted by Judge L. F. S. Foster, began the 5th day of October, and on the 30th they certified that the deficiency in its assets amounted to $50,000. The total assets were estimated by the company at $1,207,598.63, by the insurance department at $577,578.12 and by the judges at $1,013,279.65 ; and the liabilities respectively at $1,073,294.16, $1,273,932.98 and $1,073,294.16. The judges refused to give an official detailed statement of their valuations, but Judge Park furnished verbal information to the commissioner from which he prepared a table. They considered the building worth $300,000 and the lease $50,000. Brighton bonds (par $26,200), Virginia Coal stock and city lots were lumped together at $50,009.54. The bonds still held by the New York superintendent were placed at $121,750.

November 22d the directors voted to increase the capital stock $50,000 and to require full payment. On the 27th the officers certified that the full amount had been subscribed and paid, and on the 29th the commissioner found the sum standing to the credit of the treasurer at the Yale National Bank.

The commissioner was compelled by the statute to assume that the findings of the judges were correct. Accordingly, though still profoundly lacking in faith, he issued a qualified circular, to the effect that on the above assumption the company was solvent.

By what legerdemain the credit of $50,000 found its way upon the books of the bank, whence it came, and whither it went, were questions quickly lost sight of in the swift whirl of events. Mr. Noyes was plotting a flank movement.

Connecticut pleased him no longer. That much-enduring person was about to turn his back upon the state. He still carried the lobby in his pocket ; he could still control in large measure legislation likely to affect his interests ; he could still hoodwink judges ; he could still command a following of uncritical, but highly respected, gentlemen. In the presence of so many blessings one form loomed up before him, ubiquitous, irrepressible, a Nemesis, threatening vengeance for the past, and warning him away from the fair and familiar fields that continued to tempt his enterprise. He saw that even the points won in the fight with the commissioners, were of negative value, and could yield no practical benefits. To find an atmosphere suited to the flights of his genius, he must get beyond the jurisdiction of that mild-mannered, but troublesome, officer. Even before the hearing, held by Judges Park and Foster, began, Noyes was not only actively prospecting elsewhere, but had already decided in outline upon a plan of future operations.

In 1873 the National Capital Life Insurance Company of Washington, D. C., having lost two-thirds of its capital, voted to reinsure, wind up, and divide the salvage among the shareholders. In two years the work was practically accomplished, all the odds and ends supposed to have any value having been converted into cash and distributed. In August, 1875, Mr. Noyes appeared on the scene, and offered to buy the charter. A committee from the board of directors agreed to fix the price at $4,000. If paid, the sum would be a clear gain, as they considered the franchise worthless. The offer was promptly accepted. Mr. Noyes then left, but promised to return soon to complete the transaction. The following December he reappeared in Washington, attended by two confidential lieutenants, Henry D. Walker and A. Goodrich Fay. A check for $4,000 was now given to the committee, and the charter was turned over to the buyers.

The scene shifts to New York city, where the inner circle held several dark seances to materialize out of the realm of shades the capital needed to clothe, with an appearance of life, the corpse thus lifted from the grave. It was natural that the magicians should seek the aid of Augustus T. Post, for in 1871 he had sold to the American Mutual Life the Brighton bonds. Mr. Post agreed to loan them for fifteen days a mixed lot of western town and county bonds, having a face-value of $50,400, and they agreed to pay $1,500 for the accommodation. By the terms of the contract, the securities were deposited in the Continental National Bank, as the agent of the lender, and they were never to pass out of his complete control. During the period Walker was to have the privilege of inspecting and showing them to others.

Another lot of bonds and stock amounting on their face to $132,000 were borrowed and deposited on similar conditions in the Central Safe Deposit Company. Simultaneously, in Washington, books were opened for subscriptions to renew the capital of $150,000 of the National Capital Life Insurance Company. A. G. Fay, for himself and others, took the whole amount. The affair was organized by the election of William H. Clagett, of that city, temporary president; A. Goodrich Fay, secretary; and Henry D. Walker, treasurer. Mr. Clagett was not admitted to the secrets of the ring. The stock subscriptions were paid to him as president in checks or certificates which he supposed to be good and which under that impression he turned over to the treasurer.

On the 17th the directors resolved,

"That Henry D. Walker, treasurer of this company, be, and he is hereby, authorized to certify as treasurer, that one hundred and fifty thousand dollars of capital stock of this company is paid in under the provisions of the 7th section of its charter.
"Attest   "A. G. FAY, *Secretary*."

In pursuance of that vote the following certificate was issued:

"This is to certify that the capital stock of the National Capital Life Insurance Company of Washington, D. C., was duly paid in on the 17th day of December, 1875, to the amount of one hundred and fifty thousand dollars, and that at the present time the same is invested in securities

(stock and bonds), the par value of which amounts to one hundred and eighty-four thousand, six hundred and five dollars, and that the same are now in my possession as treasurer.
"December 20, 1875."
"HENRY D. WALKER,
"*Treasurer of National Capital Life Insurance Company.*"

The managers of the Washington company now invited a committee from the board of directors of the New Haven Company to inspect the securities fraudulently deposited in New York city. The invitation was accepted and Joseph A. Smith selected. December 23d Smith was taken by Walker to the Continental Bank and Central Safe Deposit Company. The borrowed securities were exhibited to him, and he made inventories of both lots.

The same day he certified to the home office:

"I have .... personally examined the schedule of assets of the National Capital Life Insurance Company of Washington, D. C., and find that said National Capital Life Insurance Company of Washington, D. C., have on special deposit in said Central Safe Deposit Company and said Continental National Bank respectively the following securities, to wit. (Here follow the inventories.)

"The gross amount of said securities being one hundred and eighty-two thousand, four hundred dollars ($182,400) with accrued interest thereon, amounting to twenty-five hundred dollars or thereabouts, the market value of which I am informed and believe to be one hundred and fifty thousand dollars, which said amount of one hundred and fifty thousand dollars constitutes the capital of said National Capital Life Insurance Company of Washington, D. C., in accordance with the terms and conditions of the charter of the said company.
"JOSEPH A. SMITH."

With the equation reduced to simplest terms, B. Noyes, as the embodiment of the Washington Company, then formally contracted with B. Noyes as the embodiment of the New Haven Company, to take the assets of the latter and assume its liabilities. At the end of the fifteen days the bogus capital of $150,000 was returned to the lenders. In the mind of the inventor the growth that sprang up, blossomed and perished within two weeks, was no more and no less genuine than the "preferred stock," "guaranty capital," and other stuff christened with imposing titles, which "learned judges," on more occasions than one, after "full consideration," had impliedly pronounced good. The wreckage gathered from New Haven afforded the enterprise as launched afresh under a change of colors, the means for coming before strangers in presentable garb.

At the annual meeting of the company, held in Washington early in May, 1876, Benjamin Noyes was elected president; William H. Clagett, vice-president; Henry D. Walker, treasurer; and J. A. Mortimore, secretary. Mr. Walker retained charge of the department of New York and New Jersey, with headquarters at 170 Broadway. A department for New England was created, with headquarters at room No. 2, Insurance Building, New Haven. The company advertised that it had over one million of dollars in assets.

In January, 1877, the National Capital Life contracted to reinsure the New Jersey Mutual Life Insurance Company, of Newark, which had over thirteen thousand policy-holders, and claimed over $1,800,000 in property. The authorities of New Jersey regarded the trade as a plot to steal the assets. Justice did not delay. In March Noyes was arrested. In May the case was called, and as he did not appear his bail of $5,000 was declared forfeited. Later he was tried, convicted and sentenced to a term of eighteen months in prison. All efforts to procure a pardon failed.

In October Judge Martin of the Superior Court, on motion of Commissioner Stedman, issued a temporary injunction restraining the National Life and Trust and the American Mutual Life Insurance Companies, their officers and agents, under a several penalty of $50,000, from proceeding further in business, except to receive any premiums tendered, and hold the same as a special deposit to abide the order of the court, to pay ground-rents and to receive proofs of losses under policies.

Commissioner Stedman also applied to have a receiver appointed for both companies. Gen. William B. Wooster, of Derby, was appointed by the Superior Court a committee to hear the testimony in the case. On all points he reported in favor of the commissioner. Accordingly, Judge Pardee granted the application. Talcott H. Russell, Esq., of New Haven, was appointed temporary receiver July 1, 1878, and permanent receiver November 9th. In addition to the ordinary functions conferred by law, he was specially authorized to bring suits to collect unpaid subscriptions to the capital stock and for installments on the same, called and improperly canceled. One year from the 8th day of November, 1878, was limited for the presentation of claims against the company, etc.

The managers had taken good care that the receiver should find very little. By an act approved July 8, 1874, the treasurer of Connecticut was authorized to receive "a bond and first mortgage" for the sum of $100,000, on the insurance building in New Haven, and to surrender to the company all other mortgages and securities held for the protection of policy-holders. The mortgages thus surrendered were duly collected, and the proceeds moved out of the state. Books, papers, everything supposed to have any value, or to throw any light on the past were spirited away. The building could not be stolen bodily, and so remained, a monument of folly and crime. If the rent was not paid promptly by the terms of the lease, the property was forfeited to the leasor. Extracts from a letter of Noyes to Walker, dated June 11, 1876, will show how closely they sometimes came to the edge:

"MY DEAR WALKER:

"We must pay to Bishop who is treasurer of Trinity Church, the ground rent due 1st May, $2,000. I have paid losses, etc., so that I am short, and we must pay $1,250 to Fay, sure.

"I have given Smith a line to Mortimer to pay over to you all he can, way down to his bottom dollar, so that you can send your check as treasurer, payable to J. A. Bishop—leaving off Treasurer—for $2000, so that the ground rent will come direct from you as treasurer, and Bishop will use the money to pay Trinity church debt with, but not credit it at present, for if the legislature at the heel of the session under Stedman's spur, should pass some damnable act of confiscation, the records will show that the building and lease is forfeited to Trinity church, when, in fact, Bishop, their treasurer, had the rent money in hand and it is not forfeited—and we fix it up anew—which, if so done, would wipe out the state deposit."

Mr. Russell fought step by step to recover what belonged to the creditors. The building realized $35,600, but back taxes and assessments reduced the net to about $20,000. About $2,000 was obtained for the Brighton bonds. Stockholders and directors were forced by lawsuits to contribute over $40,000. Some suits failed through the death or insolvency of the parties. Efforts to hold Post and others pecuniarily responsible for the fraud practiced through their aid, also failed through the death and reputed insolvency of the principal parties. In February, 1893, the receiver closed the trust, having paid two dividends of 5 per cent. each, aggregating $66,875.76.

On the release of Mr. Noyes from prison late in September, 1879, many citizens of New Haven gave him a reception at the Elliott House. From the tenor of the remarks on that occasion, a visitor unfamiliar with the history of the guest, would have supposed that a hero, persecuted by malice to the verge of martyrdom, had returned at last triumphant, to find among friends of happier days, if not fresh chances for the exercise of rare gifts, at least a retreat for an honored old age. But the blaze of welcome quickly died away. The last dozen years of fruitless struggle were brightened by few gleams of light. Deserted by nearly every one, Mr. Noyes died in the hospital at New Haven, August 31, 1891, dependent for comforts in his last illness on the kindness of a few old friends.

CHAPTER IX.

INSURANCE IN CONNECTICUT—Continued.

THE CONNECTICUT HEALTH (HARTFORD LIFE) INSURANCE COMPANY.

DURING its brief existence this company twice changed its name and twice the essential character of its risks. By the act of incorporation, passed in 1848, its business was confined to health insurance. As at a later date could have been foreseen the scheme proved a failure. Facts had not been sufficiently collected and classified to afford a basis for rates. Again, the border lines of ailment that must be crossed to entitle policy-holders to benefits, like isothermal lines across the continent, shadowy at best, grew more tortuous from prospects of indemnity.

The next year the company was empowered to make insurance predicated upon lives, to increase the capital from the limit of $50,000 to $100,000, and to change the name from the Connecticut Health to the Hartford Life and Health Insurance Company, which in 1852 was razeed to the Hartford Life Insurance Company, the health department, except for early issues, having been entirely abandoned.

It had been formed as a sort of offshoot from the Connecticut Mutual to occupy a field from which this was excluded, but now came into direct competition with its foster-father. For a time the company prospered under the new departure, but in an evil hour tried the experiment of insuring negro slaves and coolies by ship-loads. Although premiums were very high they were still far from remunerative. As a rule the worst masters took out policies and in the most hazardous occupations. Negroes were described as Cæsar or Cato, Jim or Tom, and identification was so difficult that if any of a gang died, names in the proofs of loss were easily fitted to them. Shippers of coolies knew the average percentage of loss, and hence had every advantage in arranging terms. After two or three years the experiment was abandoned, but not till incurable wounds had been left behind. The company withdrew from New York and Massachusetts in 1857, and wound up its affairs with convenient dispatch. It built and occupied the block on Pearl street, now owned and occupied by the State Savings Bank.

The company was well officered, and hence its mistakes are the more surprising. Its president, James Dixon, a winsome, tactful, scholarly gentleman, member of Congress 1845–49, United States senator two terms, 1857–69, succeeded better in politics than with insurance. Conservative by temperament he had little sympathy with measures of reconstruction contrived to secure party supremacy, and hence sided with President Johnson, whose eccentricities brought swift disaster to his cause and its supporters. William T. Hooker, afterward president of the Guardian Mutual Life Insurance Company of New York, was vice-president, and Henry L. Miller, secretary.

THE CHARTER OAK LIFE INSURANCE COMPANY (HARTFORD).

This institution at one time held the promise of a brilliant career, but reckless investments brought its affairs to a crisis from which the fall was not less swift than sad. By the charter the capital was limited to $200,000, ten per cent. to be paid in cash and ninety in stock notes. The issue of policies on the lives of husbands for the exclusive benefit of wives and children was authorized. Three-fourths of the funds must be invested either in mortgages on real estate of double the value of the debt secured, in the stocks of the United States or of the several states, or in the bonds of New York, Boston and the cities of Connecticut. One-fourth might be loaned upon indorsed promissory notes not having more than twelve months to run. The directors were forbidden to make dividends to stockholders exceeding eight per cent. per annum on the capital.

Books for subscription were opened by the commissioners August 3, 1850. There was such a rush for the shares that nine thousand six hundred and nine ($969,000) were taken and the first installment paid. The total was reduced by allotment to two thousand ($200,000). On the 24th of the same month the subscribers organized by adopting by-laws and electing the following directors: Gideon Welles, William T. Lee, Calvin Day, Tertius Wadsworth, Thomas Belknap, Erastus Smith, James G. Bolles, Charles Seymour, Jr., John A. Butler and L. F. Robinson. The board met the same evening and elected Gideon Welles, president; William T. Lee, vice-president, and Samuel Coit, secretary. Archibald Welch, M.D., was appointed consulting physician. He was killed in a railway accident at Norwalk in 1853. Dr. Samuel B. Beresford was then appointed. To his care and skill the company was largely indebted for the excellent character of its risks.

Mr. Welles, an able writer on current political topics, in early life a stalwart advocate of Jacksonian Democracy, a frequent member of the legislature, comptroller of the state, postmaster at Hartford, and Secretary of the Navy under Presidents Lincoln and Johnson, retired from the presidency in March, 1852. He was succeeded by A. Gill. John L. Bunce was elected vice-president, and James C. Walkley, secretary.

To increase the cash assets to $100,000, the board voted in June, 1852, to sell to William T. Hooker stock-notes amounting to $74,340, for the sum of $67,025, the proceeds to lie as a special deposit at five per cent. interest in the Connecticut River Bank till February 28, 1853. In February, 1853, the notes were repurchased from Mr. Hooker at the original price. Early in March the process was repeated on a smaller scale. Notes of a face value of $50,390 were sold for $50,000, and the proceeds deposited as before.

The difference in the sums realized from the two sales was made up in the cash assets of the company from the profits of the year. In July, 1854, a different device was adopted to meet the legal requirements of certain states that excluded outside companies unless they could show a given amount of paid-up capital, invested in approved securities. Instead of selling the stock-notes and making a special deposit of the proceeds for a definite period, at the expiration of which they were to be repurchased, and so on in a round of concentric circles, the secretary was authorized at discretion to sell them and with the proceeds buy bank, state or city stocks to stand in the name of the company. The institution further agreed to buy back the notes whenever requested by the purchaser at the "full amount thereof," and, to provide the means, the secretary with the consent of the president was authorized to sell any of the stocks in the treasury.

As parties bought and sold, the stock-notes changed, but care was taken to accept none unless good. As we have seen, this feature played a very important part in early insurance when the country was comparatively poor. In some other states the device was used fraudulently to launch companies without resources beyond a few chairs and other furniture. In Hartford, from first to last, both makers and endorsers expected to meet the obligations in full if need arose. When the Protection failed two or three tried to evade payment on technical pleas, but were beaten in the courts. The war against stock-notes that began about the middle of the century in several states was not provoked by any abuse of the system in Hartford.

In March, 1855, James C. Walkley was elected president, and Elias Gill secretary. Up to this time the position of president had been honorary rather than active. He now became the real head, and was expected to devote his energies to the work. At the end of the fiscal year Mr. Gill resigned, and was succeeded by Samuel H. White. Few changes occurred in the office corps during the next decade. Thomas W. Russell, elected vice-president in '59, was succeeded by Noyes S. Palmer in September, '64. Z. A. Storrs followed Mr. Palmer, and was succeeded by Mr. White in '72. Halsey Stevens became secretary in January, '73. While secretary and vice-president, Mr. White also acted as treasurer.

In March, 1867, the board voted that the president and secretary notify the stockholders to pay up in cash twenty-five dollars per share, within thirty days after demand, and the secretary was directed to indorse the same upon the stock-notes. Two reasons are given ; first, the legal requirement in several states of a paid-up capital in the sum of $150,000 ; and second, the ability to loan on the best bond and mortgage security at eight per cent. a year, " so that the maximum dividend of eight per cent. semi-annually, as specified by our charter, can be declared and paid regularly when $150,000 are paid upon the capital stock."

A year later, in March, 1868, another vote was passed in substantially the same language calling in the final twenty-five dollars per share, so as to raise the paid capital from $150,000 to $200,000, and directing the secretary to surrender to the makers the stock-notes in the treasury.

That in both instances the money for paying the instalments was furnished by the company, the record omits to mention, possibly on account of the provision in the charter which made it unlawful for the directors to make dividends exceeding eight per cent. per annum upon the capital. By a curious lapse each vote refers to the charter as permitting a maximum dividend of eight per cent. semi-annually.

Whether the reasons given for the transactions were addressed to possible visitors from the insurance departments of other states, or were thrown in to beguile the historical inquirer of the future, must be left to conjecture.

At the close of 1863 the company had in force 3,047 policies insuring $5,909,011, with gross assets amounting to $657,387, exclusive of $100,000 in stock-notes. For the next nine years growth was rapid and apparently solid. Among the agents of the Charter Oak was a large infusion of men of high character and wide influence, who secured for it a very desirable clientage. In 1869 over seven thousand two hundred new policies were issued, insuring over $18,000,000. Though this was the most fruitful year in its history the three that preceded and the three that followed indicate great activity on the part of its agents and great confidence on the part of the public.

In the face of superb labor in the field the home management was weak and wasteful. As from the walls of a reservoir too flimsy to resist the pressure from within, all at once both patrons and the public saw the contents of the treasury pouring to waste through several bad breaks.

The first official warning of danger came from John W. Stedman, insurance commissioner of Connecticut, in his first annual report, dated June 9, 1875. After describing the charter provisions of the company he says:

"Only ten dollars a share was ever paid up on the capital stock. The remaining ninety dollars were paid in dividends. On this full paid stock a dividend of eight per cent. is regularly paid according to law, and in addition to this the commissions on the business in the home office are divided among the stockholders, amounting in some years to as high as fourteen dollars a share. Certainly nothing of this kind could have been contemplated by the legislature in granting the charter of the company, and I think it wholly unwarranted." .... "I have thus made a full and fair presentation of the embarrassments of this company. There has been a weakness of judgment in its confidences, and a carelessness in loaning its money and scattering it in gratuities, amounting to a moral delinquency."

The embarrassments were more serious than could then be known. Early in 1875 the banking house of Allen, Stephens & Co. failed, owing the Charter Oak $944,816. A part of the indebtedness grew out of a joint interest in a silver mine in Utah, and other ill-defined speculations. The claim has since yielded very little except trouble and expense.

Early in the seventies the Valley Railway was built from Hartford to Saybrook on the west bank of the Connecticut. Mr. Walkley, who lived down the river, was father and president of the company. Hartford subscribed half a million toward the stock, which was increased by subscriptions, mostly from other towns, to a little over a million. First mortgage bonds were issued to the extent of another million. In 1873 the cost per mile for construction was given as $58,858, and for equipment, $5,834. The excess, furnished almost exclusively by the Charter Oak, was carried as floating debt to the extent of $1,177,564. For convenience this, including, perhaps, other items, was funded in second mortgage bonds to the amount of $1,250,000, which were lodged with the insurance company as security for loans aggregating $1,083,456. As the railway, coming eight months out of twelve in competition with a navigable river, was earning little, if anything, above current expenses, the outlook for the junior bonds was extremely dismal.

To build up business for the road $235,874 were loaned to a manufacturing concern in Higganum, and $75,000 upon a summer hotel in Saybrook, with $25,000 additional on the furniture. Mining property in West Virginia absorbed another half million of cash, and the returns from this also have come chiefly in the form of bills and worry.

While the sky was still cloudless the company erected, at a reported cost of $844,380, its home office at the corner of Main and Athenæum streets, moving in early in '71. Hot disputes afterwards arose at intervals over the value of the property. Sixteen years later it was sold to the Ætna Life for $231,000.

Minor embarrassments are passed by not because they were trivial in themselves, but trivial in comparison.

Great alarm followed the official disclosure of this condition, and a lively hunt for some mode of relief. At this juncture an officer of the New York Chamber of Insurance, and an expert in the business, brought the agents of the company into relations with Henry J. Furber, vice-president of the Universal Life of New York, who had already taken a hand in winding up the affairs of several that in the wild extravagance of the time had been driven into close corners. Mr. Furber had recently won the good-will of the insurance department of New York, by saving for the North American Life a large line of bonds and mortgages, liable to forfeiture from taint of usury. After several interviews with the commissioner and other prominent citizens of Connecticut, and, with their approval, Mr. Furber purchased the stock of the Charter Oak in the name of himself and his friends.

From the progress then made in his investigations the commissioner thought that a contribution of half a million of dollars in fresh funds would make good the impairment and restore technical solvency. Mr. Furber agreed to give that amount outright. He was to be indemnified by monthly payments of seven and one-half per cent. on all premiums collected, and by one-half the salvage on all policies purchased during the next five years. It was further agreed that at the option of the company the contract might be liquidated at any time before the expiration of the term, after Furber had received $500,000 with interest from the proceeds of the contract, and in addition such further sum for services and risks, as the parties might agree upon. In case of disagreement upon the terms of liquidation the matter was to be referred to three disinterested arbitrators, one selected by each party, and the third by the persons so chosen. Their decision was to be final.

The commissioner took the view that the $500,000 should not be charged as a liability, as it was to be repaid gradually from the loading of premiums. On the other hand, the special commission afterwards appointed contended that it became an immediate liability, and hence did not technically help at all to repair the gap in the assets.

A point less open to dispute was the extreme improbability that a man in reality making a contract with himself would have serious trouble in fixing the compensation for "services" and "risks," or that he would harm his bank account by "liquidating" it prematurely.

The affairs of the company passed into the hands of the new management late in 1875, Edwin R. Wiggin having been elected, December 9th, acting president for the rest of the year.

At the next annual meeting, January 25, 1876, James C. Walkley, S. H. White, Nelson Hollister and Daniel Philips were re-elected directors, while Edwin R. Wiggin and A. H. Dillon, Jr., were added. The same day Edwin R. Wiggin was elected president; S. H. White, vice-president and treasurer; A. H. Dillon, second vice-president; Halsey Stevens, secretary; and William L. Squire, assistant-secretary. J. C. Walkley was appointed advisory counsel, and Henry J. Furber, financial manager. Furber and Wiggin were not old associates, but were first brought together in this venture.

Mr. Furber, whose ability no one ever questioned, went to work at once to introduce order and system, in the place of disorder and confusion. He soon found that he had been greatly deceived as to the condition of the company. Assets had been overstated, and liabilities under-stated. In June he put Thomas M. Smith, an expert, on the premium note account, with instructions to ascertain and report its exact condition. Edmund A. Stedman, actuary of the State Insurance Department, went over the same ground, starting later. Both labored for months, and their final footings differed by less than $20 ($18.03). But the amount was nearly $1,000,000 less than claimed in the previous annual statement. The result was promptly reported to the department, and embodied in the next return.

Meanwhile, the large debt of the Valley road, the Higganum shops, the Saybrook Hotel, the West Virginia mines, the claims against Allen, Stephens & Company, to say nothing of minor "investments," were not only yielding no income, but several at best were sources of vexatious expense. The only light ahead came from the excellent quality of the insurance risks scattered over the country. And now the insured were learning how their premiums had been locked up in ominous speculations.

One cannot help admiring the courage and fertility of resource with which Furber met the crisis. The company had a mortgage for $800,000, taken in 1875, on eight parcels of property in New York city, owned by Edward Mathews, one of the largest holders of real estate in the city. He was greatly pressed for cash. In December, 1876, Mr. Furber bought from him the eight pieces, nearly all located on Broadway, for $3,030,000, releasing the company's mortgage of $800,000, assuming prior mortgages to the amount of $948,000, turning in the second mortgage bonds of the Valley road ($1,250,000), at $1,047,000, and paying $235,000 in cash. The trade was conducted under the eye of Commissioner Stedman, who sent to the New York department for an official appraisal. The superintendent of that state selected Thomas Knowlton Marcy, who made his report December 9th. Mr. Marcy went over the records and accounts of each piece with great care. He found the total annual expenses for taxes, insurance, repairs, etc., to be $47,887, the income from rooms actually rented, $235,480, and the net income, $187,593. He fixed the appraisal at $3,000,000, on which the property was yielding net yearly revenue at the rate of over six per cent. (6.24). Rooms then vacant were estimated to be worth $28,500 additional.

Similarly Mr. Furber traded the Higganum mortgage, amounting, with interest, to $250,000, for productive property in the heart of New York city.

It should be remembered that the winter of 1876–7 was the most dismal part of the long period of depression which followed the great financial panic of 1873. An undecided contest for the presidency of the Republic was then piled on our other troubles.

The New York property received in the trade is now estimated to be worth over eight millions. Instead of holding it for better times the company placed a price on each parcel, and sold as the market rose to its figures, the best going first. On the other hand the Valley bonds never yielded a dollar of revenue, and in the subsequent reorganization of the road were wiped out utterly.

In January, 1877, a petition signed by eleven influential policy-holders was presented to the General Assembly, asking that the affairs of the company be investigated. This was but a symptom of the distrust that pervaded the community. Through the Guardian and the Universal Mr. Furber had reinsured many weak companies. Thousands of poor people had been induced to sell or exchange policies for fractions of the reserve charged against them. This process was justly regarded in Connecticut, and especially in Hartford, as one of the most heartless and cruel contrivances ever devised for fattening the few at the expense of the many. Large local interests in the business had educated the people to regard the custody and management of life insurance funds as a most sacred trust. With such convictions, many felt that the intrusion of the methods in vogue in Mr. Furber's New York companies must be prevented at all hazards. In March, 1877, the superintendent of that state began an exhaustive examination of the Universal. In July his report, severely condemnatory, was made public. While the work was in progress various scraps of fact and inference found their way across the border, adding fuel to the flame.

As a result of the agitation a law was passed creating a special commission to investigate the life companies of the state. It consisted of Origen S. Seymour, H. M. Cleveland and David P. Nichols. During his life Judge Seymour, the chairman, filled with distinguished credit a seat on the bench of the Supreme Court of the state. He was a man of sound judgment and unquestioned probity. The special commission made a preliminary report to Commissioner Stedman, June 21, 1877, finding a deficit of $2,063,412.38. In reaching the result they reduced the appraisal on the two

New York city purchases from $3,030,000 and $800,000 to $1,845,000 and $505,000 respectively. The special commission discovered nothing not already known to Mr. Stedman. But the point of view and animus differed. Mr. Stedman saw that the situation was desperate, and in his anxiety to save the institution from ruin and its patrons from loss, gave the management the benefit of every doubt. On the other hand, the special commission (and we may safely concede that both were equally sincere) drew its inspiration from prevalent distrust and hostility.

The law relating to the winding up of insurance companies passed in 1875 left it optional with the commissioner when he found the assets of any such company impaired to notify it to cease the issue of new policies and the payment of dividends until the deficiency should be made good, but in case the assets were found to be less than three-fourths of the liabilities he was required to apply to the courts for the appointment of a receiver and the annulment of the charter. The commissioner consulted eminent counsel and hesitated. At length, borne down by overwhelming pressure, on the 14th of July, he applied to Dwight W. Pardee, one of the judges of the Supreme Court, for the appointment of a receiver. An injunction was accordingly issued. After several adjournments, July 30th, by common consent the injunction was dissolved. During the pendency of the petition plans were arranged for the transfer of the company to other hands. On the 28th, the old directors resigned *seriatim*, and the vacancies were immediately filled by the election of Marshall Jewell, William W. Eaton, George F. Bissell, Robert E. Day and Elisha Johnson. George E. Hatch held over, and J. M. Allen was added later. Simultaneously the old officers resigned. The new board at once organized and elected Marshall Jewell president of the company.

One of the last acts of the old regime before issue of the injunction was to borrow two hundred thousand dollars of the Ætna Life by mortgaging the Charter Oak building.

There is no evidence that Mr. Furber by word or deed ever tried to deceive either the commissioner or the special commission. His ways, avowedly dictated solely by self-interest, were bold and open. He did not pose as a Christian, or shed tears to be seen of men over the woes of deceived and defrauded policy-holders. Masterful in resource, if let alone he would have saved the company because its rescue was clearly for his interest. Yet, whether it was to live or die, the part of the community who believe that life should be something higher and nobler than a game of grab, breathed more freely when this adept in the game departed.

Early in July an influential committee was raised to see whether the ratio of assets to liabilities would justify an attempt to save the company from a receivership. A sub-committee, consisting of Colonel Jacob L. Greene, Thomas O. Enders, Gustavus F. Davis, and John M. Holcombe, after making as thorough an examination as the time permitted, on the 25th of July reported that economy and efficiency of management, supported by confidence on the part of policy-holders, would probably enable the company to pay all claims in full and regain solvency.

Marshall Jewell had a national reputation. He was not only successful in business, but had been governor of the state, minister to St. Petersburg, and postmaster-general. His purchase of a large majority of the stock and acceptance of the presidency promised to supply the essential conditions of recovery suggested by the sub-committee. But the change came too late. New business had ceased. Many policy-holders, taking advantage of the terms of the contract, demanded paid-up insurance to the value of their claims. While revenues were cut off, death losses and expenses continued to pour in.

In September the directors voted to scale the capital forty per cent., and to pay no dividends on the balance for five years. They also asked policy-holders to scale the liability on that account forty per cent., also promising to restore the amount so relinquished, if possible, from gradual sales of unproductive property. Claims from deaths and endowments were scaled to the same extent.

Many policy-holders consented and many held back. Meanwhile demands upon the treasury far outran income. The gentlemen who had undertaken the work of rescue became discouraged. At their suggestion, commissioner Stedman in January, 1878, again applied for a receiver. The legislature was in session, and all parties in interest now united in asking for such amendments to the charter as would enable the policy-holders to re-organize on a purely mutual basis. The act was passed and approved March 15.

On the 18th of April the policy-holders met, accepted the amendments to the charter, and elected a board of twenty-one directors. After much persuasion, George M. Bartholomew took the presidency, June 3d. Halsey Stevens continued as secretary till succeeded by Charles E. Willard in June, '79.

In December, 1878, Messrs. Wiggin, Furber, Walkley and White were tried at Hartford before Judge James A. Hovey for conspiracy. For the state appeared William Hamersley, L. F. S. Foster and John R. Buck; for the defense, Leonard Swett, of Chicago, Governor Dorsheimer, of New York, Daniel Chadwick, of Lyme, Conn., with Charles E. Perkins, A. P. Hyde and Lewis E. Stanton, of Hartford. The trial lasted twenty-four days and resulted in a verdict of acquittal for all the defendants. A witness, whose testimony before the grand jury had been decisive, meanwhile had met with a change of heart and put himself beyond reach of the court.

After the return home of the invaders from New York city Wiggin presented to Governor Jewell, for adjustment, a contract made with President Walkley, without the knowledge of Furber, to run for five years, and calling for two and one-half per cent. on all premium receipts. According to Wiggin the consideration was his share in persuading Furber to put up the famous $500,000. Mr. White had a like contract. Generosity, even colossal generosity, in handling the money of others, is not an uncommon trait. The claim was pressed, but defeated.

Mr. Bartholomew's consent to take the presidency renewed the courage of all parties in interest. Gifted with quick and keen perceptions, he was a man of affairs, accustomed to handle large transactions without neglecting details. He had the full confidence of the community and was much in demand for positions of trust. But, as can be seen now, the fight for life was hopeless from the start. The forlorn condition of the company had been widely advertised. No upright and competent agent would canvass for a concern visibly doomed. No one intelligent enough to make a desirable risk would take a contract from it. Following a lead started, but soon abandoned, by President Winston, of the New York Mutual Life, the Charter Oak years before had cut rates about twenty per cent., and thus on live policies was deprived of the margin available for repairs. Maturing claims constantly exceeded income. One piece of property after another was sold and the proceeds applied to meet current demands. Its credit withered. To raise funds Mr. Bartholomew from time to time gave his personal indorsement to the amount of over $2,250,000. With the moneys thus procured the company in a single year saved $340,000 by buying up claims. Between July, 1878, and July, 1886, $6,311,165.17 were paid to policy-holders, the number of whom was reduced from about twenty-two thousand to less than ten thousand. Yet heroic treatment failed to arrest the progress of the disease. With steady step creeping paralysis drew near the vitals.

At length, in September, 1885, Ephraim Williams, insurance commissioner, applied for a receiver on the ground that the impairment of assets exceeded the legal limit of twenty-five per cent. The case, tried before Judge Granger, turned on valuations—a question prolific of wide diversities of opinion. After a contest of two months the suit was withdrawn.

A year after the application for a receiver, or in September, 1886, the final explosion came with a sudden and dreadful shock. Heavy embezzlements from the Hartford Silk Company and from the Union Manufacturing Company of Manchester, were brought to light by the flight of the person who was both president of the Silk and treasurer of the Union. Mr. Bartholomew was president of the Union Company, a director in both and personally a heavy endorser of their paper. At a special meeting of the directors of the Charter Oak, held September 18th,

"Mr. Bartholomew stated that for some time he had had in his hands, as a matter of protection from annoying attachments, a large amount of the company's funds; that he had held himself ready to pay over these funds to the company as needed, although he had not kept them distinct and intact; that now, owing to his embarrassment growing out of the troubles of the Hartford Silk Manufacturing Company, for which he was a heavy endorser, he found himself unable to pay this company the amount due them; that he had handed to the secretary, as collateral security for this debt, certain securities which he believed would in time, at least, be worth the full amount of his indebtedness. Mr. Bartholomew said further that he deemed it necessary to make some temporary arrangement for protecting the company and continuing its business."

Possessing unlimited credit, reticent, self-centred and, till awakened too late to the error, confident of ability to meet every demand upon him as occasion arose, Mr. Bartholomew suddenly found himself unable to do so. During a long career he had signed many bonds of indemnity, especially for young men, and had indorsed paper to the amount of many millions.

September 20th Mr. Bartholomew resigned. The board directed its counsel, Charles E. Gross, to apply for a receiver. There was no opposition. Judge Pardee selected in succession Jonathan B. Bunce and Robert E. Day. Both declined. He then appointed Isaac Brooks, of Torrington, and Edmund A. Stedman, of Hartford, who both qualified.

Thus from mortal wounds inflicted twelve or fifteen years before, an institution once strong and promising, was brought to the grave.

After many delays a dividend to policy-holders of fifteen (15) per cent., amounting to $458,775.49, was paid. January 22, 1897, the court made a final order distributing the rest of the assets ($105,747.21) in payment of sundry expenses and fees, and a last dividend of three and one-fourth per cent. to policy-holders.

When the impairment of assets, caused by the recklessness of the Walkley-White *regime*, was first brought to light, both the company and a large percentage, if not the full amount of claims of policy-holders, could have been saved had the law been less mandatory and left a wider range to the discretion of the commissioner. Had it come within the power of the office to substitute a competent for an incompetent management, and to enforce such slight scaling of claims as would have restored technical solvency, the beneficiaries under its contracts would have received nearly their full dues instead of the beggarly driblets that finally reached them.

CHAPTER X.

INSURANCE IN CONNECTICUT—Continued.

THE ÆTNA LIFE INSURANCE COMPANY (HARTFORD).

THE year after its incorporation, in 1819, the Ætna (Fire) Insurance Company obtained an amendment to its charter, authorizing it to grant annuities, upon an additional capital not exceeding $150,000, to be held as a separate guaranty for the liabilities arising under the business. The privilege was never exercised. In 1850, by a second amendment, the ancillary company was empowered to grant insurance upon lives, and thirty years after the inception of the original plan, organized as the Ætna Insurance Company Annuity Fund. Rights to subscribe were distributed among the owners of the parent company in proportion to their holdings. Officers of both were the same, certain directors, with Eliphalet A. Bulkeley as chairman, having been delegated to manage the affairs of the new department.

After a brief experience, it was thought best that the control of the two institutions should be made separate and distinct, and accordingly, in July, 1853, by still another amendment to the charter, the child was launched on its independent career under the name of the Ætna Life Insurance Company. Original directors were E. A. Bulkeley, Austin Dunham, H. Z. Pratt, Lawson C. Ives, Mark Howard, John Warburton, Roland Mather, S. L. Loomis, J. W. Seymour and W. H. D. Callender. E. A. Bulkeley was chosen president, and John W. Seymour, secretary.

During the first decade of its existence the company developed slowly. It will be remembered that a period of long, and at times severe, financial depression preceded the war—a condition that bore heavily upon new enterprises, and brought to both new and old widespread mortality.

Till 1861 all contracts for insurance made by the Ætna Life were written on the proprietary plan. It then began to issue participating policies, and established a mutual department under the same control, but with entirely distinct books, accounts, and investments. Since then applicants have had their choice between the two methods. Till 1868 patrons on the mutual side were allowed to pay a part of the premiums by note, a system once quite popular, but under plans then matured all subsequent contracts have required payments in cash.

One of the first effects of the war was to aggravate the depression previously existing. As it went on, and issues of paper currency stimulated speculation and extravagance not less than legitimate business, the life companies already in the field soon began to profit from changed conditions. Large numbers of men rushed into hazardous ventures, and amid the uncertainties of their private affairs, made provision for their families by taking out heavy lines of insurance. Others of more prudent habits were influenced by the example to investigate the merits of the system, and to avail themselves of the same protection. Inquiry could not fail to satisfy the mind that the principles were sound, or that any well-managed company must always be in a position to meet maturing obligations. The sudden popularity of life insurance was due partly to more urgent need of its benefits, and partly to more thorough comprehension of the subject.

Nowhere is the greatness of the change in the attitude of the public towards

E. A. BULKELEY, Prest. 1850-1872.
Prest. Conn. Mutual Life Ins. Co.,
1846-48.

THOS. O. ENDERS,
President 1872-79.

JOHN C. WEBSTER,
Vice-President 1873.

MORGAN G. BULKELEY,
President 1879.

JOEL L. ENGLISH,
Secretary 1873.

H. W. ST. JOHN,
Actuary 1878.

G. W. RUSSELL, M. D.
Medical Director 1850.

ÆTNA LIFE INSURANCE COMPANY.

life insurance more clearly reflected than in the records of the Ætna. In 1863, thirteen years from the date of organization, its assets amounted to $310,492. In 1866 they had risen to $2,036,823. The impetus then given to the development of the company was stimulated and multiplied by the energy of the management. Its subsequent growth in resources and surplus, in reputation and popularity, has never for an instant been checked by adversities of any nature, or troubles from any quarter. It has been singularly fortunate, too, in avoiding the errors of judgment which intelligence and prudence may, without discredit, be expected to make under the law of averages. In 1868 its assets had increased to $7,538,612; in 1878, to $24,141,125; in 1888, to $32,620,676; and in 1897, to $45,557,272. Its surplus January 1, 1875, was $1,561,810; and gaining each year during the next two decades, reached $6,711,502, on January 1, 1897.

Success far transcending the dreams of the founders, and on the whole, perhaps, unsurpassed in the records of life insurance, viewed in the light of strength rather than size, either in Europe or America, is easily explained. One of the postulates of the business demands that investments shall yield an annual income of four per cent., the excess being available either for immediate distribution among the insured, or for building up a fund held in reserve to meet claims maturing possibly many years later, when the rate of interest on approved security will certainly fall below that figure. The Ætna Life was a pioneer in loaning to western farmers, having entered the field under highly favorable conditions. At the time when its treasury began to be distended by the volume of inflowing premiums, the Illinois Central Railway had a large number of outstanding contracts with settlers on their lands, agreeing to convey titles on payment of the purchase money. Both sides desired the completion of the contracts. At this juncture the Ætna Life came forward and furnished the needful funds, taking mortgages on the farms as security. All the early loans bore interest at ten per cent. The arrangement proved highly advantageous to both lender and borrower. The fertility of the soil attracted heavy immigration, with consequent enhancement in the value of the properties. While the company had abundant reason to be satisfied, thousands of farmers rose from poverty to wealth by the aid thus afforded them. As the region grew rich and the loans were paid off, the company pushed westward into Iowa, repeating the process on the same terms. Employing only trained and faithful agents, it seldom met with defaults, and when compelled to foreclose, generally succeeded, by patience, in drawing a profit from the transaction. The perils of growing competition were met by increase of carefulness, one of the rules being to loan in no case in excess of the value assessed for taxation.

In view of the good fortune that has attended the farm loans of the company, it is not singular that this has continued to be with it a favorite form of investment. On January 1, 1897, it had, thus placed, $25,200,422, secured by over seventeen thousand mortgages on as many separate blocks of real estate, representing a total value of over $105,000,000. On the few foreclosures that have occurred the books show a balance for the credit side.

While loanable funds were much less abundant than now, the Ætna Life also invested largely in the bonds of prosperous cities at the West, bearing seven and seven and three-tenths per cent. interest. On transactions involving many millions the losses were few and small. The surplus annually accruing from investments of extraordinary productiveness enabled the company to return generous dividends to the participating policy-holders, which in turn stimulated growth in new business, and added to the tide of inrolling premiums.

Its risks have been confined to the healthiest parts of the northern states and Canada, where the death rate is comparatively small.

The capital remained at $150,000 till 1878. With over twenty-four millions of assets and nearly two and three-fourths millions of surplus, the company then petitioned the General Assembly for authority to increase the capital to an amount not exceeding $750,000, and the charter was amended accordingly. The act required the increase to be made from such surplus funds as were derived from business done upon the non-participating stock plan of insurance, and to have the approval of the state commissioner. Dividends were limited to ten per cent. per annum, and contributions for this purpose from the mutual department were limited to $9,000 per annum. The capital stood at $750,000 from 1878 till 1883, when the General Assembly again amended the charter authorizing a further increase to $2,000,000. It was increased May 16, 1883, to $1,000,000; January 1, 1887, to $1,250,000; July 13, 1892, to $1,500,000; and July 1, 1895, to $1,750,000.

Eliphalet Adams Bulkeley continued at the head of the company from its inception till his death February 13, 1872. He was born in Colchester, Conn., June 20, 1803, graduated at Yale College in 1824, studing law with William P. Williams, of Lebanon, and about 1830 opened an office in East Haddam, where he was also president of the local bank. Thence he was elected to both branches of the General Assembly. In 1847 he moved to Hartford, where he formed a law partnership with Henry Perkins under the firm-name of Bulkeley & Perkins. He was first judge of the local police court, school fund commissioner, and in 1857 speaker of the House of Representatives. He was one of the organizers and first president of the Connecticut Mutual Life. Later the Ætna absorbed his energies, while incidentally as director he was connected with many other corporations. He was noted for punctuality and for the personal care given to all matters which legitimately claimed his attention.

Thomas Ostram Enders, immediate successor of Judge Bulkeley, was born in Glen, N. Y., September 21, 1832. He became interested in insurance through John G. North, of Meriden, who employed him as solicitor. He moved to Hartford, and at the age of twenty-two took a clerkship in the Ætna Life, and was elected secretary four years later. His industry, fidelity and remarkable aptitude for the business contributed largely to win phenomenal success for the company. To build this up he sacrificed himself. Severe toil, carried often late into night, broke down his health, and shortened his days. In 1879 he resigned, and rested for two years. In 1881 he took the presidency of the United States Bank, then called the U. S. Trust Company. At the time it was suffering from old losses, and the stock was quoted at sixty or less. Under his guidance it shot rapidly ahead. When he resigned in 1892, the bank, in percentage of surplus, value of shares, and ratio of deposits to capital, held the lead in the city by a long interval. Mr. Enders had his residence over the line in West Hartford. He represented that town in the General Assembly for the sessions of 1889 and 1891. He died June 21, 1894.

On the retirement of Mr. Enders, Morgan G. Bulkeley, son of the founder, became president. Born December 26, 1837, and educated in the public schools of Hartford, he began his business career in a mercantile house of Brooklyn, N. Y., in 1851, rising in seven years from the grade of errand boy to partner. When the war came, he enlisted in the Thirteenth New York regiment, and went to the front. On the death of his father in 1872, large local interests brought him back to Hartford, where he served in both branches of the city government, and for eight years as mayor, looking closely and intelligently after the financial and other interests of the public. In 1888 he was elected governor of Connecticut, and, owing to the deadlock between the two branches of the General Assembly that convened in January,

1891, he held over, under the Constitution, for a second term of two years. While Governor Bulkeley has devoted much time to the public, figures show that the interests of the Ætna Life have not suffered.

Vice-presidents have been: J. W. Seymour, 1856-7; John Warburton, 1857-60; S. L. Loomis, 1860-63; Austin Dunham, 1863-77; W. H. Bulkeley, 1877-9; and J. C. Webster, since 1879. The position was honorary till 1879. Mr. Webster has served the company since 1865, having been general agent and superintendent of agencies before taking the vice-presidency. Secretaries have been: J. W. Seymour, 1853-5; Samuel Coit, 1855-8; Thomas O. Enders, 1858-72; and since 1872, J. L. English, whose entry into business was made with the company in 1867. The position of assistant-secretary was created in February, 1890, and was filled by George W. Hubbard, an employee for a quarter of a century, till his death, October 13, 1893. He was succeeded by Charles E. Gilbert. Dr. Gurdon W. Russell, as examining and consulting physician, has been connected with the medical department from the start. Dr. James Campbell was elected medical examiner, February 13, 1894, working in connection with Doctor Russell. Howell W. St. John, the present incumbent, was appointed actuary in October, 1867. Except from death, very few changes have occurred in the official corps.

Under the general statutes the Ætna Life opened an accident department, January 1, 1891. Just six years later it had in force eighteen thousand, five hundred and thirty-two policies, insuring $79,083,850. Vice-president Webster has immediate charge of this branch; Walter C. Faxon, also connected with it, was made assistant secretary in October, 1893.

RECEIPTS TILL JANUARY 1, 1897.

Premiums $123,971,464.75
Interest 45,866,940.55

Total $169,838,405.30

DISBURSEMENTS TO POLICY-HOLDERS.

Death losses $42,833,641.22
Matured endowments 17,623,658.64
Surrender values paid 20,650,164.27
Dividends to policy-holders 18,590,343.88

Total $99,697,808.01

Number of policies in force January 1, 1897, eighty-seven thousand, six hundred and fifty-eight, insuring $145,635,940.

In economy of management the Ætna Life ranks with the first three or four of American companies. It began upstairs in a small room on State street under the wings of its elder brother, the Ætna Fire.

John C. Webster, vice-president, was born at Kingfield, Me., May 24, 1839. Equipped with a good English education, he learned the printer's trade, and before reaching the age of twenty-two was at the head of one of the largest printing offices in Concord, N. H. In 1864 he became agent of the Ætna Life in that city, and soon after general agent for the state of New Hampshire. In 1873 he was made superintendent of agencies, when he moved to Hartford. He has been vice-president since July, 1879. For fifteen years, up to 1895, he edited the *Ætna*, a quarterly publication devoted to the interests of the company. He organized and has had throughout special supervision of the accident department.

Joel L. English, born October 1, 1843, at Woodstock, Vt., in 1867 entered the Hartford office of the Ætna Life as a clerk, and was appointed secretary in 1872. In this single company his life has been devoted to the performance of a ceaseless round of duties. While a life of quiet work may be bare of dramatic incidents, Mr. English is regarded by the profession as one of its most accomplished members.

Howell W. St. John, actuary, was born at Newport, R. I., in April, 1834. After graduating from Yale University as a civil engineer, he pursued the profession in the South and West until October, 1867, when he became actuary of the Ætna Life. He is one of the charter members of the Actuarial Society of America, was its president in 1893 and 1894, and one of its delegates to the International Convention of Actuaries held at Brussels in September, 1895.

Charles E. Gilbert, assistant secretary, was born in Wallingford, Conn., November 8, 1836. During the war he was employed in the offices of the mustering officer and the military commandant of Connecticut and Rhode Island. In 1868 he was made cashier of the Ætna Life and assistant secretary in February, 1895.

With customary good fortune in 1888 the Ætna Life acquired for $231,000 the commodious and elegant building erected by the Charter Oak Life, at a cost by the books of $844,380. The home offices were transferred to the new quarters in the summer of that year. The marvelous growth of the Ætna Life cannot be repeated in the future by any similar organization, because the conditions which rendered the process possible have passed never to return.

THE PHŒNIX MUTUAL LIFE INSURANCE COMPANY (HARTFORD).

Proceeding on the theory that total abstainers from the use of alcoholic drinks could safely be insured at lower rates than miscellaneous risks, accepted, without close regard to personal habits, a number of men, connected for the most part with the temperance reform, in 1851 secured a charter for the American Temperance Life Insurance Company. The incorporators were: Barzillai Hudson, a prominent leader in the crusade against alcohol; Benjamin E. Hale, editor of the *Fountain*, a cold-water sheet; Thomas S. Williams, ex-chief justice of the Connecticut Supreme Court; Francis Gillette, a noted abolitionist in the formative period of the party, and for a year in the United States Senate; James B. Hosmer, philanthropist, who left large sums for public uses; Francis Parsons, a prominent lawyer; and Edson Fessenden, keeper of the Eagle Hotel.

The capital was placed at $100,000, divided into shares of $50 each, with power to increase to $200,000. Ten per cent. was required at the time of subscribing, six per cent. within twenty days after organization, and the balance was allowed to rest in stock-notes.

Books were opened July 22d by H. S. Ramsdell, Andrew T. Judson and A. M. Collins, commissioners, and were closed at noon the next day when it was found that twenty-three hundred and forty-three shares of $50 each had been taken. The number was scaled to two thousand. On the 24th the subscribers met at the *Fountain* office and elected for directors B. Hudson, J. B. Hosmer, T. Wadsworth, F. Parsons, Albert Day and John H. Goodwin. B. E. Hale was elected secretary for the year ensuing on the same ballot. In the afternoon the directors chose B. Hudson president, and Tertius Wadsworth vice-president. On the 28th the board already elected chose four additional members, viz.: W. W. Hoppen, Noah Wheaton, Francis Gillette and Edson Fessenden.

August 4th by-laws were adopted. The distinctive article provides that the company shall take no risks upon the lives of persons addicted to the habitual use of intoxicating liquors as a beverage.

Moved by strong convictions, advocates of temperance gladly accepted an opportunity to subject their beliefs to a practical and perhaps decisive test. Accordingly, tables were prepared graduating the cost of insurance about ten per cent. below current rates, and the issue of policies began. All premiums were at first required in cash. Had the scheme met with popular favor perhaps the correctness of the theory would have been demonstrated. However, persons interested in the cause did not hasten to seize the privilege, and others did not care to sign a pledge of perpetual abstinence in consideration of the discount. Solicitors found the restrictions placed upon the freedom of the individual an ever-present obstacle, blocking the persuasive force of their eloquence. Satisfied after a fair trial that, however correct the principle might be, the attempted application of it ran counter to the inclinations of human nature, the managers abandoned the temperance feature in 1861, conformed the rates and contracts to the common practice, and with legislative permission, changed the name to the Phœnix Mutual Life Insurance Company.

Many of the risks taken under the original plan still remain on the books, and as a whole have perhaps justified the opinions of the founders in regard to the greater longevity of those who entirely avoid spirituous drinks.

October 5, 1852, Benjamin E. Hale was chosen president for the rest of the year, and James H. Holcomb, secretary. Mr. Hale resigned February 23, 1853, to take the general agency of the company, and was succeeded by Edson Fessenden. Mr. Holcomb also resigned, and declining a re-election, was succeeded by J. Augustus Wright, March 14th. W. H. Hill was secretary, April, '57–July, '65, and James F. Burns, July, '65–June, '75. The company decided to conduct its business on the mutual principle and to treat the stock as a guaranty capital, entitled only to six per cent. a year, the legal rate of interest.

The early progress of the company was slow. In June, 1861, when the experiment of insuring only the strictly temperate was abandoned, its gross assets amounted to $262,088.40. For the previous year premiums reached $48,704.02 and income from investments, $10,749.81. With change of method and the stimulus given to all activities by the Civil War, came rapid growth. Imitating a popular feature of the time, it gave up the wholly cash requirement, accepting part payment in notes.

The panic of 1873, followed by six years of sore depression, brought ruin upon many insurance companies both life and fire. All interests suffered. Even the savings banks of New England and of our older states, though placed by law under severe restraint and strict supervision, sustained heavy losses from shrinkage of securities, and the strongest were forced to reduce the rate of dividend from six to four per cent. a year. Some failed. Some pulled through by scaling their liabilities. As prices soared skyward during the outpour of inconvertible paper currency giving to business of all kinds a delusive appearance of prosperity, so they sank again toward the cold bed-rock of reality, when the financial drunk came slowly to an end.

The Phœnix suffered not only from general causes, but from the payment of excessive dividends, or return premiums to policy-holders. For a long period these were fixed at thirty-three per cent. on the temperance and fifty per cent. on the other tables. Managers sought to win business by giving patrons larger returns than their rivals. At times the strife became fairly frenzied. When pushed to extremes the policy took away the main resource for making good the general shrinkage of prices that fell upon all interests, and often from unexpected quarters.

For the above reasons the situation of the Phœnix in 1875 was serious, but not alarming. The statement of its condition on December 31, 1874, showed admitted assets of $10,011,876, including $16,000 paid in on capital account and a surplus as regards policy-holders of $339,866.

Secretary Burns was the real executive officer. His methods were not approved by Aaron C. Goodman, with one exception the largest stockholder, and long a non-resident director. In early manhood Mr. Goodman was a bookseller and book-publisher in Hartford. Later he opened a paper warehouse in New York city and carried on a large and lucrative business. In 1873 he returned to Hartford. He now became a constant attendant at the meetings of directors, where his free criticisms provoked the ire of the secretary and occasionally ruffled the temper of the president.

A plan was arranged to displace the obnoxious director at the annual meeting in June, 1875. The proposed victim got wind of the plot and resolved not to be sacrificed in that way. He offered his shares to several prominent directors, and failing to get a bid, took the opposite course and so added to his interests as to secure practical control. His purchases included a block of three hundred and ninety-seven shares from Mr. Fessenden. At the election a few days later Mr. Goodman was chosen president; Jonathan B. Bunce, vice-president; and John M. Holcombe secretary. Heretofore the vice-president had held an honorary title. He was now made a member of the working staff.

Under the rigid scrutiny of the new officers, an alleged surplus of over $300,000 before the end of December was changed into a deficit of $79,000—a change very painful to the incoming management, and due not to current shrinkages, but to the correction of past errors. To fill the gap the directors required payment of the stock notes, amounting to $84,000.

The affairs of the company were found to be in great confusion. Many months of arduous labor passed before its exact condition was reached. Not only had a great deal of worthless stuff been carried to the credit of assets, but still larger sums on sundry classes of policies had been dropped from the liabilities, though the company was responsible for the claims. As the truth was reached the books were corrected. Troubles came to light one by one, and hence were more easily borne.

The statment of December 31, 1875, represented the financial condition as then understood. Many policy liabilities were afterwards discovered and restored. New by-laws were framed and adopted. A department for insuring at lower rates on the stock plan was put in operation. Real estate taken by foreclosure was gradually sold, and for the most part without loss. After the annual statement of December, 1878, the chief drain on resources came from the restoration of policies that under the previous management had dropped from acknowledged liabilities. From these causes, several years elapsed before the management could claim with confidence a solid surplus.

When the crisis was safely passed, it became manifest that the company had fallen into a chronic habit of attending to repairs instead of new construction. While the volume of assets from 1875 to 1888 remained nearly stationary, the surplus grew from $4,679 to $1,318,537, and the insurance in force fell from over sixty-nine to less than twenty-five millions.

President Goodman, who owned one thousand and two shares, and thus a controlling interest, desired to sell on account of ill-health. Early in 1889, William Barnes, ex-superintendent of the insurance department of New York, after various preliminary negotiations, introduced John J. McFarlane, of Philadelphia, to Mr. Goodman. Mr. McFarlane offered $500 a share for Mr. Goodman's holdings. He claimed that as he had decided to go into life insurance on a larger scale, he could afford to spend this sum for a well-established plant, as the outlay would be much less than the cost of reaching equal strength from fresh beginnings. He brought letters of indorsement from reputable people. His backers described him as an ex-member of the State Senate of Pennsylvania, an elder in the Presbyterian Church, a Prohibitionist; in short, as variously virtuous. At the above figures for a limited time he obtained an option on the entire block.

Inquiries on the part of persons interested in the company and in the city satisfied them that the proposed purchaser was not a man to whom could safely be committed the custody of many millions of trust funds. As the discussion proceeded the conviction deepened that a large body of assets controlled by a handful of stock that bore to the mass a ratio of less than one per cent., like a tall pyramid inverted, must be in constant danger of fall. The accumulation of cash in bank, amounting to three-fourths of a million, was also a sore temptation to schemers. If to-day one assailant with honeyed words, but evil designs, was detected and repulsed, another as bad or worse was likely to appear on the skirmish line to-morrow or next month.

Both stock and policy-holders united to eliminate the peril. Mr. Goodman, the largest owner, expressed a willingness to make concessions from the estimate he placed on the value of his shares. Others took similar ground. An appeal was made to the legislature, then in session, to furnish, by charter amendments, the machinery for extinguishing the stock. That body promptly passed an act providing for the retirement of the capital and the transfer of ownership and control to the insured when duly accepted by the parties in interest.

A meeting of policy-holders to be held on or before December 3, 1889, was empowered to purchase all the capital stock of the company at a price not exceeding $250 per share, with interest at the rate of five per cent. from July 1st, to be paid out of the surplus, provided such price be first approved by the insurance commissioner as not impairing the reserves, and that no less than a majority be purchased at any price. Transfers were to be made to the commissioner and his successors in office, in trust for the insured, till all the stock had been bought, when the certificates were to be surrendered to the company for cancellation and retirement. The existing directors were to hold office and fill vacancies till the meeting in December. Meanwhile on the stock standing in his name, as trustee, the commissioner was authorized to vote for directors. Great power and a wide discretion were lodged in his hands.

These proceedings put an end to the schemes of operators like Mr. McFarlane. On the 7th of May Mr. Goodman gave to Charles E. Gross, his assignees and appointees, an option for ten days on one thousand and two shares for $250,000, one-half of the sum offered by the Philadelphian. The offer was accepted on the 11th, and the stock was delivered and paid for July 3d, a syndicate of directors and appointees of Mr. Gross assuming the load. On the same day Mr. Goodman resigned as president and director. The block was transferred to John C. Parsons to hold in trust and transfer to the company, provided the policy-holders voted to buy at the price paid. At the meeting in December they so voted by a large majority. All the other shares except ten which remained out for a year or two longer were taken at the same price. Since then the company has been mutual in methods and in interests as in name.

The meeting also chose a board of fifteen directors, who completed the reorganization, by electing J. B. Bunce, president; John M. Holcombe, vice-president, and Charles H. Lawrence, secretary.

The commissioner demanded repayment of dividends in excess of six per cent., for the years 1882 and 1889, inclusive, and all the old directors, except Mr. Goodman, complied. He refused and was sued, but the suit was at length withdrawn.

In 1890 John J. McFarlane, having played leading part in wrecking the American Life Insurance Company and the Bank of America, both of Philadelphia, fled the country, while three confederates in crime went to prison. In the spring of 1893 he returned from Brazil, surrendered to the authorities and was sentenced for four years, preferring, as he said, "punishment in jail to the endless misery of a wanderer in exile."

Renewing its youth the Phœnix Life, under the new *regime*, has advanced steadily in every element of strength. The number of policies written increased from 1,224 in 1889, to 5,193 in 1896, and premium receipts from $650,777 to $1,430,228. Although the cost of securing new business makes its rapid increase a heavy drain on resources, the net surplus grew meantime from $534,000 to $571,552, where we might reasonably have looked for retrogression. Belonging now wholly to the policy-holders, the company has taken a secure place among the solid institutions of the state and country. Its gross assets January 1, 1897, were $10,658,042.71.

In 1896-7 the company built a home-office on the south side of Pearl street, near Main, seventy by one hundred and twenty feet, six stories high in front and three in the rear, exclusive of the basement. The floors and roof are built after the new Columbian system, an American adaptation of the more clumsy French concrete method, combining, as modified, lightness, strength and safety. It is fire-proof throughout. It has a high-speed electric elevator, gas and electric lights, direct and indirect steam heat, sanitary plumbing, with abundant ventilation and light for all the rooms. The front is in the Italian renaissance style.

For its own use the company occupies the entire second floor with the rear of the third. On the first floor, flanking the entrance on each side, are two large rooms with fire-proof vaults, suitable for banks. The rest of the building will be rented for offices. Around the elevator is a flight of iron stairs with platforms and treads of Italian marble. The rooms occupied by the company are finished in East India mahogany, and the rest of the interior in oak. There are nine fire and burglar-proof vaults constructed with the most approved devices.

Jonathan B. Bunce, born in Hartford, April 4, 1832, passed from the high school of his native town to the Sheffield Scientific School of New Haven, whence after a course of eighteen months, he moved to New York city as a member of the firm of Dibble & Bunce, commission merchants. In 1860 he was recalled to Hartford by the death of his father, and succeeded him in the wool business, entering into partnership with the surviving member of the firm, Drayton Hillyer. At the outbreak of the war Gov. Buckingham, in searching for a suitable person to reorganize the department, tendered to Mr. Bunce the position of quartermaster-general. He accepted, and for six months devoted himself untiringly to the work, equipping for the field nine infantry regiments, a battalion of cavalry and a battery of artillery. Feeling that he could no longer in justice to himself withhold attention from his own business which was expanding rapidly under the stimulus of war expenditures, he then resigned. The partnership of Hillyer and Bunce continued for fifteen years. At its expiration in 1875 he entered the Phœnix Mutual as vice-president, and at the reorganization in 1889 became president. He is identified with many of the financial and humane institutions of the city.

Mr. Holcombe was born in Hartford, June 8, 1848, graduated at the Public High School in 1865, and at Yale University in 1869. While studying law he was turned aside by fondness for mathematics into the actuarial department of the Connecticut Mutual Life, and in October, 1871, was appointed actuary of the insurance department of Connecticut. Of the Phœnix he became assistant secretary in 1874, secretary in 1875, and vice-president in 1889.

As a citizen and as a member of both branches of the municipal government

Mr. Holcombe has labored indefatigably to improve local sanitary conditions, among other things securing the passage of an ordinance establishing the Board of Health, on which he is now serving as commissioner a third term. He is chairman of the committee which laid out the intercepting sewer for draining the Park river valley.

Charles H. Lawrence, secretary, was born in New York city, Aug. 23, 1845. Passing from the public schools to the then Free Academy, he came to Hartford in 1866 as shipping clerk for Smith, Bourn & Co. He entered the Phœnix Life, January 1, 1871, and was chief clerk of the investment department at the time of reorganization in June, 1889, when he was elected secretary. He has taken deep interest in municipal affairs, and in addition to other services was three months acting mayor.

CHAPTER XI.

INSURANCE IN CONNECTICUT—Continued.

THE CONTINENTAL LIFE INSURANCE COMPANY, HARTFORD.

CHARTERED in 1862 the Continental was organized in the spring of 1864, with a capital of $150,000, divided into six thousand shares of $25 each. In July, 1866, the capital was increased to $300,000. Forty per cent. was paid in cash, and sixty per cent. was represented by stock notes. May 16, 1864, was elected the first board of directors, consisting of John S. Rice, Lucius J. Hendee, James L. Chapman, Samuel E. Elmore, Horace Cornwall, Buel Sedgwick and Ezra Hall. Three months later Allyn S. Stillman, H. K. W. Welch and Abner Church were added. The original seven met May 23d and elected John S. Rice, of Farmington, president, and Samuel E. Elmore, secretary.

It was a period prolific in the birth of life insurance companies. In New York, under a general statute, many sprang into being about this time. After struggles variously prolonged most of them passed away. Meanwhile intensity of competition enhanced expenses and diminished profits.

At the annual meeting in 1870 a plan to capture the management took form. Several of the old directors were displaced. James S. Parsons, as representative of the assailants, was elected vice-president, with the duties ordinarily assigned to the superintendent of agencies. Mr. Elmore succeeded Mr. Rice in the presidency. Francis D. Douglass, assistant secretary since July 1, 1869, was made secretary.

At the next annual meeting the intrusive element dropped out. Lucius J. Hendee, was elected vice-president, and the by-law attaching certain duties to the office was rescinded. May 1st Mr. Hendee retired, and John S. Rice was elected in his place, with the special assignment of examining all claims for losses.

At the annual meeting in March, 1873, the assault, partially successful in '70, but foiled in '71, carried the position. The new directors were: John C. Tracy, Edwin Bulkeley, George C. Johnson, Ansel Arnold, Thomas Ramsdell, John S. Wells, J. G. Martin, James S. Parsons, H. B. Freeman and Robert E. Beecher. One-half of the new board resided in the town of Windham. They elected James S. Parsons president, and Robert E. Beecher secretary.

January 1, 1873, the statement claimed assets of $2,735,394 (of which $1,330,315 were in premium notes), and a surplus over all liabilities of $355,357.

In the statement for December 31, 1874, the capital is first reported as full-paid.

It was done thus. John C. Tracy, a director in the Continental, was also president of the Farmers' and Mechanics' Bank. For friends he did illegal acts which in the end brought heavy losses upon the bank and punishment upon himself. December 31st, a package of stock notes having a face value of $180,000 was deposited in the bank, and a credit for the same amount entered on the pass-book of the Continental. January 19th the package was withdrawn, and the credit cancelled.

As more fully described in the history of the Charter Oak a special commission was appointed in 1877 to investigate the life companies of Connecticut. Judge Origen S. Seymour, chairman, examined the home affairs of the Continental, taking as a point of departure the annual statement to the commissioner, dated December 31, 1876. The return and the books of the company were found to correspond. Still, strange outcroppings perplexed the mind of the Judge and led him to probe deeper. At first the dance of ghostly figures without substance grievously bewildered him. Weeks of hard labor passed before the real situation took form in his mind.

After the revolution of 1873, the new management, to entrench itself more securely, bought with the funds of the company from hostile interests 4670 shares of its own stock at a cost of $125,482.90, or $5,482.90 more than all the cash paid into the treasury on capital account. The block stood December 31, 1876, in the name of John C. Tracy, trustee, by whom as trustee also the accompanying stock note of $70,050 was signed. It is apparent that the money thus paid out and the note given to itself had no value whatever as security for creditors.

Various large sums were credited by President Tracy on the pass-book of the Continental which were nowhere to be found in the accounts of the bank. The first was an item of $186,907.16, which represented to the extent of $180,000 the stock-notes, including the one for $70,000 virtually given through its trustee by the company to itself. From time to time the Continental had advanced $133,534.90 to Sharps' Rifle Company. The vouchers were handed to Mr. Tracy, and he entered on the pass-book a credit for the same amount. His act was wholly illegitimate. Whether the property was worth more or less than the face of the vouchers would depend of course upon the outcome of the venture. The $125,482.90 paid out for its own stock appeared in two items, one of $20,966.40, credited on the pass-book, and the other in a certificate of special deposit for $104,516.50. The latter went toward making up the sum reported as cash deposited in bank. There was still another credit of $35,000 which represented not even the shadow of a shadow. Against this aggregate of $480,924.90, but two offsets can be allowed; the notes for sixty per cent. on the 7330 shares in the hands of the public ($109,950) and the equity in Sharps' Rifle Company.

United States bonds, par $205,000, market value $230,625, and Windham town bonds, $35,000, were included in the same return among the assets owned by the company December 31st. It is true that December 27th the president of the Continental wrote to the bank requesting it to buy on account of the company $200,000 United States bonds. From the 5th to the 10th of January inclusive the bank made the purchases on the general credit of the company, using its own funds for the purpose, holding the bonds as security with power of attorney to sell, and again disposed of them all between February 10th and March 2, 1877, repaying itself with the proceeds. Yet to keep up the show the insurance company as if in payment drew checks upon the unreal credits entered on the pass-book, but not on the bank ledger. The ownership of the Windham bonds seems if possible even more mythical. Mr. Tracy left the bank in February, 1877. In the adjustment that followed, the spectral assets, evoked from the realm of shadows by his aid, returned to the nothingness whence they seemed to spring.

The special commission submitted its report to the General Assembly January 15, 1878, but no adverse action was taken. Commissioner Stedman required the company to restore the money used in the purchase of its own shares. Thereupon the officers represented to certain stockholders that on account of the disturbance created by the special commission there was need of a temporary increase of assets. Supposing that the emergency would soon be passed, the parties appealed to gave their notes, with collaterals, for sums that amounted altogether to $125,482.90. No interest was collected from the makers, and all dividends on the securities entrusted to the officers were paid over to the actual owners.

In the summer of 1887, a local firm of brokers, with which the president of the Continental had had extensive dealings, failed. Within a few days the affairs of the concern were published in detail. Among the securities hypothecated to the firm to reinforce speculative margins, and in several cases rehypothecated elsewhere, the parties, who had filled the gap of $125,000, recognized some of their own stocks. Others had vanished. Stocks and bonds, once the property of the Continental, and supposed by the directors to be securely stored in the vaults of the company, turned up to their surprise in the same place.

Commissioner Fyler at once began an examination, taking as a basis the statement for December 31, 1886. By the 17th of November he had progressed so far as to feel called upon to issue an order, under the statute, forbidding the issue of new policies and the payment of dividends. After further progress he became satisfied that the impairment exceeded twenty-five per cent. of the assets, and on the 30th of November applied to Judge Carpenter, of the Supreme Court of Errors, for the annulment of the charter, and the appointment of a receiver. The application was resisted, and the case adjourned till December 23. At the second hearing, the petition was not opposed, and the Court appointed Lorrin A. Cooke and John R. Buck receivers.

Under the scrutiny of the commissioner, the volume of admitted assets shrank from $2,113,356.68 to $1,235,680.97, including $391,064 in premium notes. He placed the direct liabilities at $2,070,045.25.

Before the second hearing the president had retired beyond the jurisdiction of the Court. The secretary was indicted for perjury, in swearing to a false return. It was claimed on his side that he had never made oath to the return, and that the certificate of the notary was false. Under a New York decision in a similar case, that "there must be proof of the oath taken, independent of the notary's certificate, signature, seal and jurat," the judge advised that the case be nolled.

THE CONNECTICUT GENERAL LIFE INSURANCE COMPANY.

The Connecticut General entered a field already crowded, not as a competitor of older institutions, but with the view of selecting at adequate rates, from risks which others rejected. Dr. Phelps, father of the Connecticut Mutual, was also the godfather of the Connecticut General, and proposed to further aid the infant enterprise with liberal slices from the excess lines of the parent company. The promoters reasoned, quite plausibly, that if fire rates could be so adjusted upon all classes of property as to be remunerative, there could be no inherent difficulty in graduating the cost of insurance for impaired lives also. It was soon found, however, that the infirmities buried in the human system were too deceptive and variable to respond to any determinate law of averages. Moreover, applicants who failed to pass the standard examinations, did not display expected alacrity in accepting the benefits of the new departure on the terms proposed. Each one's confidence in his own destiny is so strong that he must either suffer from "malaria," or be clearly nearing the grave, before he will admit that his chances of longevity are less than those of his neighbor. Happily the error in the theory was soon shown by the perplexities encountered in attempts to apply it, and in two years the feature was abandoned, and the business of the company thenceforth confined to first-class risks.

It is worthy of note that the Universal and the American Popular Life Insurance Companies, organized about the same time on the same theory, persisted in adhering to the plan, and paid the penalty a few years later by dying bravely in the last ditch.

In view of the extra hazards and untried conditions to be met, the capital was placed by the charter at not less than $500,000. Ten per cent. was required at the time of subscription, a second installment of 10 per cent. was called at the first meeting of directors, and a third, of 30 per cent. in cash, June 9, 1866. When the experiment of insuring impaired lives was given up, the need of a large capital to guarantee the performance of contracts also vanished. Hence, by permission of the Legislature, it was reduced in 1874 to $250,000, the amount actually paid in. The reduction was effected by the cancellation of stock notes. In 1880 it was again cut down to $150,000, by taking up two-fifths at par, the growing strength of the institution having rendered a larger guaranty needless. This was the first life insurance company in Connecticut of which the capital was wholly paid in cash.

The first board of eighteen directors, twelve from Hartford and six from other cities, was elected July 20, 1865. A week later John M. Niles was elected president; Edward W. Parsons, vice-president, and Thomas W. Russell, secretary. Mr. Niles held the place but a few weeks, having been succeeded by Mr. Parsons in September.

With others the Connecticut General suffered from the shrinkage of values that followed the panic of 1873. Loans made on real estate at inflated values defaulted, throwing upon its hands large blocks in several cities, notably in Washington, D. C. The distress to all interests was severest during the winter of 1876-7. The annual statement for December, 1876, showed an impairment of capital on a four per cent. basis of $12,607.67, or, throwing out items not admitted by the commissioner, of $18,265.41. Total assets then amounted to $1,272,298. But the turning point had been reached. From that date onward the company has steadily gained in every element of strength, though compelled from time to time to charge off losses arising from the old transactions above referred to.

In May, 1876, Thomas W. Russell, an expert in life insurance, succeeded Mr. Parsons as president, and at the same time Frederick V. Hudson was elected secretary.

In 1872 the company began to issue policies on the tontine plan in a modified form for terms of ten and twenty years. In July, 1887, the scheme was abandoned in disgust, partly from conviction that the theory was injurious and misleading, and partly from the incessant complaints of the unfortunates who fell by the wayside. It seemed impossible to print conditions in type sufficiently conspicuous to attract the attention of the insured to the terms of the contract. On the other hand, those who have held out to the end have had no ground for fault-finding. The funds belonging to separate classes have been kept distinct, and have been charged only with their proportionate share of expenses. On long-term policies the company is paying fifty-nine per cent. of estimated results, and on short term, eighty-eight, as the latter are less affected by the continuous fall in rates of interest, which dropped fully one-third during the progress of the experiment. These results are from fifty to over one hundred per cent. better than results attained by some of the largest companies in the country, which about the same time went into the scheme on a grand scale with promises as alluring as experts in the manufacture of advertising literature could produce.

May 22, 1894, President Russell reached the age of three-score years and ten. From the young men in the office, whose welfare he has studied with the solicitude of a father, came the suggestion that the company take some appropriate notice of the event. The idea was approved by the directors. At a complimentary dinner given on the 29th of June, officers, directors, employees and general agents, with a few invited guests, came together to express their regard for one who had served the institution continuously from its birth. Three others were present who had also been connected with it from the beginning: Doctor Melanchthon Storrs, vice-president, toastmaster and medical examiner; Leverett Brainard, mayor of the city at the time, and a continuous director; and Walter H. Tilden, agent at Philadelphia, and an original stockholder.

Mr. Russell was born at Greenfield, Mass. From 1846 till 1852 he was a merchant at Mystic Bridge, Conn., and incidentally acted as local agent for the Charter Oak Life Insurance Company, which in the latter year, when he represented the town of Stonington in the General Assembly, persuaded him to move to Hartford and take a traveling agency. In 1857 he was elected vice-president. He resigned in 1864, while its sky was still unclouded, and after a year with the Connecticut Mutual, aided in launching the company to which he has devoted the energies of three-fifths of his business life. Since his accession to the presidency it has enjoyed not only uninterrupted, but in regard to solidity, conspicuous prosperity. Others have grown faster in accumulations, but few now surpass it in strength.

January 1, 1897, the company had gross assets amounting to $2,944,747.97, with a net surplus of $388,862.35 exclusive of its capital of $150,000. Of the surplus, too, $260,058 belongs to a special class of policies. There have been few changes in the official corps.

Frederick V. Hudson, secretary, was born in February, 1838, in Cincinnati, O., where, in 1867, he became local agent for the Penn Mutual, and the next year state agent for the Hartford Life and Annuity. After a short term he accepted the general agency of the Connecticut General in October, 1868, and was elected secretary in 1876.

Edward B. Peck, assistant secretary, was born in Galveston, Tex., January 31, 1840; was educated in the schools of St. Louis, Mo., taught several years, a part of the time as principal of one of the public schools of Bridgeport, Conn., engaged in mercantile business in Alabama, whence he moved to Hartford, where he was made cashier and accountant of the Connecticut General in May, 1868, and assistant secretary in May, 1882.

Robert Watkinson Huntington, actuary, was born in Norwich, Conn., November 9, 1866; graduated at the Hartford High School in 1885, at Yale University in 1889, and in November of the same year entered the office of the Connecticut General, of which he was appointed actuary June 29, 1893.

THE HARTFORD LIFE AND ANNUITY INSURANCE COMPANY.

This company was chartered in 1866 as the Hartford Accident Insurance Company, primarily to make insurance connected with loss of life or personal injury through accidents of every description, and with the privilege also of making ordinary insurance upon lives. August 14th, of the same year, the subscribers chose the following directors, viz.: Daniel F. Seymour, Jasper H. Bolton, Stiles D. Sperry, E. Thomas Lobdell, John A. Butler, Alvan P. Hyde, Chester Adams, John W. Danforth,

Elisha P. Smith, Jacob Knous, Hiram Bissell, Thomas J. Vail, Joshua R. Lord, John B. Russell and David A. Rood.

T. J. Vail was elected president; C. C. Kimball, vice-president; and September 10th, W. S. Manning, secretary. The capital was placed at $300,000.

Little was then known about accident insurance, and the unprofitableness of the attempt soon became apparent. In 1867 the name was changed to the Hartford Life and Accident Insurance Company, and in 1868 the descriptive words were changed to the Hartford Life and Annuity.

For the first two years money was lost rapidly. Changes now occurred in both *personnel* and policy. The accident business was dropped. In May, 1868, Chester Adams consented to act as president *pro tem.* till a suitable person could be found. After much importunity C. C. Kimball took the position in January, 1869. With a keen sense of the needs of the situation he cut off excrescenses, reformed old methods and soon put the concern on a money-making basis. James P. Taylor, later cashier and president of the Charter Oak Bank, served as secretary from May, 1867, till May, 1874.

With the improved outlook certain parties in the directory were seized by a sudden and singular desire to obtain control for the sake of the supposed honors and emoluments. No resistance was offered from within. On the contrary, a large block of stock was indirectly and kindly supplied to them at high prices. At the next annual election in May, 1870, Wareham Griswold was chosen president, and D. F. Seymour, who had been vice-president since February 8, 1869, became the active manager.

Affairs now took another turn. Expenses grew, and business became unprofitable. The book value of the shares fell from eighty-eight in the spring of 1870, to fifty-five within the next five years. Mr. Griswold died in 1876, and was succeeded by E. H. Crosby. Stephen Ball, who was elected assistant secretary October 28, 1867, and secretary May 12, 1874, saw that a change of method was imperative. Under his guidance new business was dropped, collections were made from the home office, and rigid economy was enforced. Meanwhile every proper claim was fully and promptly met. So great are the recuperative energies of life insurance that in a few years the technical solvency and general credit of the company were fully restored, the capital having been reduced meanwhile to $250,000. It was now ready to re-enter the field aggressively.

In January, 1880, the company adopted a form of natural premium insurance combining low cost and security, devised by Henry P. Duclos, formerly of St. Albans, Vt. At the same time a contract was made with Duclos and his associate, A. T. Smith, to manage the agency department. The system requires policy-holders to pay only for the actual mortality among members as it occurs, in quarterly periods. Applicants for insurance pay a single admission fee, which varies according to the amount required, but not with the age of the person. For collecting and distributing the funds and all other expenses of management, a yearly charge of $3.00 per $1,000 of insurance is made, and the rate cannot be increased. The safety fund, which gives the system its name, is made up exclusively of contributions of $10.00 per $1,000, required of each member once only, and placed in the hands of the Security Company of Hartford as trustee for the policy-holders. In July, 1894, it reached the contract limit of one million of dollars. Till then semi-annually the entire net income from the fund was divided pro rata among the holders of certificates in force, who, five years before or earlier, contributed to it their full share, and the dividends thus accruing were applied to the reduction of subsequent dues and mortality-calls. Since that date the contributions from new members are semi-annually added to the income from it, when the entire surplus thus accruing is distributed in like manner.

The principal, placed by a deed of trust beyond the control of the company, remains at an even million, as a guaranty that death claims shall always be met in full, even if the membership for any cause be so reduced that stipulated mortality-calls fail to produce enough to satisfy the claims.

By mathematical computation the rates are so fixed that the amount of insurance in force must fall below one million dollars to cause an insufficient membership. Should such contingency occur, the trustee is required, from the principal of the safety fund, to pay all outstanding policies in full, without waiting for death to mature the claims. Had the condition arisen in the early stages of the venture, and before accumulations were sufficient to meet all liabilities in full, the deed provided for the division of the fund pro rata among the holders of certificates in force. This was the first company in the country doing business on the assessment plan, where an ample fund was built up to protect the insured against adverse possibilities, liable to occur in the distant future.

Several modifications of the original plan have been adopted, but none which alter its essential character. Mr. Duclos died in March, 1885. Mr. Smith continued to manage the agency department till his resignation in September, 1896, when he was succeeded by W. B. Warner, who had been in the service of the company fourteen years, and assistant superintendent of agencies, ten.

Since 1880 the business of the company has been confined to the "safety fund plan."

Late presidents have been E. H. Crosby, May, 1876-1882; Frederick R. Foster, May, 1882-1889; H. A. Whitman, May, 1889-1893; R. B. Parker, since 1893.

January 1, 1897, assets were, ... $2,465,152.65
Liabilities, ... 1,893,922.34
Number of policy-holders. 44,297

Rienzi B. Parker, president, was born in South Coventry, Conn., February 15, 1838. Soon after leaving the High School in Ellington, he engaged in the manufacture of cotton goods, an industry in which his father had long experience. In 1873 he established the Ravine Mills Company, at Vernon, Conn., and is still its treasurer. A stockholder in the Hartford Life and Annuity from the first, he was elected president in May, 1893.

Stephen Ball, secretary, was born in 1839, in New Haven, Conn. He came to Hartford in 1867, from New Orleans, where he had been employed in the service of the government. In August of the same year he was made assistant secretary of this company, and in 1874, secretary. He was largely instrumental in rescuing the institution from its early dangers and in building it up afterwards.

W. A. Cowles, an employee of the company since May, 1872, was elected assistant secretary, May 13, 1874.

After plans prepared by Frederick R. Comstock, at the corner of Asylum and Ann streets, in 1897, the company will complete, mainly for its own use, a building of five stories, with a frontage of sixty-two and a depth of one hundred and two feet. The style is a modification of the Italian renaissance. The first story of the exterior has a base course five feet high, of granite with a hammered dress face, surmounted by Indiana limestone laid in courses. This is crowned by a continuous and highly-ornamented cornice of terra-cotta, slightly lighter in color than the limestone. The stories above are laid in buff-colored press-brick and cream-colored terra-cotta. The entire superstructure is supported by steel columns and steel beams encased in solid walls of brick. On the level with Asylum street are two stores, with the printing department of the company in the rear, opening into Ann. The second and third floors are occupied wholly by offices of the company. Each has a fireproof vault, eight and one-half by eighteen feet. The fourth and fifth floors will be leased till the room is required by the owners. Hot water is used for heating, and electricity for light. Much attention has been given to ornamentation both on the exterior and interior.

CHAPTER XII.

INSURANCE IN CONNECTICUT—Continued.

MISCELLANEOUS INSURANCE.

ASIDE from marine, fire and life insurance, attempts have been made in Connecticut from time to time to extend the business to various other classes of risks. Several health companies were chartered about the middle of the century, and the reason of their failure is given in our account of the Connecticut Health. A little later the notion became suddenly prevalent that money could be made by insuring live stock. A few experiments proved the futility of the scheme. Somehow the cow or the ox that died belonged to the part of the herd that happened to be covered by the policy. The question of identity often arose to the bewilderment of agents, if not of owners. It was soon discovered, too, that less care was taken of horses when heavily insured. On our canals and in other pursuits where consumption was rapid, the records showed the exact ratio of loss so that managers took out policies only when sure of saving money by the operation.

Two institutions in Connecticut, each entering as a pioneer a field not previously trodden in America, have won eminent success.

THE TRAVELERS INSURANCE COMPANY.

In 1863, when passing through England, James G. Batterson, of Hartford, became interested in the subject of casualty insurance, and after examining the methods pursued there and on the Continent, was convinced that the system could be advantageously transplanted into the United States. On his return home the scheme was talked over with influential friends, but at first met with little encouragement or sympathy. However, the personal force of the projector, backed by arguments which grew in number and cogency as the discussion went on, began to win valuable converts, and the enterprise soon materialized in tangible form. Outside of the charmed circle skepticism still prevailed, but a nucleus had been formed and a charter was secured in June, 1863.

By the terms of the charter the capital was placed at not less than $100,000, with the right to increase it at will to any sum not exceeding $250,000. An installment of ten per cent. was required at the time of subscription, a second installment of like amount within sixty days after organization, and the remaining eighty within the same period in stock notes properly secured and payable at the call of the directors.

At first the business of the incorporation was limited to "the insuring of persons against the accidental loss of life or personal injury sustained while traveling by railways, steamers, or other modes of conveyance in the United States and other countries."

At the City Bank of Hartford, a book for subscriptions was opened by the commissioners, James G. Batterson, George M. Bartholomew, Gustavus F. Davis and William L. Collins, January 28, 1864, when two thousand shares of $100 each were taken and the first installment paid. The first meeting of stockholders, held at the same place February 23, voted to issue the remaining fifty thousand dollars of capital stock, and elected the following directors: James G. Batterson, Ebenezer Roberts, W. H. D. Callender, Thomas Belknap, Jr., James L. Howard, Charles White, George W. Moore, Cornelius B. Erwin, Marshall Jewell, Hugh Harbison, G. F. Davis, George S. Gilman, and Jonathan B. Bunce. The next day the board elected James G. Batterson president. March 4th G. F. Davis was elected vice-president, and Rodney Dennis secretary.

Finding the powers first granted too narrow, the managers by an amendment to the charter one year later obtained authority " to make all and every insurance connected with accidental loss of life or personal injury sustained by accident of every description."

To the substantial nucleus of president and secretary were added in time several other young men who manifested capacity for the assimilation and mastery of complex details, and the gifts of all were put to a severe test in the early struggles of the company for existence. Severe labor, rigid economy, and especially quickness and accuracy in the interpretation of facts, carried the enterprise safely through the perils of infancy. Not a penny was wasted on superfluities. The first office, located on the second floor to save rent, was furnished with two chairs and a second-hand pine desk set on a cheap table. A carpet was an extravagance not to be thought of. For a while the officers did all the work alone, writing the letters, keeping the books, instructing agents in the mysteries of the craft, and running on errands for exercise. The first luxury to be introduced was an office-boy, who became assistant secretary.

For eight generations children have read with unabated interest of the pilgrimage of Hooker and his flock through the trackless forest, from Massachusetts Bay to the banks of the Connecticut, with only the compass and north star for guides. On starting into the wilderness the Travelers had the benefit of neither compass nor star. At home no one had gone before to cut a bush or blaze a tree ; while the conditions underlying the casualty business in England differed so widely from those in America that the scanty generalizations formulated in tables by the pattern-company proved treacherous and misleading. From the bottom stone in the foundation to the flagstaff on the tower, the officers constructed as they went, without aid from architectural designs or preformed plans, necessarily making many mistakes, and costly mistakes too—tearing down, changing, rebuilding, adding here and discarding there —till from a chaos of materials grew the present solid, stately, and enduring edifice, the despair of rivals, and the delight of friends.

No kind of business, and especially no branch of insurance, can be carried on with safety till its laws have been generalized from a wide range of experience. In the case of the Travelers, it was necessary to get the experience and to deduce the governing principles simultaneously. The process of adjustment demanded frequent and radical changes in classifications and rates, introducing confusion into methods, annoying and losing patrons, and exciting in faithful agents ebullitions of sore displeasure. The knife of the surgeon was in constant requisition. Meanwhile the executive officers did not sleep on beds of roses, at least till the small hours of the morning, for midnight often found them at headquarters, toiling over the solution of changeful problems or anxiously discussing what should be done next.

The palpable benefits of the system, the disbursement over a wide area of many small sums to injured persons who fortunately held policies in the Travelers, the gratuitous advertising given to the business by its relations to destructive railway accidents, though productive of a copious inflow of premiums, damaged the company at a certain stage of growth in two ways. Men engaged in dangerous pursuits insured in large numbers before the actual cost of the hazard had been determined, and, in fact, bought indemnity much too low. Perils from this source passed away as enlarged experience enabled the officers to correct the tables. The other danger came from the opposite quarter, and though serious enough in the thick of the fight, now seems almost ludicrous when viewed in connection with the mental conditions which preceded and followed in swift succession. Reversing the normal sequence of development, the age of skepticism yielded place to an age of faith, and before the doubting Thomases near home had ceased to hum, with a slight accent of derision, "what will the harvest be?" a swarm of casualty companies, organized in 1865 and 1866, rushed wildly into the field. With ample powers of destruction all lacked the art of construction, and after emulating the feats of the historic bull in the china shop, sank one by one into unremembered graves, and though mourners were many, the only monuments of the departed are the death records in the state insurance reports.

During the winter of 1864 five western states chartered over a dozen accident companies. Elsewhere others were striving with frenzied haste to reach fields that were supposed to glow with golden harvests. Nearly all began to issue railway accident tickets, bringing such confusion upon the business that obviously some form of combination could alone save strong and weak alike from common ruin. To pave the way, in May, 1865, the managers of the Travelers procured a Connecticut charter for the Railway Passengers Assurance Company for risks by travel alone, amended the following year to include general accidents and life insurance. The first meeting of presidents and representatives was held at Cincinnati, O., June 15, 1865. Others followed. At length, in 1866, seven companies united to prosecute the work for their joint benefit under a single management and a uniform system extending over the whole country. The instrument was the Railway Passengers Assurance Company, in which each as a corporation took stock and had representation in the directorate. It was organized on a capital of $260,000, with $44,800 more allowed for equipments taken or canceled, making a total of $304,800, of which the Travelers held $128,600. James G. Batterson was elected president, and headquarters were located in Hartford. By a singular fatality all the others found the losses from the residue of their business too great to be repaired by the dividends from their common offspring. A kind of cholera infantum carried off most of the lot in 1867. At the end of five years the Travelers was left sole survivor, residuary legatee and reinsurer of the rest. Having bought the shares of its late associates, the company in 1878 turned the Railway Passengers into the ticket department of its own office. In 1871 not an American rival was left, for the concerns which declined to enter the union had perished even more summarily.

As a rule the officers and employees of the Travelers have been singularly loyal to its interests. At the end of three decades there had been few removals from the official corps by death, and few withdrawals from the office force from any cause whatever. An element of discontent seceded in 1874, having carefully prepared for the event. The assistant secretary and the actuary went out to take the vice-presidency and the secretaryship respectively of the Hartford Accident Insurance Company, which was chartered in June, 1874, and soon began business on a capital of $200,000.

Richard D. Hubbard, afterwards governor, was induced to take the presidency. A noted humorist, in a speech industriously circulated, procured for the new concern no small amount of gratuitous advertising. Yet in two short years the fledgeling was dead and buried with every dollar sunk. Luckily the jokes were let loose before the first course of the barmecide feast.

October 25, 1865, the directors voted to introduce and prosecute the life department of insurance. The business was conducted on the purely stock plan and was pushed as fast as due regard to the requirements of a legal reserve would permit. Although the loss ratio was exceptionally small, the rates charged were so low and the business grew so rapidly that not until 1873 did the balance sheet of the life department show a technical profit. For a number of years so great was the popularity of its life policies that the company was forced to reject many first-class risks in order to avoid swelling the deficit to figures that to the uninformed might be made to appear alarming. Yet from the start the prosperity of the department far exceeded estimated results as embodied in tables of mortality. In the early stages the Travelers skillfully used the profits of the Accident to promote and protect the growth of the life department. Behind both was the security afforded by a sound capital.

At the first meeting the stockholders voted to increase the capital from $200,000 to $250,000. March 19, 1864, 50 per cent. of the subscriptions, inclusive of previous payments, was called in cash. In June, 1864, by an amendment to the charter, an increase to an amount not exceeding $1,000,000, was authorized. The following October the directors voted to increase it to an amount not exceeding $400,000. December 4, 1865, the board declared from surplus earnings, a dividend of 25 per cent., payable in the stock of the company at par. For the benefit of owners, unadjusted fractional shares were sold at auction at the Merchants' Exchange, and brought 157½ @ ¾. Meanwhile, the balance of the stock notes given for subscriptions had been paid in cash in convenient installments. The capital remained at $500,000 from December, 1865, till January 1, 1875, when $100,000 was added by a dividend from surplus. Similarly it was raised from $600,000 to $1,000,000, April 1, 1892.

Having outgrown rented rooms, the Travelers purchased, in 1872, the historic mansion at the northeast corner of Prospect and Grove streets, built in 1820 by Henry L. Ellsworth, first commissioner of patents, and occupied among others, by Oliver Wolcott, secretary of the United States Treasury under Washington, governor of Connecticut, etc.; Professor Charles Davies; Roswell C. Smith, manufacturer of school-books; Isaac Toucey, governor, secretary of the navy, etc. In 1891 the company added a third story to the original building, a new wing on the northwest corner, and, in the rear, running parallel to Grove street, a new wing one hundred by twenty-five feet, three stories high. Four fire-proof vaults were added to the five already in use. Granite steps, surmounted by a portico of granite, appropriately symbolize the solidity of the institution to which they lead.

A very great proportion of the losses in the accident department of the Travelers come from the ordinary casualties daily occurring all over the country, which attract little attention beyond a limited circle; the large sums which the company is often required to pay to the injured and to the heirs of the killed after notable disasters, making but a small fraction of its disbursements. Still, death claims alone amounted to $32,000 from the railway accident at Angola, January, 1868; to $43,000, at Carr's Rock, April, 1868; to $20,000, at New Hamburg, February, 1871; to $13,000, steamer "Metis," September, 1872; to $52,000, at Ashtabula, January, 1877; to $15,000, at Chatsworth, Ill., August, 1887.

At the time of the great conflagration, one hundred and eighty-one Chicago firemen held policies in the Travelers, and not one was injured, though over $20,000 had previously been paid there on this single class of risks.

The *Travelers Record*, established in 1865, and issued monthly from the home office, by giving wide currency to facts and arguments showing the benefits of casualty insurance, has aided materially in enlightening the public, and thus extending the business. Edwin G. Barrows, first editor, was succeeded at his death, in 1875, by William M. Pearl. Forrest Morgan followed in November, 1882. Mr. Morgan retired in March, 1896, and was succeeded by George William Ellis, a son of the secretary, and a recent graduate of Trinity College. Under the editorship of Mr. Morgan the company, in 1889, issued, as a souvenir, in five volumes, the collected writings of Walter Bagehot.

Why has the Travelers prospered while all rivals, save two or three late entries, have perished? Many minor reasons might be given, but they all run back to a common source—differences of management. The company was not started as an asylum for failures in the struggle for existence, but from its inception has been guided by men of great capacity, with definite and inflexible aims.

It can be said of James Goodwin Batterson, the president, that he has done much on many different lines, and has excelled in every field of effort. Only a person of extraordinary strength, physical and mental, could so break through the limitations that defy the ambition and hinder the success of all save a favored few. He was born in Bloomfield, Conn., February 23, 1823, spent his boyhood in New Preston, fitted for college in the academy at Warren, served an apprenticeship in a printing-office in Ithaca, N. Y. ; returning home, studied law with Judge Origen S. Seymour, and then entered the marble works of his father in Litchfield. Five years later, the headquarters of the house were moved to Hartford. From making monuments the operations of Mr. Batterson soon extended to the construction of buildings, at first at home, and then over a rapidly-broadening area. Among the structures thus erected may be mentioned, in Hartford, the marble building of the Phœnix National Bank, the granite and marble work of the home-office of the Connecticut Mutual Life, the State Capitol ; in New York city, the Worth monument, built in 1857, the stone and marble work of the Mutual Life, of the Equitable Life, of the Manhattan and other banks, of the Waldorf and Imperial Hotels, of the Vanderbilt houses, both there and at Newport; in Providence, of the City Hall ; in Washington, of the new congressional library, etc. His marble works in New York city, established about 1860, in normal times give employment to five hundred hands. His granite quarries in Westerly, R. I., grade among the first in the country. Mr. Batterson was the first person in the United States to use machinery for polishing granite. The upbuilding of the Travelers has been another integral part of his varied career.

With so many practical affairs continually pressing upon him, Mr. Batterson has somehow found time to become a finished scholar, writer and speaker. His studies embrace Greek, Latin, the modern languages, Egyptology, political economy, science, philosophy, sociology and general literature, and he is proficient in all. He is also a connoisseur in art, and the owner of a large and choice collection of paintings.

Rodney Dennis, secretary from the beginning till March, 1896, was born at Topsfield, Mass., January 14, 1826, came to Hartford when sixteen years old, and, having served an apprenticeship in the grocery trade, established the house of Dennis & Ives at the age of twenty-one. A few years later his partner fell sick and never returned to work, while he was disabled for months by a serious accident. He now sold his interest, and going to Augusta, Ga., entered the employ of the historic firm

TRAVELERS INSURANCE COMPANY.

of Hand, Williams & Wilcox. After two years there and two in Albany he returned to Hartford in 1855, and was connected with the Phœnix Bank till he took the secretaryship of the Travelers in 1864. At first he attended to all the details of the business without assistance of any kind, toiling till late into the night, and keeping up the habit with few relaxations for many years. There was a constant struggle between physical endurance and consecration to work. Other employees caught his spirit and followed his example. Thus largely was success won.

A man of public spirit and great heart Mr. Dennis has opened his purse with notable freedom to aid a great variety of enterprises that held out a promise of promoting the welfare of the city, and to charities, organized and private, has given unstintingly of money, time and effort.

Looking to both sides the company has always dealt fairly and justly in settling with claimants. By holding old and attracting new patrons the policy has been fruitful in benefits.

George Ellis, secretary, was born in Hartford September 17, 1843, educated as a civil engineer at the Rensselaer Polytechnic, Troy, and entered the navy in November, 1861, as an officer of the engineer corps, remaining till 1868, when he resigned to enter upon the practice of his profession in connection with railway construction in Minnesota. In 1871 he removed to New York city to act as professional consulting engineer in railway enterprises in which his friends were engaged. He became actuary of the Travelers in June, 1874, and was elected secretary January 27, 1897.

John E. Morris, assistant secretary, was born in Springfield, Mass., November 30, 1843, came to Hartford in the spring of 1860, was connected with the Charter Oak Bank till September 20, 1862, when he enlisted in Company B, Twenty-second regiment Connecticut Volunteers, and remained in service till the expiration of the term of enlistment, July 7, 1863. He was the first clerk employed by the Travelers, having taken his place at the head of the column July 6, 1864. In May, 1874, he was elected assistant secretary.

Edward V. Preston, superintendent of agencies, was born in Willington, Conn., June 1, 1837, moved to Hartford in 1850, and followed mercantile pursuits till the outbreak of the war. In July, 1861, he was appointed quartermaster of the Fifth Connecticut, with the rank of first lieutenant. After various services he was commissioned by the president, February 19, 1863, as additional paymaster United States Volunteers, with the rank of major, and so continued till honorably discharged July 31, 1865. He at once entered the Travelers, and, after working two years as special agent, was appointed superintendent of agencies—a position which he has since held continuously.

John B. Lewis, M. D., surgeon and adjuster, was born in Suffolk county, N. Y., March 10, 1832; graduated on his twenty-first birthday from the University Medical College of New York city; settled at Vernon, Conn.; was commissioned as surgeon of the Fifth Connecticut, July 3, 1861; in the spring of 1862 was commissioned as brigade surgeon United States Volunteers, and was soon after made medical director of Shield's division; and from 1863 to '65 was in charge of the United States general hospital at Cumberland, Md. He remained till after the close of the war, having been present in thirteen battles and skirmishes, including Antietam.

Since 1869 he has devoted his time and talents to the medical department of the Travelers, writing meanwhile numerous papers on historical, medical and medico-legal subjects. His most elaborate work is a large volume prepared under the joint authorship of himself and Dr. C. C. Bombaugh, of Baltimore, describing the many plots and stratagems for defrauding life insurance companies and the manner of their detection.

Sylvester C. Dunham, counsel, was born in Mansfield, Conn., April 24, 1846; was educated at the State Normal School, New Britain, Conn., and at Mount Union College, Ohio; studied law with Charles E. Mitchell, of New Britain; and on admission to the bar moved to Hartford in 1871, where he was engaged in general practice for twelve years. In 1885 the interests of the Travelers Insurance Company in Colorado irrigation enterprises became involved in litigation through the operations of The Colorado Loan and Trust Company. Accounting proceedings were commenced in the United States Circuit Court by which it was sought to recover a judgment against the Travelers for more than $1,000,000. Mr. Dunham was employed to devote his entire attention to this litigation, for which purpose he visited Colorado eighteen times. The litigation continued seven years and resulted in the recovery by the Travelers, and companies associated with it, of absolute title to some seventy thousand acres of land and the canals built to supply it with water, and a judgment in favor of the Travelers and against the plaintiffs for about $94,000. Mr. Dunham has since had the general oversight of the properties so acquired, which are held by five Colorado land and canal companies of which he is the secretary and treasurer, the Travelers being the principal stockholder. He is also the general counsel of the Travelers, having charge of its legal affairs at the home office, and is a member of the board of directors.

January 1, 1897, the total assets of the Travelers amounted to $20,896,684.63, with a surplus to policy-holders of $2,976,424.36, of which $1,000,000 is in capital stock.

THE HARTFORD STEAM BOILER INSPECTION AND INSURANCE COMPANY.

As remarked already two attempts in Hartford to introduce novel and untried forms of insurance have proved notably successful. In both cases the result, made more striking by the failure of imitators and short-lived rivals, is clearly due to intelligence and skillfulness of management.

In the mind of the projectors the conception of the above company was several years in taking form. At the time water was still largely used to drive machinery in manufacturing villages, but in towns steam, from necessity, was taking its place. Change to the new motive power was hastened by the inevitable concentration of skilled labor in cities. But the transfer was attended by great destruction of life and property. Conspicuous among casualties was the almost daily record in newspapers of steam-boiler explosions. Engine makers and users had not learned how to handle with safety the mighty agent. In not a few instances criminal carelessness came to the help of ignorance in inviting disaster.

There was no legal and little moral restraint to hold in check the recklessness. The notion prevailed that a certain waste of life and property in the use of steam was unavoidable. Attention, too, was diverted from responsible agents by the habit of speaking of disastrous explosions as the "act of God," or by otherwise hiding the human element under similar euphemistic expressions.

In the year 1857 a coterie of young men in Hartford, drawn together by congenial aims, organized the "Polytechnic Club," with the view primarily of investigating and discussing questions of science in relation to practical utilities. Among the members were Elisha K. Root, who succeeded Colonel Colt in the presidency of the armory, Francis A. Pratt, Amos W. Whitney, E. M. Reed, Professor C. B. Richards, of Yale; Charles F. Howard, Joseph Blanchard, J. M. Allen and others. Several members of this earnest but unpretentious club have since won international fame.

As a power coming more and more into use, but then under very imperfect control, steam became a favorite topic in the club. The results of foreign study and experiment were eagerly appropriated. Members discussed the causes of boiler explosions and means of prevention. It became known that the Manchester Steam Users' Association had already been organized in England with the view of preventing such accidents by periodical inspection. Under the system as started there the manufacturer paid a certain sum annually for examination, receiving in return either a certificate of the safe condition of his boiler or a report condemning it, but the certificate, like those in some places since issued by direct appointees of the state, involved no pecuniary obligation whatever, and if disaster occurred, the paper, while relieving the holder from the charge of carelessness, entitled him to no indemnity.

Although not one of the members of the Polytechnic Club was connected with insurance, the body unconsciously drew inspiration from the local predominance of the interest, which was then making Hartford famous as the home of skilled underwriters. In the course of the debates on the subject the attention of members was attracted to the feasibility of combining a guaranty with the inspection, thus giving both parties to the contract a pecuniary interest in the safety of the boiler. So far as known, the conception had not at that time materialized elsewhere. Although distinctly evolved in the club, the seminal idea waited several years for further development on account of the intervention of the Civil War.

A charter was procured in June, 1866, incorporating The Hartford Steam Boiler Inspection and Insurance Company, "for inspecting steam boilers, and for insuring against loss or damage to property arising from explosions or other accident in the use of steam boilers." The capital stock was to be not less than two hundred thousand nor more than one million of dollars, of which ten per cent. was required in cash at the time of subscription, and ten per cent. more within sixty days after organization.

August 31, 1866, the commissioners met and decided to open books on the 10th of September at the office of the Connecticut River Banking Company for subscriptions to the capital, which they fixed at five hundred thousand dollars. The shares having all been taken, the stockholders met, October 6th, and elected the following board of directors: Henry Kellogg, Richard W. H. Jarvis, Frank W. Cheney, John A. Butler, Charles M. Beach, Jonathan B. Bunce, Daniel Phillips, George M. Bartholomew, James G. Batterson, Marshall Jewell, Edward M. Reed, all of Hartford; George Crompton, Worcester; Daniel L. Harris, Springfield; Earl P. Mason, Providence; George Ripley, Lowell; F. Ratchford Starr, Philadelphia; Edwin D. Morgan, New York.

There was some delay in completing the organization. As an initial step the board desired to secure J. M. Allen as president. Although then a young man of thirty-three, Mr. Allen had become known as an earnest investigator in the fields of science. Indirectly the discussions in which he took a leading part had led up to the formation of the company. At this juncture, however, he had made an engagement for a year in New York city and was forced to decline. October 13th H. H. Hayden was elected secretary, and November 10th Enoch C. Roberts, president.

At the outset, strangely enough, the enterprise suffered from open lack of faith on the part of those who appeared before the public as its sponsors. After a trial of a few weeks, Mr. Roberts sent in his resignation, but was induced to let it rest without action till the following summer. Director after director sold his stock and followed the example of the president. Others with difficulty were induced to step into the vacancies. General demoralization prevailed. The question of retiring from business was seriously discussed.

In its troubles the board again turned to Mr. Allen. He was now free to listen to overtures, and, on the report of the committee appointed to confer with him, was elected president, September 16, 1867.

At the annual meeting of the stockholders in 1868, the condition of the company had so improved that a special vote was passed expressive of their gratification, and their confidence in the future.

For a long time the process was slow, the toil incessant, and the way wearisome. Most seemed to regard the new departure as a useless novelty, that must soon run its short-lived course. What will Hartford people undertake to insure next? was a question often asked in tones of undisguised derision. In the hands of a manager less firm in conviction, or less conciliatory in manner, the prophecy of disaster must have wrought its own fulfillment. Mr. Allen met the flavor of sarcasm with the antidote of pleasantry, and toiled on to create a demand which it should be his future business to supply.

For the first five years the company occupied a single room, sixteen by eighteen feet square, and for the same period the floor of the vault was spread with papers for the protection of the books, from the unwillingness of the officers to go to the extravagance of fitting it up with shelves. In a moment of self-indulgence, the president did invest $14 in a desk for his own use, but such outbreaks of luxury seldom occurred.

It is an open secret that all the successful insurance companies of Hartford practiced the most rigid economy till their business became thoroughly established, while those which set out with the theory that success could be hastened by a liberal scale of expenditure, invariably dropped into the sleep that knows no awakening. Other beginners may profit by the lesson.

Although the income of the company was at first small, the thoroughness of its inspections saved it almost wholly from losses. The cost of testing far exceeded any other item of outlay. For several years state insurance departments, recognizing the exceptional character of the business, and noting the infrequency of losses, did not require any charge to be made to liabilities for reinsurance-reserve. Hence savings over current expenses appeared on the books as net profits. Ten per cent. in dividends on the cash capital was paid in 1869, eight in 1871, and since then never less than ten. Besides, in 1872, $20,000 from profits were indorsed on the stock notes, $30,000 in 1873, $25,000 in January, 1874, and $15,000 the following October. In less than three years, out of surplus earnings, the cash capital had grown from $100,000 to $190,000. Meanwhile laws had been passed in several states excluding stock notes from admitted assets. Under the head of capital these were charged as a liability, and, hence, instead of a help, became a dead weight, burdensome in the ratio of volume. Accordingly, in October, 1874, under an act amending the charter, the capital was reduced from $500,000 to $200,000, and the par of the shares from $100 to $40. The stockholders were called on for $10,000 to make it fully paid at once. In 1883 the General Assembly empowered the company to restore the capital to the amount authorized in the original charter by increasing either the number or par of the shares. In February it was increased to $250,000 by a dividend of $50,000 from profits. Here it remained till the annual meeting in 1887. Meanwhile the yearly business had grown thirteen-fold since, in October, 1868, the board saw fit to spread on the record a vote of congratulation over brightening prospects. Numerous failures in all kinds of insurance had taught the public to demand strength on the part of those to whom they looked for indemnity. Rivals came and went, and, during their brief sojourn in the land of the living, often sought patronage by a vain show of wealth. To meet the situation, the company early in 1887 raised the capital to $500,000 by allowing each stockholder to take his proportion at par in cash.

During the first year of his incumbency, Mr. Allen started the *Locomotive*, a monthly which has built up a body of valuable literature concerning the steam boiler and cognate subjects. In it, after exhaustive investigation, are treated, with various illustrative aids, particular cases of explosion, with the view of explaining the exact cause. From the multiplicity of inquiries thus pursued, generalizations of the utmost value have been formed. Thirty-two thousand copies are distributed each month, and the paper is highly prized, not only by practical men, but also by students of science. A. D. Risteen, a graduate of the Worcester Polytechnic School, is associate editor.

In the prosecution of the work the energies of the company are mainly directed to the cure of defects and the prevention of disaster. Boilers under its care are visited by experts at stated periods, and thoroughly examined, while the appliances intended to secure safety are put in complete order. During the year 1896, twelve thousand, nine hundred and eighty-eight dangerous defects were reported, and six hundred and sixty-three boilers were condemned. From the outset the company has made two millions, one hundred and seventy-seven thousand and forty-five inspections, discovered one hundred and ninety-six thousand and forty-six dangerous defects, and condemned ten thousand, four hundred and sixty-three boilers. Had these been allowed to go undetected, the neglect in bad cases would have borne fruit hereafter in the needless destruction of life, limb, and property. This part of the work is performed by two hundred and twenty-five skilled and trained inspectors.

Some defects are beyond the reach of human scrutiny, and hence, with the resources now at our command, the element of danger cannot be completely eliminated. In case of explosion or rupture, the company makes good all loss or damage to property, with indemnity for loss of life or personal injury, to an amount not exceeding the sum insured.

The home office is a magazine of statistics and information, collected from all parts of the country, and relating to every phase of the business, and of the whole patrons have the benefit free.

The company furnishes to the insured plans and specifications for boilers, settings, and piping; also for steam chimneys, and when desired, supervises the erection, at reasonable expense. These embody the principles taught by scientific research and approved by experience, as made to subserve the attainment of the highest degree of economy, efficiency and safety. Many large plants thus built in a few years have saved the original cost in fuel alone. Suggestions in the way of economy, care and management make a part of the ordinary inspections.

Calls upon the company for structural plans long ago became so numerous as to require a separate department for attending to this branch of the work. Advice is asked on all kinds of mechanical and engineering questions connected with the use of steam both for power and heating. Of special value are the studies here prosecuted in regard to the material, form, setting and riveting of boilers. The matter of riveting joints has been worked out with great care. As each hole weakens the plate, the problem is to find the frequency and size that assure the highest attainable strength. After solving the problem mathematically, President Allen caused joints to be made in exact conformity with the theory thus deduced. These were then tested at the United States arsenal at Watertown, Mass., when the strength was found to be within two-tenths of one per cent. of his computation. He foretold, too, the exact place of fracture when the resistance of the joint was finally overcome.

The company has a chemical laboratory under immediate charge of George H. Seyms, for the analysis of water. In some parts of the country water apparently good is found to be wholly unsuitable for steam, depositing a scale and corroding the interior of boilers. In each case the company points out the counter-agents which remedy the trouble.

No officer or employee is permitted to have a pecuniary interest in any boiler or boiler appliance. While the best advice is given, an attitude of impartiality towards the trade is strictly maintained.

They now insure about sixty-two thousand boilers, the annual explosions averaging about one one-hundredth of one per cent. The imagination alone can deal with the saving of life, of suffering, and of property, through the methods which have been elaborated and introduced to the world by a company which might, without violence to language, be classed among the beneficent institutions of the country.

Up to January 1, 1897, the company had returned to patrons in losses paid and cost of inspections, nearly $4,000,000. During the year 1896, gross premiums reached $910,054.34, and income from investments, $84,422.30. There was disbursed in losses only $87,078.11. The company pays out a great deal to prevent trouble, and hence comparatively little in the way of indemnity. On the same date gross assets, inclusive of the capital of $500,000, reached $2,119,096.69, with unadjusted losses of $10,885. As the outgo is used largely to defray cost of inspection, the reserve ($1,291,858) may be regarded from the standpoint of the layman as technical rather than essential.

It should be borne in mind that the expansive force of steam is sufficient to rend any boiler in use. Hence none but competent engineers should be employed. Once in a while, in case of sudden sickness or some other emergency, a green hand is put temporarily in charge, and from this cause have come the most distressing casualties that have occurred under the policies of the company.

In 1873 the company moved into the present Ætna Life Insurance building, where its rooms are equipped with all scientific appliances for the conduct of the business. It occupies the entire second, and a large part of the third floor.

The history of this company is also the story of the life-work of its president, Jeremiah Mervin Allen. Born at Enfield, Conn., May 18, 1833, of a lineage wherein love of science and mechanics has been hereditary, his early studies and predilections seemed to lead up directly to the calling which fell to him unsought. While a teacher for four, and a fire insurance adjuster for two years, he attended to his duties with a fidelity that attracted attention, and at the same time gave his leisure to study. When Mr. Allen accepted the presidency there was no demand for the policies of the company. To convince steam users of the utility of the system, he made frequent and arduous journeys, often traveling by night, and using honeyed words of persuasion by day. A change, complete and universal, and having its sources in this early missionary work has since taken place. Regular inspections are now regarded as hardly less indispensable than fuel and water.

Mr. Allen's methods are rigidly scientific. He has prepared many formulæ that express with mathematical precision the rules of construction and criticism constantly observed. Love of their chief, born of fatherly courtesy and kindness, explains in good part the loyalty of employees to the company.

Outside of his profession Mr. Allen has been of great service to the public by his skill in applying scientific principles to practical affairs. He is often called upon to discover hidden causes of trouble and to find a remedy. He has written much and delivered many addresses on scientific subjects. He holds many positions of trust.

INSURANCE IN CONNECTICUT.

When the Hartford Board of Trade was organized in 1888, Mr. Allen was elected president, and by public importunity has been almost forced to retain the position ever since. Towards its usefulness in promoting the solid growth of the city his tact and judgment have very largely contributed.

The office of first vice-president is honorary, its incumbent not belonging to the active force. It is filled by Gen. William B. Franklin, late of the United States Army.

Francis Burke Allen, second vice-president, was born in Baltimore, Md., June 1, 1841; served the Illinois Central Railroad in the department of mechanical engineering, 1857–1861; served as an officer in the engineer corps of the United States Navy, 1862–1868; resigned in 1868 to become foreman of the Novelty Iron Works of New York; in 1871 accepted the position of assistant to the superintendent of motive power on the Northern Pacific Railway; in 1872 entered this company as special agent in the New York department; in 1882 was invited to Hartford as supervising general agent, and in 1887 was made second vice-president. Incidentally he has been a leading spirit in various military and naval associations.

Joseph Bancroft Pierce, secretary, was born in Thomaston, Conn., October 13, 1835, and after a short experience in manufacturing entered the insurance field in Hartford in 1860 as bookkeeper for the North American Fire, with which he remained as general agent, adjuster, assistant secretary and secretary till its extinction in the Chicago fire of 1871. He then became general agent of the National Fire of Hartford, and in March, 1873, secretary and treasurer of the Steam Boiler Inspection and Insurance Company, where he has since remained.

Lyman Bushnell Brainard, assistant treasurer, was born March 27, 1856, in Westchester, Conn., and at the age of twenty began to acquire experience in insurance as a canvasser. For a year from April, 1878, he solicited for the State Mutual of Hartford, giving up the position to become general agent and adjuster for the Jersey City, with which he continued till August, 1886, when he accepted a more lucrative position with the Equitable Mortgage Company of New York city, which he served as secretary and head of the bond department. He resigned March 2, 1894, to take his present place.

INSURANCE IN CONNECTICUT LOCALIZED.

With the exception of a few scattered mutual fire companies the business of insurance in Connecticut is now almost confined to Hartford. From time to time about one hundred and thirty separate institutions have received charters from the General Assembly of the state giving authority to engage in various forms of underwriting. Many tried the experiment and failed. Not only large fires, but long periods of mercantile depression have brought great fatality.

In Hartford towards the close of the eighteenth century a number of leading merchants and others, with the view primarily of protecting vessels and cargoes sailing from the river towns to the West Indies, undertook the work in constantly changing partnerships. In 1803 they formed a chartered company, which, though prosperous at first, withered during the Napoleonic wars and the War of 1812. While this venture was still struggling with perils of the sea the Hartford and the Ætna took up the work on land. Success attracted others. A profession was gradually formed to discover correct theories to which practice may, in the long run, safely be made to conform.

Here leadership has been gained, not by luck or accident or favoring circumstances, but by profound study of the facts and principles involved in the business, by high native intelligence, sharpened to a keen edge in frequent adversities, by patient endurance through periods of misfortune, by heroic courage in meeting exceptional calamities, and not least by scrupulous integrity in dealings with the public.

The business, too, is conducted in a cosmopolitan spirit. Present managers have won their places not through favoritism or inherited influence, but through merit alone. Ability, character, technical skill, special gifts are welcomed from every quarter. The sketches above given show the breadth of area and the wealth of experience now brought together in the different offices of the city. In a word, conspicuous success has been won by intelligence and integrity. The decisive way in which occasional lapses from rectitude have been treated emphasizes the general truth by vividness of contrast.

STATE COMMISSIONERS.

The office of commissioner of insurance was created by a law passed in 1865, but singularly enough his duties were defined by a law enacted in 1864. The department was not established till 1871.

COMMISSIONERS.	TERMS OF SERVICE.	COMMISSIONERS.	TERMS OF SERVICE.
Benjamin Noyes	1865–1871	Orsamus R. Fyler	1886–1893
George S. Miller	1871–1874	*John S. Seymour	1893–
John W. Stedman	1874–1880	Burton Mansfield	1893–1895
John W. Brooks	1880–1883	Frederick A. Betts	1895–
Ephraim Williams	1883–1886		

*John S. Seymour held the office from March 4th to April 11th, 1893, when he resigned to take the office of commissioner of patents at Washington.

POSTSCRIPT, JULY 1st, 1897.

ÆTNA INSURANCE COMPANY.—The foregoing history was brought down to February, 1897. During the interval several important changes have taken place. March 19th James F. Dudley, vice-president of the Ætna Insurance Company, while absent on a business trip, died suddenly of apoplexy at New Orleans. April 7th E. O. Weeks was promoted to the vice-presidency and A. C. Adams and Henry E. Rees were elected assistant secretaries. Mr. Adams was born in Barnstable, Mass., April 9, 1847. He entered upon insurance work in 1865, and since 1891 has been special agent of the Ætna in the New England field. Mr. Rees was born in Macon, Georgia, April 29, 1857, and has been engaged in insurance since 1881, having served as special agent of the Ætna at the south since 1889. F. C. Bennett, general agent of the Western Branch office at Cincinnati, Ohio, since 1870, died May 25th, aged sixty-seven. N. E. Keeler, the assistant general agent and Thomas E. Gallagher, a valued special agent of the company in New York, have been appointed to fill the vacancy under the firm-name of Keeler & Gallagher. President William B. Clark, having served as president also of the National Board of Underwriters, in May declined a re-election to that honorable position, owing to pressure of duties connected with his own company.

HARTFORD LIFE INSURANCE COMPANY.—At the last session of the Connecticut Legislature the name of the Hartford Life and Annuity Insurance Company was changed to the Hartford Life Insurance Company.

INDEX.

ABBOT, William G. 66
Ackley, Elijah 60
Adams, A. C. 118
Adams, Chester 104
Adams, Demas 18
Adams, John T. 11
Ætna Insurance Company:
  Why started, 22; organization, 22; modest beginnings, 23; Henry L. Ellsworth, 23; re-insurance of the Middletown Fire Insurance Company, 23; labors and vigilance of directors 23; extension of the agency system, 24; a cautious secretary, 24; sore trials overcome by courage of directors, 24; companies saved by united action, 25; Isaac Perkins, 25; fire losses a gauge of general conditions, 25; panic of 1837, 25; trip of the president, 26; first fire policy in Chicago, 26; travels of directors, 26; Joseph, Junius S., and J. Pierpont Morgan, 26; inland insurance, 26; fire of 1845 in New York City, 27; turning the half century, 27; business from the Protection, 27; rapid growth, 28; increases of capital, 28; Thomas K. Brace, 28; Edwin G. Ripley, 28; Thomas A. Alexander, 29; contest over re-insurance reserves, 29; classification of losses, 29; first chromo poster, 29; introduction of outline charts, 29; in 1819 a book of instructions, 30; losses at Chicago, 30; Lucius J. Hendee, 30; Jothan Goodnow, 30; E. J. Bassett, 31; A. C. Bayne, 31; William B. Clark, 31; James F. Dudley, 31; William H. King, 31; Egbert O. Weeks, 31; assets, 32; A. C. Adams, 118; H. E. Rees, 118.
Ætna Life Insurance Company:
  Origin, 90; first directors, 90; early development slow, 90; war stimulus causes rapid growth, 91; productive investments, 91; farm loans, 91; large returns to policy-holders, 91; increases of capital, 92; Eliphalet A. Bulkeley, 92; Thomas O. Enders, 92; Morgan G. Bulkeley, 93; officers, 93; statistics, 93; accident department, 93; John C. Webster, 93; Joel L. English, 93; Howell W. St. John, 94; Charles E. Gilbert, 94; home office, 94.
Alcott, Samuel 3
Alexander, David 18
Alexander, Thomas A. 29
Allen, Francis B., Sketch of ... 117
Allen, J. M. 87, 112, 113, 114, 115, 117
  Sketch of 116
Allen, Stephens & Company 84
Allyn, T. C. 18, 21
Alsop, Joseph 8
Alsop, Richard 3
American Mutual Life & American National Life and Trust Company of New Haven:
  Formation and first officers, 69; incorrect and fatal assumptions respecting rates of interest and mortality, 70; commissioner Elizur Wright puzzled 70; high character of President Silliman, 70, 71; Benjamin Noyes, president, 70; also insurance commissioner, 71; a prophet more honored at home than abroad, 71; a faithful trustee banished, 71; swapping scrip, 71; an attack from Norwich, 72; a new charter, 72; legislative stupidity or criminality? 72; long gestation, 72; change in name only, 73; action of new commissioner, 73; re-insurance of National Life of New York, 73; a bad bargain and unexpected obstacles, 73; John W. Stedman, insurance commissioner, assailed by complaints 73; his examination and its discoveries, 73; application for appointment of trustee, 74; flexible decision of court, 74; a "guaranty capital" of words only, 74; securities mostly mythical, 75; unconscious share-holders, 75; phantoms treated as realities, 75; report of commissioner to the General Assembly and reply of directors, 76; action of the legislature, 76; sudden conversions, 76; plain talk from commissioner, 77; over $27,000 for the lobby, 77; second trial and miscarriage, 77; a vanishing bank credit, 77; plotting a flank movement, 77; purchase of a Washington charter, 78; dark seances, 78; borrowed bonds, 78; born again, 78; re insurance of a New Jersey company, 79; "Jersey justice," 79; appointment of receiver, 80; scant assets, 80; Noyes in prison, 80; triumphant return. 80; darkness at the end, 81.
Atlas Insurance Company, Hartford:
  Succeeds the Charter Oak and retires after a struggle of eight years 57
Averill, Eliphalet 33
Ayrault, James 63

BACKUS, Asa 11
Backus, Joseph 60
Baker, William E. 36
Baldwin, Simeon 11, 21
Baldwin, Simeon E. 74
Ball, Stephen 101, 105
Barnes, Jonathan, Jr. 22
Barnes, William 65, 96
Barrows, Edwin G. 110
Bartholomew, George M. 88, 89
Bassett, Erastus J. 31
Batterson, James G. .. 50, 106, 107, 108
  Sketch of 110
Bayne, Andrew C. 30, 31
Beecher, Robert E. 109
Belden, H. K. 21
Bennett, F. C. 32, 35, 118
Bennett, J. B. 35

119

INDEX

	PAGE
Bennett, Martin	38, 39
Foreign agencies	57
Sketch of	57
Beresford, Samuel B.	82
Betts, Frederick A.	118
Bill, Elijah A.	60
Billings, Coddington	8
Bishop, J. A.	75
Bissell, George F.	18
Bissell, George P.	87
Bliss, Lewis	15
Boardman, H. F.	60
Boardman & Spencer	32
Bodwell, George B.	56
Bolles, Armin	56
Bolles, James G.	16, 20, 54
Bombaugh, C. C.	111
Bowers, Caleb B.	21, 36, 54
Bowers, William N	54
Brace, Jonathan	6
Brace, Thomas K.	12, 23, 26, 27
Sketch of	28
Brainard, Leverett	36
Brainard, Lyman B.	117
Breed, Shubael	12
Brewster, Augustus	12
Brewster, Augustus O.	12
Brewster, James H.	57
Sketch of	57
Bridgeport Fire and Marine Insurance Company: Organization, 36; exclusion from New York, 36; padding assets, 36; a frightened director, 37; insolvency, 37; officers, 37.	
Bristol, Willis	36, 48, 70, 72
Brooks, Isaac	89
Brooks, John W.	55–118
Browne, John D.	24
Sketch of	39
Buck, Daniel	12
Buck, Daniel	54
Buck, John R.	88–104
Bulkeley, Eliphalet A.	63–90
Sketch of	92
Bulkeley, Morgan G.	92
Sketch of	92
Bulkeley, William H.	93
Bull, Michael and Thomas	3
Sketch of	6
Bunce, Edward M.	66
Sketch of	69
Bunce, Jonathan B.	89, 96, 97
Sketch of	98
Bunce, John L.	82
Burdick, George H.	42–43
Sketch of	44
Burns, James F.	95–96
Burt, Charles R.	38, 39
Sketch of	40
Bushnell, Cornelius S.	47
Buswell, John	12
CALDWELL, John	2, 3, 5, 6, 7, 3?
Sketch of	4
Calhoun, Philo C.	37
Callingham, W. J.	56
Camp, John N.	60
Camp, William S.	60
Campbell, James	93
Cannon, Henry L.	37

	PAGE
Carter, Buswell	77
Catlin, Julius	60
Chadwick, Daniel	88
Chamberlin, A.	56
Charter Oak Fire and Marine Insurance Company: Formation, 52; chronic impairment, 52; reduction of capital, 52; destruction by Chicago fire, 52; officers, 52.	
Charter Oak Life Insurance Company: Charter requirements, 82; large over-subscription, 82; first directors and officers, 82; Gideon Welles, 82; stock notes, 82; early officers, 83; votes for the eyes of examiners, 83; good agents outside, bad management inside, 83; warning from Commissioner Stedman, 84; failure of Allen, Stephens & Co., 84; building a railway, a summer hotel, a costly office, etc., 84; Henry J. Furber, 84; his contract, 85; reorganization, 85; discoveries of experts, 85; Furber's fertility of resource and advantageous purchases, 86; distrust of Furber, 86; a special commission, 86; in the courts and another reorganization, 87; Marshall Jewell president, and departure of Furber, 87; investigations, 87; liabilities scaled, 88; reorganization on mutual basis, 88; trial for conspiracy, 88; secret contracts, 88; George M. Bartholomew, president, 88; large reduction of liabilities, but hopelessness of the case, 88; appointment of receivers,89; final distribution, 89.	
Chase, Charles E.	24
Chase, Edwin S.	59
Chase, George L.	18
Sketch of	18
Chatfield, H. W.	37
Chenevard, John	3
Sketch of	6
Chew, Colby	8
City Fire Insurance Company (Hartford): Changes of name and policy, 36; careful management and prosperity, 36; destroyed by Chicago fire, 36; officers, 36.	
City Insurance Company (New Haven): Early prosperity, 37; turn of the tide, 37; retirement after the Civil War, 37; revival after long dormancy, 37; second retirement, 37.	
Clagett, William H.	78, 79
Clark, Daniel W.	33, 34
Clark, Joseph N.	36
Clark, L. W.	39, 56
Clark, William B.	28, 30, 42, 118
Sketch of	31
Cleveland, H. M.	86
Coffin, O. Vincent	60
Cofran & Bissell	21
Coit, George M.	21
Coit, Samuel	82, 93
Colt, David	8
Commissioners' insurance, of Connecticut	118
Comstock, Frederick R.	105
Condict, H. D.	36
Connecticut Fire Insurance Company: Organization and first directors, 37; cautious policy, 38; extinguishment of stock notes, 38; Benjamin W. Greene, 38; John B. Eldredge, 38; heavy losses in the Chicago fire, 38; charter saved, 39; good fortune following, 39; increase of capital, 39; J. D.	

Browne, 39; home office, 39; statistics of growth, 40; Charles R. Burt, 40; L. W. Clark, 40.
Connecticut General Life Insurance Company: Insurance of impaired lives, 101; changes of capital, 102; first directors and officers, 102; shrinkage after the panic, 102; in 1876 permanent turn, 102; Tontine policies, 102; Thomas W. Russell, 103; a notable banquet, 103; statistics, 103; Frederick V. Hudson, 103; Edward B. Peck, 103; Robert W Huntington, 103.
Connecticut Health Insurance Company: Health insurance a failure, 81; change of name and aim, 81; insurance of slaves and coolies, 81; incurable wounds, 81; officers, 81.
Connecticut Mutual Life Insurance Company: Local studies in insurance half a century ago, 62; a charter regardful of all rights, 62; organization and first directors, 63; guarantee fund provided, 63; dissensions provoked by economies, 63; defeat of the disaffected, 64; new directory and peace, 64; retirement of guarantee notes, 64; situation in 1861, 64; the premium note, 64; official impertinence defied, 65; no booty for blackmailers, 65; equitable distribution of savings, 65; plots, onset and failure of land speculators, 66; Guy R. Phelps, 66; James Goodwin, 66; successive officers, 66; Jacob L. Greene, 67; John M. Taylor, 67; conservative methods of the company, 67; discussion and action in regard to fall in rates of interest, 67; to tontine frauds, 68; statistics, 68; Edward M. Bunce, 69; Daniel H. Wells, 69; John D. Parker, 69.
Connor, William 21, 33
Continental Life Insurance Company: Organization, 99; the time prolific in new life insurance companies, 99; first directors and officers, 99; revolution with change of officers, 99; how sixty per cent. of capital was reported as paid, 100; examination by special commission, 100; bewildering confusion of fictitious credits, 100; disappearance of securities loaned to plug up a hole, 101; appointment of receivers, 101; shrinkage of assets, 101.
Cook, Howard W. 56
Cooke, Lorrin A. 101
Cooper, Samuel 60
Courant, The Connecticut 6
Courtney, Thomas E. 37
Cowles, W. A. 105
Cowles, E. B. 56
Cowls, Samuel 14
Crosby, E. H. 104, 105
Cross, Isaac 61

DAGGETT, Alfred 48
Danforth, J. W. 54
Davis, Gustavus F. 87, 107
Davies, J. C. 35
Day, Isaac C. 42
Day, Robert E. 54, 87, 89
Denison, Austin 8
Denison, Charles 21
Denison, Elihu 8
Denison, John L. 12, 71
Dennis, Rodney 107
Sketch of 110

Devotion, John L. 61
Dewell, J. D. 55
De Witt, J. 61
De Witt, John H. 61
Dickson, Robert 40
Dillon, A. H. 85
Dixon, James 28
Sketch of 81
Dodge, David S. 63, 64
Doolittle, Tilton E. 47
Dornin, George D. 52
Dorsheimer, Gov. 88
Duclos, Henry P. 104, 105
Dudley, James F. 30, 118
Sketch of 31
Dunham, Austin 93
Dunham, Sylvester C. 112
Douglass, Francis D. 99
Dwight, Timothy 8

EATON, William W. 87
Eldredge, John B. 38
Sketch of 39
Ellis, George, sketch of 111
Ellis, George W. 110
Ellsworth, Henry L. 23, 109
Ellsworth, Pinckney W. 61
Ellsworth, William W. 7
Sketch of 32
Elmore, Samuel E. 99
Embargo and non-intercourse acts 9
English, J. L., sketch of 93
Enders, Thomas O. 87, 93
Sketch of 92
Erving, D. D. 60
Erving, R. A. 60
Erving, William A. 60

FAXON, Walter C. 93
Fay, A. Goodrich 78
Fessenden, Edson 95, 96
Fillmore, C. J. 61
Fisher, Augustus F. 59
Flower, Ebenezer 64, 66
Foote, John P. 33
Foreign trade of Connecticut 9
Foster, E. K. 46, 47
Foster, Frederick R. 105
Foster, L. F. S. 77, 88
Franklin, William B. 50
French, B. W. 76
Furber, Henry J. 84, 85, 86, 87, 88
Fyler, Orsamus R. 101, 118

GALACAR, Charles E. 44
Gallagher, Thos. E. 118
Galpin, Philip S. 36
Galpin, John 59
Gleason & Cowles 5
Gilbert, Charles E. 93
Sketch of 94
Gill, A. 82
Gill, Elias 83
Gillett, Ralph 36, 52
Sketch of 61
Glover, Thomas 12
Goodman, Aaron C. 96, 97
Goodnow, Jotham 31
Sketch of 30
Goodrich, Elizur 11

	PAGE
Goodwin, James	63, 64
Sketch of	66
Goodwin, James J.	26
Goodwin, James L.	33
Goodwin, James M.	25
Goodwin, Jonathan, Jr.	28
Grant, David	59, 60
Green, Nathaniel	37
Greene, Benjamin W., Sketch of	38
Greene, Jacob L.	66
Sketch of	67
Greenslit, David	59
Griffing, John S.	36
Griswold, Wareham	104
Gross, Charles E.	89–97

HAMERSLEY, William	88
Hammond, Asael	59
Hale, Benjamin E.	94, 95
Harris, C. W.	60
Harrison, Justus	8, 36
Harrison, Henry B.	74
Harrison, Lynde	76
Hartford Bank	1, 6, 13, 15, 16, 17, 19, 59.

Hartford County Mutual Fire Insurance Company:
Limit of operations and premium note, 59; modest start, 59; in 1842 a crisis safely met, 59; effects upon it of Chicago fire, 59; business confined to Connecticut and to safer class of risks, 60; officers, 60.

Hartford Insurance Company (Marine):
In 1803 organized, 6; merger in the Protection, 7, 10, 32.

Hartford Fire Insurance Company:
Organization, 12; difficulty of investing, 12; first purchase, 13; laws of average, 13; capricious rates, 13; character and care, 13; pay of agents, 14; spirit of Puritanism, 14; slow growth, 14; causes, 14; indemnity for losses the primary object, 14; novelties unpopular, 14; planting early agencies, 14; who, not where? 15; gratuities, 15; city watch, 15; re-insurance of the New Haven Fire Insurance Company, 15; salary of officers, 15; first clerk, 15; income and outgo, 15; impairment 15; paying losses by loans 15; in early days no reserves laid by, 16; Eliphalet succeeds Nathaniel Terry, 16; meeting a crisis, 16; reward of courage, 16; extraordinary losses, 17; action of directors, 17; increases of capital, 17; Hezekiah Huntington, 17; T. C. Allen, 18; George L. Chase, 18; a more aggressive policy, 18; new departments, 18; the great Chicago fire, 18; the Boston fire, 19; President Chase and the Ocean Bank of New York, 19; successive offices, 20; present building, 20; small stock liability, 20; secretaries, 21; P. C. Royce, 21; Thomas Turnbull, 21; Charles E. Chase, 21; departments, 21; large assets, 21.

Hartford Life and Annuity (now Hartford Life):
Chartered to do accident as well as life insurance, 103; first directors and officers, 103; changes of name and abandonment of accident feature, 104; impairment of capital, 104; recovery under the presidency of C. C. Kimball, 104; after changes, 104; scheme of Henry P. Duclos, 104; presidents, 105; statistics, 105; Rienzi B. Parker, 105; Stephen Ball, 105; home office, 105; name changed, 118.

	PAGE
Hartford and New Haven Insurance Company, 2,	
3, 5, 32.	

Hartford Steam Boiler Inspection and Insurance Company:
Transition from water to steam power, 112; frequency of casualties, 112; the Polytechnic club, 112; first directors and organization, 113; lack of faith with failure imminent, 113; J. M. Allen accepts the presidency, 114; his tact and carefulness, 114; rapid and solid growth, 114; *The Locomotive*, 115; aims, cure of defects and prevention of disaster, 115; magnitude of the work, 115; home office a bureau of scientific information, 115; furnishing plans for steam plants, 115; responses to scientific tests, 115; chemical laboratory, 116; impartiality toward the trade, 116; statistics, 116; J. M. Allen, 116; General William B. Franklin, 117; Francis B. Allen, 117; Joseph B. Pierce, 117; Lyman B. Brainard, 117.

Hartford, supremacy in underwriting	4, 117
Hastings, A. F.	54
Hastings, W. C.	54
Hatch, George E.	87
Havens, Walter H.	60
Hayden, H. H.	113
Hazard, Augustus G.	27, 29
Hendee, Lucius J.	99
Sketch of	30
Hill, W. H.	95
Holcombe, James H.	95
Holcombe, John M.	87, 96, 97
Sketch of	98
Hollister, Nelson	85
Homans, Shepard	65

Home Insurance Company (New Haven):
Formation, 53; capital increased to one million, 53; dividends from capital, 53; reckless zeal, 53; reduction to one-half million, 53; bankruptcy, 53; indignation of Commissioner Noyes, 53.

Hooker & Brewster	14
Hooker & Chaffee	3
Hooker, William T.	63, 81
Hopkins, Ian	3
Hough, Timothy	37
Howard, James L.	61, 62
Howard, Mark, courage and foresight	34, 35, 49, 52
Sketch of	50
Howe, Edmund G.	67
Howe, William	3
Hoyt, John W.	60
Hubbard, Elijah	22
Hubbard, George W.	93
Hubbard, Gurdon S.	26
Hubbard, Richard D.	50, 100
Hubbard, Thomas	22
Hudson, B.	52, 94
Hudson, Frederick V.	102
Sketch of	103
Hudson & Goodwin	3
Sketch of	6
Hudson, Henry	12
Huntington, Charles P.	12
Huntington, Ebenezer	12
Huntington, Edward B.	57
Huntington, Hezekiah; Sketch of	17
Huntington, John G.	12
Huntington, Levi	11

INDEX

	Page
Huntington, Richard	60
Huntington, Robert W.	103
Huntington, Zachariah	11
Hyde, A. P.	88
Hyde, Lewis	12
IMLAY, William, policy	2, 30, 43
JAMES, Fred. S.	52
Jenness, F. W.	31
Jewell, Marshall	42, 87
Jewett, George D.	54
Jillson, Asa	42
Sketch of	43
Johnson, Elisha	76, 87
Johnson, Robert A.	54
Jones, Daniel	3
KEELER, N. E.	118
Kellogg, Henry	10, 41
Sketch of	43
Kimball, C. C.	104
King, Hezekiah	33
King, William H.	30
Sketch of	31
Kingsbury, Ephraim	14
Kinney, J. W.	11
Knox, John	3
Knox, John B.	44
Knox, Normand	3, 6, 7
LAMB, Joseph G.	71
Law, Richard	8
Lawrence, Charles H.	97
Sketch of	99
Lawrence, Samuel	3
Lathrop, Barrel	11
Lathrop, Thomas	12
Learned, Ebenezer, Jr.	12
Learned, Joshua C.	8
Leavitt, Hooker	14
Lee, William T.	82
Leete, Charles S.	36
Lewis, H. G.	75
Lewis, John B.; Sketch of	114
Lewis, William	36
Lester, George S.	55
Lester, George W.	36, 55, 56
Life Insurance, beginnings of	61
" " Denounced by Elder Swan	62
Lobdell, E. Thomas	49
Loomis, Simeon L.	25, 26, 41, 42, 93
Lyman, C. C.	16, 21
Lynde, John H.	21
Lyon, R. F.	72
Lyon, William	8
MACK, Samuel E.	35, 41
Magill, H. M.	35, 44
Magill, R. H.	41, 44
Maltby, C. S.	75
Manning, W. S.	104
Mansfield, Burton	118
Marcy, Thomas K.	86
Marine Insurance (early)	3
Mason, E. J.	37
Mason, James M.	37
Mason, H.	36, 37

	Page
Matthews, Edward	86
MacFarlane, John J.	96, 97
Merchants' Fire Insurance Co. (See National)	
Meriden Insurance Company:	
Retirement after a fairly successful career, 56.	
Merritt, George S.	57
Merwin, S. E.	53
Middletown Insurance Company	7, 8
Reinsured	22
Middlesex Mutual Assurance Company:	
Largest of state mutuals, 60; methods and progress, 60; officers, 60.	
Miller, Asher	8
Miller, George S.	72, 118
Miller, Henry L.	81
Milligan, Edward	44
Miscellaneous insurance	106
Mitchell, J. C.	35
Mitchell, J. H.	44
Mitchell, Walter	12, 15, 16, 22
Morgan, Forrest	110
Morgan, John	2, 3, 32
Sketch of	5
Morgan, Joseph	26, 66
Morgan, Junius S.	26, 66
Morgan, J. Pierpont	26
Morgan, Nathaniel H., sketch of	41
Morgan, N. D.	64
Morgan, Samuel	12
Morris, John E., sketch of	111
Morris, Luzon B.	48
Mortimore, J. A.	79
Mutual Assurance Company of the City of Norwich	11, 58
Mutual Assurance Company of New Haven	11
Mutual Insurance Companies, dates of incorporation and gross assets	58
NATIONAL Fire Insurance Company (successor to Merchants'):	
Organization and first directors of the Merchants', 49; experience of Mark Howard, president, 49; stock fully paid in cash, 49; overwhelmed by Chicago fire, 49; all assets distributed pro rata, 50; revival in the National, 50; first directors, 50; Mark Howard, 50; his instruction book, 51; James Nichols, 51; home office, 52; statistics of progress, 52; Ellis G. Richards, 52; Benjamin R. Stillman, 52; departments, 52.	
Naval victories won by sailors trained in merchant marine	10
Nevers, George	52
New England Fire and Marine Insurance Company: Formation, struggles and death	54
New Haven Fire Insurance Company	3, 7, 15
Reinsured	21
New London County Mutual Insurance Company: Officers	60, 61
Nichols, David P.	86
Nichols, James	49, 50
Sketch of	51
Niles, John M.	102
North American Fire Insurance Company: Organization, 53; depletion by dividends and death, 54; officers, 54.	
Northrop, Frederick W.	47, 48
Norton, Ebenezer F.	44
Norwalk Marine and Fire Insurance Company: Sale to a foreign company	54

	PAGE
Norwich Fire Insurance Company	7, 8, 10
Sketch of	11
Noyes, Benjamin, 45, 47, 53, 69, 70, 71, 72, 73, 75, 76, 77, 78, 79, 80, 118.	

OCEAN Bank receivership 19
Ocean Insurance Company, of New Haven 8
Orient Fire Insurance Company (Hartford):
Successor of the City Fire Insurance Company, 55; organization and first directors, 55; Boston fire, 55; increases of capital, 55; Charles B. Whiting, 55; panic of 1893, and its effects on insurance, 56; statistics, 56; officers, 56; James C. Taintor, 56; Howard W. Cook, 56; departments, 56.

PALMER, James C.	59
Palmer, John	59
Palmer, Noyes S.	83
Park, John D.	77
Parker, E. F.	60
Parker, John D.	66
Sketch of	69
Parker, Reinzi B., sketch of	103
Parsons, Enoch	8
Parsons, Edward W.	102
Parsons, James S.	99, 101
Parsons, John C.	97
Parsons, S. G.	54
Passing the hat	10
Patten, Nathaniel	12, 13
Pearl, William M.	110
Peck, Edward B.	103
Perkins, Charles E.	88
Perkins, George L.	12
Perkins, Isaac	23, 24
Sketch of	33
Perkins, Thomas C.	25, 32
Sketch of	33
Perkins, Thomas S.	8
Peterson, Charles	36
Phillips, Daniel	85
Phelps, Anson G.	15
Phelps, Elisha	59, 60
Phelps, Guy R.	61, 63, 65, 101
Sketch of	66

Phœnix Fire Insurance Company:
An inspiration of Henry Kellogg, 40; organization and first directors, 41; Nathaniel H. Morgan, 41; agents and business from the Protection, 41; occupation of the Pacific coast, 41; no prolonged infancy, 41; increases of capital, 42, 43; payment by Marshall Jewell of first loss after Chicago fire, 42; reaction from despair, 42; forest fires, 43; successive quarters, 43; Henry Kellogg, 43; D. W. C. Skilton, 43; J. H. Mitchell, 44; statistics of growth, 44; G. H. Burdick, 44; Charles E. Galacar, 44; Edward Milligan, 44; John B. Knox, 44; departments, 44.

Phœnix Mutual Life Insurance Company:
Temperance theories, 94; organization and first directors, 94; adoption of regular plans, 95; early officers, 94, 95; panic of 1873, and excessive returns to policy holders, 95; change of policy and officers, 96; Aaron C. Goodman, 96; repair of assets, 96; appearance of John J. McFarlane, 96; results, 97; by retirement of stock the company made

	PAGE
mutual, 97; statistics, 98; new office, 98; Jonathan B. Bunce, 98; John M. Holcombe, 98; Charles H. Lawrence, 99	
Pierce, J. B.	54
Sketch of	117
Post, Augustus T.	78
Post-Revolutionary poverty and isolation, 1; activities, 1.	
Pratt, Elisha B.	61, 63, 64
Pratt, Francis A.	112
Pratt, Henry Z.	31, 64
Prentice, Amos	54
Preston, Edward V., sketch of	111
Preston, Selden C.	55
Preston, Zephaniah	67

Protection Insurance Company:
Lineal successor of the early underwriters of Hartford, 7, 10; fall of its business to the Ætna 28; inherits a stock of traditions and good-will, 32; first directors, 32; William W. Ellsworth, 32; Thomas C. Perkins, 33; work of Ephraim Robbins, 33; his success, 33; Cincinnati office a club room of whig chiefs, 33; Mark Howard, first special agent, 34; profits scattered in dividends, 34; St. Louis fire, 34; a spicy interview, 34; a constricted treasury, 34; struggles and collapse, 35; lessons from the failure, 35; residuary legatees, 35.

Putnam Fire Insurance Company:
Intestine war, 54; unjustifiable presumptions, 54; general mismanagement, 54; struggles and destruction by Chicago fire, 55.

QUINNIPIAC Insurance Company (New Haven:
Return of capital to shareholders and retirement, 55.

RANSOM, Amos	12
Redfield, S. B.	8
Rees, Henry E.	118
Rice, John S.	99
Rice, O. P.	54
Richards, Ellis G.	51
Sketch of	52
Richardson, Joseph	37
Ripley, Edwin G., Sketch of	28, 31
Ripley, David	12
Ripley, G. B.	11
Risteen, A. D.	117
Roath, William	61
Roberts, Enoch C.	113
Robertson, John B.	50, 72
Robins, Ephraim, Sketch of	33
Robins, W. B.	34
Robinson, David F.	33
Robinson, Vine	58, 59
Root, Elisha K.	112
Root, Ephraim	6
Royce, Philander C.	21
Ruggles, Samuel B.	36
Russell, Gurdon W.	93
Russell, Talcott H.	80
Russell, Thomas W.	83, 102
Sketch of	103
SAGE, Ebenezer	8
Sanford, Elihu	8
Sanford, Peleg	4

INDEX. 125

	PAGE
Sanford, Thomas	3
Sanford & Wadsworth	2, 5, 32
Satterlee, D. R.	53
Security Insurance Company (New Haven): Escapes the great fires at Chicago and Boston, 35; changes of policy, 35; successive officers, 36; its prosperity, 36.	
Sexton, Julius M.	52
Seymour, Daniel F.	104
Seymour, James S.	14
Seymour, John S.	118
Seymour, John W.	90, 93
Seymour, Origen S.	86, 100
Seyms, George H.	116
Shepard, Charles	59, 60
Sherman, Roger	8
Shipman, Elias	2, 5, 8, 32
Shipman, John	8
Shultas, James B.	60
Silliman, Benjamin	69, 70, 71
Simrall, J. W. G.	35
Skilton, D. W. C., sketch of	43
Skinner, Roger S.	15, 21, 23
Smith, A. T.	104, 105
Smith, Joseph A.	60
Smith, Joseph L.	75, 79
Smith & Tatley	44
Smith, Thomas M.	85
Southworth, Wells	37
Sprague, Joseph H.	52, 57
Squire, William J.	85
Stanton, Lewis E.	88
Starr, Jared	8
State Fire Insurance Company (New Haven): Mysterious origin, 45; adding zero to zero, 45; unconscious beneficiaries, 45; entry into Massachusetts, 45; disappearance of the secretary, 46; Elizur Wright, commissioner, deceived, 46; talk on a steamboat, 46; discoveries, 46; anger of Mr. Wright, 46; call upon the State's attorney to prosecute, 46; correspondence, 47; Benjamin Noyes elected secretary, 47; a test suit, 47; penalty for being caught in bad company, 47; list of assets, 47.	
State Mutual Insurance Company (Hartford).	61
Stedman, Edmund A.	85, 89
Stedman, John W., 73, 76, 79, 80, 84, 86, 87, 88, 101, 118.	
Steel, George T.	77
Steere, W. T.	12
Stevens, G. Farnham	56, 57
Stevens, Halsey	83, 85, 88
Stillman, Benjamin R.	51
Sketch of	52
St. John, Daniel	60
St. John, Howell W.	93
Sketch of	94
Stock notes	7
Storrs, Aaron H.	59
Storrs, Z. A.	83
Sugden, William E.	60
Sumner, George	64
Swan, Elder	62
TABER, Job	8
Taintor, James C., sketch of	56
Taylor, Charles	20
Taylor, James P.	104

	PAGE
Taylor, John M.	66
Sketch of	67
Taylor, Stephen	60
Terry, Eliphalet	15, 16
Sketch of	17
Terry, Nathaniel	12, 13, 15
Sketch of	16
Thames Fire Insurance Company: Formation, misfortunes and retirement, 54; officers, 54.	
Thomas, Simeon	12
Thorp, P. M.	37
Totten, Gilbert	8
Tomlinson, Isaac	21
Toucey, Isaac	63, 109
Towner, Theron	56
Tracy, Henry B.	11
Tracy, John C.	100
Travelers' Insurance Company: Inception of the scheme, 106; first directors and officers, 107; hard work, severe economy and close study of new problems, 107; making paths without precedents, 107; generalizing laws, 107; diversified dangers, 108; birth and death of new accident companies, 108; loyalty of employes, 108; secession, jokes and funeral, 108; addition of a life department, 109; increases of capital, 109; purchase for home office of an historic mansion, 109; character of casualties, 109; The Travelers' Record, 110; causes of success, 110; James Goodwin Batterson, 110; Rodney Dennis, 110; George Ellis, 111; John E. Morris, 111; Edward V. Preston, 111; John B. Lewis, 111; Sylvester C. Dunham. 112; statistics, 112.	
Trezevant & Cockran	56
Turnbull, Thomas	21
Twining, A. C.	71
UNION Fire Insurance Company (Hartford): Returns capital to share holders and retires, 54.	
Union Insurance Company of New London	7, 8
VAIL, Thomas J.	104
WADSWORTH, Daniel, sketch of	4
Wadsworth, Jeremiah	2, 4, 32
Sketch of	4
Wadsworth, Tertius	94
Wales, George	15
Wallace, J. A.	54
Walkley, James C.	82, 83, 84, 85, 88
Walker, Henry D.	78, 79, 80
Waite, C. C.	36
War of 1812 followed by commercial distress	10
Washburn, J. H.	37
Waterman, Nathan M.	54
Watkinson, David	12, 15
Watkinson, Edward B.	67
Webster, Charles T.	55
Webster, J. C., sketch of	93
Weeks, E. O., sketch of	31, 118
Welch, Archibald	82
Welch, George M.	54
Wells, Daniel H., sketch of	69
Wells, James H.	12
Welles, Gideon	82

	PAGE		PAGE
Wheaton, B.	59	Williams, Joseph	11, 12
White, Adams	59	Williams, J. F.	61
White, Joel W.	10	Williams, Thomas S.; Sketch of	7
White, Samuel H.	83, 85, 88	Williams, William	12
Whiting, Charles B.	13, 21, 51	Wilmarth, A. F.	21, 28
Sketch of	55	Wilson, Charles	53
Whiting, Spencer	3	Windham County Mutual Insurance Company:	
Whitman, H. A.	105	Incorporation, methods and assessments, 58;	
Whitney, Amos W.	112	pay of officers and directors, 58; officers, 59.	
Whittemore, B. B.	54	Winters, Charles J.	60
Whittlesey, Chauncey	8	Wolcott, Oliver	109
Wiggin, Edwin R.	85, 88	Woodbridge, Samuel	12
Wilcox, Jedediah	56	Woodbridge, Ward	12
Willard, Charles E.	88	Woodruff, Samuel	54
Willard, William D.	60	Woodward, Truman	8
Williams, Abram	40	Woodward, William	60
Williams, Benjamin	8	Wooster, William B.	80
Williams, Ephraim	89, 118	Wright, Elizur	46, 47, 70
Williams, Ezekiel, Jr.	3, 7, 32	Wyman, William H.	32, 35
Sketch of	5	Young & Hodges	21

www.ingramcontent.com/pod-product-compliance
Lightning Source LLC
Chambersburg PA
CBHW030337170426
43202CB00010B/1155